JORDAN AND
THE HOLY LAND

JORDAN AND THE HOLY LAND:

Editors: ROBERT C. FISHER, LESLIE BROWN
Assistant Editor: DIANA NICHOLSON
Drawings: SANDRA LANG
Maps and City Plans: DYNO LOWENSTEIN
Photographs: KAY SHOWKER

FODOR'S

JORDAN
and the
HOLY LAND
1979

by
KAY SHOWKER

DAVID McKAY COMPANY, INC.
New York

*The following Fodor Travel Books (English language) are current in 1979.
(Selected Fodor guides are also available in French, Hebrew, Hungarian,
Italian, Japanese and Spanish languages.)*

AREA GUIDES:

EUROPE
EUROPE ON A BUDGET
AUSTRALIA, NEW ZEALAND
   AND THE SOUTH PACIFIC
CANADA
CARIBBEAN, BAHAMAS
   AND BERMUDA
INDIA AND NEPAL

JAPAN AND KOREA
MEXICO
PEOPLES REPUBLIC
   OF CHINA
SCANDINAVIA
SOUTH AMERICA
SOUTHEAST ASIA
SOVIET UNION
U.S.A. (1 vol.)

COUNTRY GUIDES:

AUSTRIA
BELGIUM AND
   LUXEMBOURG
BERMUDA
BRAZIL *
CZECHOSLOVAKIA
EGYPT
FRANCE
GERMANY
GREAT BRITAIN
GREECE
HOLLAND
HUNGARY *

IRAN
IRELAND
ISRAEL
ITALY
JORDAN AND THE
   HOLY LAND
MOROCCO
PORTUGAL
SPAIN
SWITZERLAND
TUNISIA *
TURKEY
YUGOSLAVIA

USA REGIONAL GUIDES:

FAR WEST *
HAWAII
MID-ATLANTIC *
MIDWEST *
NEW ENGLAND *

NEW YORK *
ROCKIES AND PLAINS *
SOUTH *
SOUTHWEST *

USA SPECIAL INTEREST GUIDES:

AMERICA ON A BUDGET
INDIAN AMERICA
OLD SOUTH *
OLD WEST *

ONLY-IN-AMERICA
   VACATION GUIDE *
OUTDOORS AMERICA *
SEASIDE AMERICA *

SPECIAL INTEREST GUIDES (INTERNATIONAL):

ANIMAL PARKS OF AFRICA
CRUISES EVERYWHERE

RAILWAYS OF THE WORLD
WORLDWIDE ADVENTURE GUIDE

CITY GUIDES:

LONDON   PARIS   PEKING

CONTENTS

AUTHOR'S FOREWORD

Jordan may possibly be the most underrated tourist destination in the world. While its name is as familiar to us as the Bible, Americans have almost no mental picture of the country. And while Jordan's King Hussein is a frequent and familiar visitor to the U.S., we have only a vague idea about the land and the people he governs.

Jordan is not only the heartland of the Middle East and the Arab world, it is the very spot where man first developed the communal life that launched Western civilization. Here, at this crossroad, three of the greatest religions of mankind—Judaism, Christianity and Islam—flowered. Here, too, the great empires—Egyptian, Hittite, Babylonian, Assyrian, Greek, Roman, Persian, Nabataean, Byzantine, Arab, Crusader—conquered and destroyed, ruled, built and created. Some of what they built can be seen today. The people and their culture are the mosaic they created.

In Jordan it is almost impossible to sink a shovel into the ground without turning up some vestige of the past. Although archeological exploration is in its infancy, Jordan has already uncovered a complete Roman town and four perfectly preserved Roman theaters—one of which is smack in the middle of Amman's downtown. Jordan has Byzantine mosaics that rival Ravenna; not one but two

Crusader castles; not one but six Umayyad palaces; and Petra—lost to the world for centuries, breathtakingly beautiful, strange and mysterious to this day. It is one of the few places in the travel lexicon that can truly be called unique.

Last but not least, Jordan is the Holy Land. From one end of the country to the other, the familiar names and settings leap off the pages of the Old Testament, seemingly little changed through the centuries. Here, too, Christ was baptized at the River Jordan, and He ministered through the highlands. There is hardly a town or village in Jordan that does not have a church, ancient or modern, commemorating His visit and marking His deeds.

But all this is Jordan past. What of Jordan present? Nothing will come as more of a surprise. Modern Jordan is something of a miracle.

Out of the Biblical hills of Gilead and Moab, the River Jordan and the sands of Arabia, a new and dynamic nation has been forged in less than 50 years. No country in history has had to struggle harder with fewer resources to overcome greater obstacles. It has been through four wars in three decades; on two occasions its population has doubled in one week.

When the new country was born in the 1920's, Jordan's mountains and countryside had been denuded of trees and animals after centuries of neglect; the desert claimed 80 percent of its land. There were almost no roads or schools or hospitals, and the great water systems of antiquity were in ruin. Modern Jordan began quite literally from scratch, and with the meagerest of resources built a nation.

Today, a network of good roads connects every part of the country, and elaborate water and irrigation systems are reclaiming the land. Jordan's industries are humming and its schools are packed. Because of its central location it is fast becoming an international center for business, which is discovering what the ancients already knew—the best route to the lucrative markets of the Gulf and Arabia is the Jordan connection.

And what else does Jordan offer?

For a start, it has the best climate in the Middle East. Warm, bright days and cool, crisp nights; rainless skies for eight months of the year.

Magnificent scenery greets the eye from every direction. From north to south, mountain peaks lightly covered with snow drop precipitously into canyons of variegated rock and ravines which blush with spring flowers. To the east, the mountains slope gently into green pastures until they meet the uncompromising desert undulating to infinity.

Here, you can witness the passing of traditional society almost before your eyes and in a panorama of paradox. The Bedouin life, free in the vastness of the desert and disciplined by its harshness, is juxtaposed against city life where comfort is gained but freedom lost. You can watch a shepherd graze his flock on the patches of green between building cranes and cement mixers. Fashionable boutiques with designer dresses have their floors polished and their windows washed by char women dressed in the traditional *thobe,* an everyday caftan—to us the height of fashion. Trucks and cars whiz down the highways, but always watch out for a stray donkey or camel, sheep or goat which might amble across the road. University girls in tight jeans and high-heeled boots stride hand-in-hand with their sisters in long dress and covered heads.

And what else is there?

Jordan's fantastic scenery isn't all above ground. The Gulf of Aqaba at the head of the Red Sea has some of the most beautiful marine life in the world. You can scuba, snorkel, or see it from the comfort of a glass-bottom boat. The sea is so clear that 150 feet down appears to be only a few feet away.

There's another sea, too—the Dead Sea, so thick with brine it is impossible to sink in it. Or, if you do not like it quite so strong, there are the hot springs where Herod took the cure, or the oasis where Lawrence took the Turks.

Most important of all, there are the Jordanians themselves—the kindest and most hospitable people in the Middle East, who have retained the finest qualities of their Arab heritage, trying hard not to lose the millenia of tradition behind them as they gallop into the 21st century.

Jordanians want you to see their country. They really enjoy having you as their guest, and they mean it when they say, "Ahlan wa Sahlan."

* * * *

As do all the countries of the Middle East, Jordan abounds with important historical and Biblical sites, any of which could be the subject of a book. But this is a guidebook, not a textbook. It is meant to be a concise and practical guide for the modern traveler.

We have tried to highlight the most important places and direct the newcomer through the maze of hills, tells, digs, temples, churches, castles, mosques, etc. that cover the country. If by using this guide your interest is stimulated to learn more, then it will have served a useful purpose.

The Suggested Reading List in the Supplement is an introduction to the vast amount of historical and Biblical literature available. I have relied heavily on these sources in preparing the book and make no claim to original historical research.

The choice of information included has been mine with no obligations whatever. Although I traveled from one end of the country to the other to obtain the data, and interviewed many people to help me evaluate my material, there will certainly be places and facilities that have been overlooked. We would welcome suggestions from readers for inclusion in future editions.

The transliteration of Arabic words into English is a continuing problem; consistency is almost impossible. The following variations will serve as examples: Moslem or Muslim; Koran or Qu'ran; Muhammad, Muhammed, Mohammed, Mohamed, Mohammad, Mehemet or Mehmet.

We have tried to be practical. Place names, shops, hotels, etc., are written as they appear locally so that a visitor will recognize them. Historical names are given in their commonly accepted forms. Terms that might be used by a traveler are rendered simply and as closely as possible to their English equivalents, without the use of symbols or diacritics. Without some knowledge of Arabic or linguistics, the use of elaborate systems is usually more confusing than helpful.

*   *   *   *

A book such as this is never a one-person effort. It requires the help of many—more than there is space to name; but I would particularly like to thank Jordan's Minister of Tourism, Ghaleb Barakat, and Director General of Tourism, Michael Hamarneh, whose interest and help made my task easier; Ali Ghandour, Chairman and President of Alia, The Royal Jordanian Airlines, whose continuing interest and enthusiasm helped me get the job done; Akram Barakat, director of the Jordan Information Center, Washington, D.C.; and Helen Khal of Doremus & Company, Washington, who was there every step of the way.

FACTS AT YOUR FINGERTIPS

 WHEN TO GO. Spring and autumn are the best times to visit Jordan; the weather is wonderful for travel throughout the country. However, we would not dissuade anyone from going at other times of the year.

The country's climate is as diverse as its scenery. Daytime summer temperatures are hot, but nights are cool. Winter often brings light snow on the mountaintops. Spring carpets the countryside with beautiful wild flowers and the valleys with pink oleander. Rain falls from November to April, but the rest of the year there is sunshine every day. Fall and spring are long and pleasant, though occasionally a strong desert wind blows in spring. July and August are hot in much of the country. From December through February Amman and the surrounding area are cool, but Aqaba on the Gulf is a warm and sunny winter resort.

AVERAGE TEMPERATURES IN MAJOR TOURIST CENTERS

		Winter		Spring			Summer			Fall		
	Dec.	Jan.	Feb.	Mar.	Apr.	May	June	July	Aug.	Sept.	Oct.	Nov.
Amman	F.50	46	48	53	60	69	74	77	78	74	69	59
Aqaba	F.62	60	62	68	75	83	89	90	91	86	80	71

HOLIDAYS. National: March 22, Arab League Day; May 1, Labor Day; May 25, Independence Day; August 11, His Majesty King Hussein's Accession to the Throne; November 14, His Majesty King Hussein's Birthday.

Moslem holidays: The Moslem (Hegira) calendar is a lunar one, the first year corresponding to the year of the Prophet Muhammad's flight from Mecca to Medina (622 A.D.). Since the Moslem year is 13 days shorter than the Gregorian year, its holidays vary from year to year, and it is difficult to know precisely on which day in the Gregorian calendar a Moslem feast will fall.

Eid el Fitr, a three-day feast, celebrates the end of Ramadan, the holy month of fasting. *Eid el Adha* (or *el Kabir*) celebrates the end of the *Haj,* or pilgrimage to Mecca, commemorating Abraham's offering of his son. The feast lasts three days and is the most important one in the Moslem faith. *Muharram I* is the Moslem New Year, the first day of the Islamic calendar. *Moulid el Nabi,* which falls on the 12th day of Rabi I, is the birthday of the Prophet. *Rajab 27* is the Feast of *al Miraj,* commemorating the Prophet Muhammad's nocturnal visit to heaven. *Sha'ban 9,* Arab Renaissance Day, commemorates the Arab Revolt against Ottoman rule.

On major feasts Jordanians tend to make a long holiday of it. Government offices and many businesses close down for several days. Businessmen in particular should try to avoid a visit during long holidays and especially during Ramadan.

Friday is the sabbath in Jordan, according to the tradition in most Moslem countries. Government offices and most but not all business offices and shops are closed.

Christian holidays: At Easter, celebrations of the Western and Eastern churches in Jordan fall according to the Eastern church date, which can be as much as a month after the Western one. These are the most impressive and moving services of the year. For Eastern Christians Easter is a bigger and more important feast than Christmas.

Christmas is observed by the Roman Catholic, Protestant and Orthodox Churches on December 25. In Bethlehem and Jerusalem special services begin on Christmas Eve, December 24, and continue through the following day. It should be noted also that the Coptic and Abyssinian Churches celebrate Christmas in mid-January.

THE MOSLEM CALENDAR

Gregorian	Moslem
January	Moharram
February	Safar
March	Rabi I
April	Rabi II

May	Jumada I
June	Jumada II
July	Ragab
August	Shaban
September	Ramadan
October	Shawal
November	Thul-Kida
December	Thul-Higga

The Moslem months have alternately 29 or 30 days, and the year has 354 days, so that they do not coincide precisely with the Gregorian calendar from year to year. For example, in 1978 Ramadan fell in mid-August, in 1979 it will be in early August, and in 1980 it will start in late July.

 HOW TO GET THERE. *By Air:* Alia, The Royal Jordanian Airlines, has had direct flights from New York to Amman since the summer of 1977. It was the first Arab airline to connect the United States with the Middle East on a regular basis and by direct, non-stop flights. As of May 1, these services are scheduled to be increased to four weekly from Houston and New York on Boeing 747's.

Several European airlines have direct flights from Europe to Jordan. Flying time is 5 hours from major European cities and 10½ hours from New York.

Alia also links Jordan with other Middle Eastern capitals, with daily flights to Beirut, Cairo, Damascus, Baghdad, and the countries of the Gulf—Bahrain, Kuwait, Qatar, Saudi Arabia and the United Arab Emirates. Most of these flights take from one to two hours. The carrier also offers service to Karachi and Bangkok, and expects to add several other destinations in the Far East in the near future.

AIR FARES

Among the more confusing aspects of travel these days is the matter of air fares, and perhaps none are more confusing than those which apply to the countries of the Middle East. The following fares were valid at the time this book went to press, but, judging from past experience, prices will probably have changed by the time the ink is dry on the page.

All prices are round-trip between New York and Amman:

Individual Fares

First Class	$1,974 available year round.
Economy Class	$1,194 basic fare (Sept. 15-May 31).
	$1,330 peak season (June 1-Sept. 14).
Youth (ages 12–22)	$ 657 basic
	$ 693 peak

7–60 day Apex (advance-purchase): Reservations and tickets must be made no later than 21 days in advance of departure. No stopovers. Basic fare (Sept.-May 31), $545; peak season (June 1-Aug. 31), $655.

14–21 day Excursion: Two European stopovers are permitted in each direction. Surcharge of $15 for weekend departure. Basic, $913; peak, $994.

14–21 day Excursion: Basic, one stopover in Europe in both directions, $754; peak, one stopover in Europe westbound only, $844.

14–21 day Middle East Excursion: No stopovers in Europe. Basic, $732; peak, $823.

21–120 days Excursion: No stopovers. $750 year-round.

22–45 day Excursion: Two stopovers in both directions. Basic, $788; peak, $891.

Group Fares

8–21 days: No weekend departures or eastbound stopovers; one westbound stopover permitted. Eight-day stay in Middle East and group of 10 persons required. Basic (Sept. 15-May 31), $657; peak, $689.

4–9 days: Minimum group of 10 persons; no stopovers. Winter only (Sept. 15-Mar. 14), $586, or $610 with one westbound stopover.

14–21 days: Six stopovers but not more than two each way in Europe; minimum group of 5 persons and $70 on land arrangements must be included in tour package. Surcharge of $15 for weekend departure. Basic, $727; peak, $835.

By car: An interesting overland route from Europe through the ancient lands of Turkey and Syria enters Jordan at Ramtha, about 70 miles north of Amman. Driving time from Damascus is about four hours (allow one to two hours for border crossings).

Regular shared-taxi service is available between Damascus and Amman and costs J.D. 2. Petra Taxi Company, with offices in Damascus and Amman, has cars leaving about every hour from Damascus for Amman. You should telephone the day before to reserve a seat. If you are planning to return to Damascus or Beirut from Jordan, be sure to obtain multi-entry visas for Syria and Lebanon.

For the return to Damascus by taxi, the companies in Amman which offer regular service are Hadad Taxi, Feras Taxi and Hilal Taxi. For long journeys by shared taxi you may want to buy two seats for yourself, since the price is so cheap. This way the car is less crowded and the ride will be more comfortable.

By bus: Between Damascus and Amman there are four coaches daily, leaving from each city at 8 A.M., 10 A.M., 3 P.M. and 5 P.M. in winter, and 7 A.M., 9 A.M., 3 P.M. and 5 P.M. in summer. The service is handled by Karnak in Damascus and by JETT in Amman. Coach service is also available between Damascus and Irbid, Jordan's second largest city. The buses depart twice daily from each town; the fare is J.D. 1. Low-cost transportation either by bus or shared taxi facilitates tourist travel to many places throughout Jordan. These are detailed later in this chapter.

By train: Jordan's only rail line is the narrow-gauge, single-track Hejaz Railway, built in the early 1900s for pilgrim traffic between Damascus and Medina. Much of it was destroyed in World War I during the Arab Revolt against the Turks led by Sherif Hussein, the great-grandfather of the present king, and Lawrence of Arabia. Sectors have been reconstructed, and a new branch has been added which extends to the port of Aqaba. It carries only freight.

By sea: With the reopening of the Suez Canal in 1975 it became possible once again to visit Jordan by ship from Europe. Several cruise lines now include Aqaba on itineraries from the Mediterranean through the Suez to the Red Sea and up the Gulf of Aqaba. These include Epirotiki Line's *Neptune,* and Royal Viking Line's *Royal Viking Sea* and Karageorgis Line's *Navarino.* Passengers visit Petra on a day tour.

A car and passenger ferry service is available between Aqaba and Suez on board a regularly scheduled ship, *Al-Kamar El-Saudi.* The ship sails weekly from Aqaba to the ports of Suez and Jeddah, on Mondays and Thursdays respectively. Rates begin at $50 to Suez and $70 to Jeddah. The line is run by the Telestar Maritime Agency (phone: 36162) with offices near Firas Circle on Jebel Hussein in Amman. Mail address: P.O. Box 9360. Cable: TELSTAR. Telex: 1604 Telstar.

 PACKAGE TOURS. In almost every case, tours from the U.S. to Jordan include other countries of the Middle East. The great majority are Holy Land tours which use Jordan as a gateway. Generally, this type of tour spends two days in Jordan, with rushed visits to Petra and Jerash.

As part of a Middle East and Holy Land tour, the following general interest, nonpilgrimage tours are samples of what is available:

Four Winds, 175 Fifth Avenue, New York City 10010, offers a 16-day tour at $1,628 and a 22-day tour at $2,038, both plus air fare. Both tours visit Egypt before going to Amman and Petra and traveling on to Jerusalem.

Atpac, 3 East 54th St., New York 10022, has an 18-day Middle East tour priced from $1,115 plus air fare. It includes two days in Jordan.

Maupintour, 900 Massachusetts St., Lawrence, Kansas 66044, has a 22-day Middle East package which starts with a week in Egypt and continues with two days each in Syria and Jordan, followed by a week in Jerusalem and environs. It is priced from $1,837 and has frequent departures throughout the year. A 29-day Egypt, Jordan, and Israel package offers three days in Jordan. It is priced from $2,268 plus air fare. A 20-day program includes a Red Sea cruise which calls at Aqaba and visits Petra.

Persepolis Travel, 667 Madison Ave, #909, New York 10021, has a 15-day package which starts in Egypt and combines two days in Jordan with Jerusalem. It is priced from $838.

Other agencies with similar programs are *Mediterranean Express Tours,*

6253 Hollywood Blvd., Los Angeles 90028: 10 days, Jordan and the Holy Land, from $399 plus air fare.

Nawas International, 20 East 46th Street, New York 10017: 15 days in Egypt, Syria, Jordan, and the Holy Land, from $995 plus air fare, or the 22-day version which adds Turkey and Greece at $1,495 plus air fare.

Sunny Land Tours, 166 Main Street, Hackensack, N.J. 07601: 15 days in Egypt, Jordan and the Holy Land, from $845 plus air fare; 22 days from $1,080, adding Greece and Turkey; two 15-day programs which visit Syria, Jordan, Turkey, and the Holy Land, from $695, or a 10-day tour combining Egypt, Jordan, and the Holy Land, from $500.

TWA Getaway Middle East, 2 Penn Plaza, New York, has a variety of programs: 10 days from $1,278; 14 days from $1,725, and three weeks from $2,395. All prices include air fare from New York.

Travcoa, John Hancock Center, 875 N. Michigan Ave., Chicago 60600: 22 days, Egypt, Syria, Jordan, Holy Land, and Turkey, priced from $1,795; or a 40-day version from $3,395 that adds Greece and Turkey.

Travelworld, 6922 Hollywood Blvd., Los Angeles, Calif. 90028: 22 days, Jordan, Egypt, Tunisia, Morocco, Holy Land, from $1,890; 22 days, Turkey, Jordan, Holy Land, Syria, Egypt, and Greece, from $1,990. Jordan and the Holy Land are also included on several round-the-world programs.

United States Travel Agency (non-government), 1730 K St., N.W., Washington, D.C. 20006, offers an 8-day extension to Jordan and Jerusalem as part of its "Treasures of Egypt" Discovery Tour. The Egypt portion costs $1,390 and the extension $895, including air fare.

Christian pilgrimage tours are offered by a number of firms who specialize in these programs. They are almost always led by a clergyman. Among the firms are Catholic Travel Center, 1730 Rhode Island Ave., Washington, D.C. 20036; Bibleland Tours, 2221 DeVine Street, Columbia, South Carolina 29205; Wholesale Tours, 387 Park Ave. South, New York, N.Y. 10016.

 PASSPORTS AND VISAS. To visit Jordan, travelers need a valid passport or a recognized travel document and a visa issued by Jordanian Consulates abroad. Tourists may also obtain visas upon arrival at Jordanian frontier posts and airports.

A multiple-entry tourist visa, valid for four years, may be issued upon request. Your visa application should be accompanied by one passport-size photograph and a stamped, self-addressed envelope. For U.S. citizens there is no visa charge; for British citizens, the cost is $3.80. Visa fees vary for citizens of other countries. Payment should be made to the Jordan Embassy by money order or certified check only.

For business visas follow the same procedure as above, with the addition of a letter from the company or employer stating the purpose of the visit.

A Group or Collective Visa is available for tour groups providing the group stays in Jordan two or more days.

Travel Between Jordan and Israel

Travel between Jordan and Israel is permitted by a two-way crossing from Jordan or a one-way crossing from Israel. (If you enter Jordan via Israel, be sure that no Israeli visa is affixed to your passport.) You must leave Jordan directly or via neighboring Arab countries; as of this writing you will not be allowed to return to Israel.

If you come to Jordan direct or via neighboring Arab countries and want to visit Israel, you are permitted after a minimum of two nights' stay in Jordan to cross over and return to Jordan.

It is important to remember that Jordan government offices are closed on Fridays, Israeli government offices are closed on Saturdays, and the American and British Consulates in Jerusalem are closed on Sundays.

Tourists going to Israel from Jordan can obtain a permit to cross over to the West Bank from the Ministry of Tourism in Amman or through a travel agent. The permit is a separate document which allows you to cross over and return. Remember, it is important that you do not allow Israeli authorities to stamp your passport in any way.

So long as you are in a group, the crossing between Jordan and the Israeli-occupied West Bank is likely to be easy and uncomplicated. Your travel agent will have already made the necessary arrangements and will have the proper documentation in hand for the group.

If you are traveling on your own and not making your travel arrangements through a stateside agent, then on your arrival in Amman you should go in person with your passport to the Ministry. You should do this immediately upon arrival, as the paperwork takes a minimum of two days. You should plan to take a taxi (J.D. 4.500) or taxi-service (J.D. 1) from Amman to the Jordanian security post, where you board a bus for the river crossing. Taxi service from Abdali station is available. The drive from Amman to the security post takes about 50 minutes.

American and other foreign tourists of Arab origin, no matter where they were born, must secure permission from the Ministry of Interior. This may take longer to process, although it can usually be speeded up if you have a good agent working on it.

The crossing itself is time-consuming and may be unpleasant and uncomfortable. The bridge closes at 1 P.M. daily and is completely closed on Saturdays, the Jewish sabbath. It's necessary to begin your journey early (via taxi) to reach the Jordanian security point, where you must board a bus, the only vehicle authorized to make the crossing. You cannot cross over in a taxi or your own car. The last bus leaves the security point (on both sides) at 11 A.M.

On arrival at the Jordanian security post you present the papers issued by the Ministry of Tourism and, after clearance, wait for the next shuttle bus to take you across the bridge. Passports are checked at the bridge itself (located approximately 2 miles from the security post) and a military escort boards the bus to accompany it to the middle of the bridge, where his West Bank counterpart takes over and gives a briefing to passengers on Israeli entry formalities.

The ride will be a memorable experience. The bus is completely full, neither air-conditioned nor cushioned, and rather old. Passengers are frequently loud and lively with lots of children, and plenty of food will be passed around—and offered to you. Local passengers try to be helpful to tourists, and they will certainly be friendly.

JETT has recently added bus service which makes the crossing directly from Amman to the Israeli military station, eliminating the need to change buses or to change from a taxi to a bus. Cost is J.D. 4.

Upon arrival on the West Bank, there are two separate security points, one for tourists and another for the local Arabs. Security officials may sometimes be unpleasant, though tourists are generally treated courteously. Your luggage (and your person) will be thoroughly searched. Some items, such as shoes, and anything suspicious are X-rayed and might even be confiscated—all a grim reminder that there is still a war on in the Middle East.

Once you have passed through Israeli security, there are taxis to take you into Jerusalem or anywhere else you may wish to visit. The crossing procedures take three to four hours.

 HEALTH REGULATIONS. Anyone coming from epidemic or endemic areas is required to have an inoculation certificate against smallpox. Although not required by Jordanian law, you may also want to be inoculated against typhoid, paratyphoid, tetanus and cholera. Cholera vaccinations are required for travelers, except children under one year of age, coming from infected areas.

 WHAT TO TAKE. Pack with a plan so that you will not be burdened with useless items. Limit baggage to what you can carry—and leave enough room for the gifts and souvenirs you are sure to buy in Jordan.

Although Jordan is thought of as having a hot climate, you will be surprised to discover how much the temperature varies within a given day or from one month to the next. Jordan has four well-defined seasons. Hence, your wardrobe should be planned according to the time of year and the extent of your itinerary.

In early summer (May, June) and fall (September, October), cotton and dacron dresses and slacks for ladies and slacks and suits for men are comfortable, provided they are made of the type of fabric that breathes. In the dead of summer (July and August) only pure cotton dresses, blouses and skirts, shirts and trousers are recommended, especially for those who suffer from the heat.

Winter (December through March) can be cold with some rain, especially in the highlands. Women will need light wool or knitted suits and dresses with long sleeves or jackets. Gentlemen should have medium-weight suits and warm sweaters. Even April can be cool, especially in the evening. Women should be sure to include a versatile dress with jacket or a polyester knit with long sleeves. Include a lightweight coat or cape, a warm housecoat, nightgown, and warm slippers, as floors are usually laid in tiles. A stole or warm wrap for evenings is useful year-round. It is amazing how even in the middle of summer, when the sun goes down after a hot day there is sometimes a chill in the air. You will feel it all the more because the day was so warm. Moreover, older houses, old hotels and guesthouses are not centrally heated, and it is frequently cooler inside than outdoors.

An adaptable long dress or skirt is useful for dinner and evenings out. Hats, except as protection against the sun, are seldom worn. A mantilla is appropriate in church.

Jordanians are accustomed to foreigners and to the bizarre ways some tourists dress. Nonetheless, it is still a conservative country as far as women are concerned. Slacks are readily accepted; shorts and bare sunback dresses are not. Unless you want to attract attention to yourself, modesty in dress and decorum in manner are wise.

For men, there is not a great deal of emphasis on formality of dress, but it is conservative.

Hotel laundry service is usually fast and reasonable, so you do not need to burden yourself with a great deal of clothing.

Useful items to include in your suitcase are small binoculars, a small flashlight, a washcloth, disposable premoistened facecloths, insect repellent, collapsible hanger, face soap (keep it in plastic bags), packaged soap powders, moisture cream and a collapsible drinking cup. Always have a generous supply of facial tissues on hand—you will be amazed at their many uses, and only deluxe hotels supply them in your room. If you do not want to be bothered with packing all these items, they are readily available in Amman.

Sunglasses are a MUST, and a shade hat for sightseeing in the open, in the desert and for the beach is advised, especially in summer. Be sure to bring comfortable, flat walking shoes, summer or winter. Sneakers are wonderful for walking and climbing around monuments and sites of antiquity, especially at Jerash and Petra. A raincoat will be necessary in January, February and March. A bathing suit for sunbathing or for swimming should be included year-round—and don't forget to pack the suntan lotion.

 USEFUL ADDRESSES. *Embassies and Consulates:* Jordan Mission to the United Nations, 866 United Nations Plaza, New York, N.Y. 10017, (212) 752-0135; Embassy of the Hashemite Kingdom of Jordan, 2319 Wyoming Avenue, N.W., Washington, D.C. 20008, (202) 265-1606; 100 Bronson Avenue, Ottawa, Ontario K1R 6G8, Canada, (613) 238-8090; 6 Upper Phillimore Gardens, London W8 7HB, England, 937-3685.

Jordan Information Center, 1701 K. Street, N.W., Washington, D.C. 20006, (202) 659-3322.

Alia Offices: New York City: 545 Madison Avenue, Tel. (212) 949-0050.
Washington, D.C.: 1925 K. Street, N.W., Suite 505, (202) 857-0401.
Atlanta: 229 Peachtree Street, N.E., Suite 2415, (404) 659-2542.
Houston:3336 Richmond Avenue, Suite 314, (713) 524-3700.
Chicago: Six North Michigan Avenue, Suite 808, (312) 236-1702.
Los Angeles: 510 West 6th Street, Suite 1132, (213) 623-3376.
Detroit: Tower 14, 21700 Northwestern Highway, Suite 998,
   Southfield, (313) 624-9233.
Toronto: 155 University Avenue, (416) 862-7527.
Montreal: 1200 McGill College Avenue, Suite 1640, (514) 879-1611.
London: Sales Office, 177 Regent Street, London, W1, 734-2557/8/9/50.

ARRIVING IN JORDAN

TRANSPORTATION INTO TOWN. Taxis and porters
are available at all times at the airport in Amman,
although passengers arriving late at night may have to
wait awhile for a taxi to be called. A taxi stand is
directly in front of the exit doors. The ride to a downtown hotel takes about
15 minutes and costs no more than JD1.500 regardless of the number of
passengers, so long as they all have the same destination.

An airport tax of JD2 is charged on departure from Jordanian airports.
Remember to leave yourself enough Jordanian currency to pay this tax on
departure. If you should run out, however, don't be concerned. You can
exchange money at the airport. It's a bit of a hassle, but not difficult provided
you allow yourself ample time.

CUSTOMS REGULATIONS. Normally, all àrticles
classified as traveling requirements are exempt from
customs duty. In addition to your personal clothing,
you are allowed the following items duty free: 200
cigarettes or 200 grams of tobacco, sporting equipment, cameras, films,
typewriter, licensed firearms and ammunition for hunting, binoculars, baby
carriage, jewelry, dog or cat (if vaccinated and properly certified), and one
liter of wine or spirits.

Printing or sound reproduction equipment, phonograph with records
(including portable and used) are subject to duty. A radio is exempted from
duty when imported for less than six months.

Generally, as a tourist you may bring in gifts in small quantities and of low
commercial value duty-free. The exemption, however, is subject to the
discretion of the customs officer.

Security Formalities: Before disembarking from a plane or on arrival at the
frontier, you are asked to fill in a standard international form to be presented
to immigration authorities. Basically, the form asks for passport information
and the length and purpose of your visit.

Baggage is subject to inspection and tourists are often requested to open luggage. If any questions should arise, Tourist Police are near at hand to assist visitors.

At the borders the Jordanian officials are generally very courteous. There is a rest house at Ramtha where one crosses into Jordan from Syria. Drinks and refreshments are sold and toilet facilities available.

Customs review is the most severe on tourists entering Jordan from Israel or returning to Jordan from there. Particularly, customs officials will confiscate books and tape which appear to them to have a political intent, even if in fact they do not.

 MONEY. The monetary unit in Jordan is the Jordanian Dinar (JD) which is divided into 1000 fils. One dinar is equal to about $2.90 or £1.83. In reverse, $1 equals about 300 fils. (The rate may fluctuate slightly from day to day depending on the market rate, but it has not changed more than a few cents over the past decade.) Ten fils are also called a piaster (pt.). Thus $1 equals 29 pt.

Jordanian money appears in the following denominations:

Banknotes: JD50, 20, 10, 5, ½ (500 fils).

Silver: 250 fils (25 piasters), 100 fils (10 pt.), 50 fils (5 pt.), 25 fils (2.5 pt.) and 20 fils (2 pt.).

Copper: 10 fils, 5 fils.

There are no restrictions on the amount of Jordanian currency, foreign banknotes, travelers cheques or gold visitors may bring into or take out of the country. Special authorization is required for the import and export of stocks and bonds.

Foreign currency, drafts, and travelers cheques should be exchanged at banks and at authorized money changers. Exchange facilities are provided in the arrival lounge at the airport in Amman and at the border guard at Ramtha. In Amman, most banks and money changers are located downtown on the main street and near or in hotels. Hotels and merchants will accept travelers cheques.

Credit cards are beginning to be used in Jordan, but their acceptance is limited. Leading hotels and restaurants and a few merchants and travel agencies will accept the best-known ones, such as American Express, but do not expect to use them to cover your costs. Also, personal checks are difficult to cash. To avoid problems, carry travelers' cheques. In out-of-the-way places carry Jordanian currency in small denominations, as change may not always be available.

 TIPPING. Most hotels and restaurants add a 10 percent service charge (12 percent in deluxe places), but the people who actually do the work expect tips. As a guide, try this formula: on departure from a hotel, your total tips should not exceed 10 percent of your bill before the service charge is added.

Taxi drivers do not expect tips, but be sure to agree on the fare before entering the taxi.

STAYING IN JORDAN

 TOURIST FACILITIES. The main organization in Jordan to facilitate tourism is the Tourism Authority of the Ministry of Tourism and Antiquities. Main Office: Jebel, Amman, P.O. Box 224. Amman, phone 42311/7. Department of Antiquities: P.O. Box 88. Amman, phone 44336.

Tourist Guides: Guides in Jordan are required to pass an examination prepared by the Tourism Ministry before being licensed to practice. You may ask to see a guide's license before engaging him. Guides who speak English are available through reliable travel agencies or the Tourism Ministry at JD7 per day. During heavy tourist seasons it is wise to ask your agent to book a guide in advance of your arrival.

Tourist Police: Jordan has well-trained, extremely pleasant and cooperative Tourist Police. They are stationed at major tourist sites and the airport to assist visitors when the need arises. Although they are trained to act as guides, this is not their primary function.

In addition, the government Rest Houses at major tourist sites act as information centers.

Travel Agencies: Any travel agency in Amman will be able to arrange automobile transportation and a guide to the major sightseeing attractions. Prices are regulated, but you should agree on the fee before departing. If several persons are traveling together, hiring a car for the day is the best way to tour the country.

For someone traveling alone, however, this is expensive. Several companies advertise individual fares for daily tours by bus or car depending on the time of year. Jordan Express Tourist Transport Company (JETT) has a bus leaving Amman for Petra on Tuesday, Friday and Sunday at 7 A.M. and returning in the afternoon. Cost is $30 per person for round trip, lunch, horse and guide. Also, there often will be other persons traveling alone who are eager to share taxi costs. As soon as you arrive in Amman, go to one of the travel agencies in town and inquire.

GOVERNMENT-LICENSED TRAVEL AGENCIES IN AMMAN

Name	Address	Telephone
Amin Ka'war & Sons	Prince Mohammed St.	22324
Apollo Tours & Travel Agency	Prince Mohammed St.	41083
Aqaba Tourist & Travel Agency	Jebel Amman-1st Circle	23607
Arab Tourist Company	King Hussein St.	24363
Atlas Travel & Tourist		

Agency	King Hussein St.	24262
Attaher Tourist & Travel Agency	King Hussein St.	22128
Aviaturist	Prince Mohammed St.	38146
Ayoub Caravan Tours	King Hussein St.	38836
Baker Travel Company	Jordan Intercontinental Hotel	41334
Bestours	Prince Mohammed St.	37171
Bisharat Tours Corporation	Jordan Intercontinental Hotel	41350
Blue Bell Tours	Grand Palace Hotel	61913
Concord Travel & Tourism	King Hussein St.	23536
Crown Tours	King Hussein St.	36919
Debbas Touring & Travel Agency	Prince Mohammed St.	30243
Fadel Deeba Travel & Tourism	King Hussein St.	25646
General Tours	King Hussein St.	24307
Guiding Star Agency	Prince Mohammed St.	42526
Halaby Tourist Company	King Hussein St.	39540
Holiday International Tours Company	King Hussein St.	23648
Holy Land Tours	Jordan Intercontinental Hotel	41446
International Holiday Planners	Prince Mohammed St.	41031
International Traders	King Hussein St.	25072
Jerusalem Express Travel	King Hussein St.	22151
Jordan Express Company	King Hussein St.	21778
Jordan Resources Company	King Hussein St.	23135
Jordan Travel Bureau	King Hussein St.	21220
Karnak Travel Agency	King Hussein St.	25174
Khoury Travel Tourist Agency	King Hussein St.	23430
Lawrence Tours	Grand Palace Hotel	61121
Nahas & Ka'war Travel	King Hussein St.	30879
National Tourist Office	King Hussein St.	23388
Nawas Tourist Agency	King Hussein St.	22184
Near East Tourist Center	Jordan Intercontinental Hotel	41906
Orient Tours	King Hussein St.	24290
Pan Pacific Travel & Tourism	King Hussein St.	21688
Petra Tours	King Hussein St.	30380
Philadelphia Travel Agency	King Hussein St.	30800
Rainbow Travel & Tourism	King Hussein St.	21656
Seikaly's Travel & Tourism	Prince Mohammed St.	22147-8
Telstar Travel & Tourism	Jebel Al-Hussein	36162
Terra Santa Tourist Company	King Hussein St.	21309
Travel Masters	King Hussein St.	24807

Name	Address	Telephone
Wazzan Travel & Tourism	King Hussein St.	23180
Ya'ish Travel & Tourism	King Hussein St.	30610
Za'atara Tourist Company	King Hussein St.	36011
JETT Tourist Buses	Abdali Street	36172

LANGUAGE. Arabic is the official language of Jordan; however, English is widely spoken at every level throughout the country, and educated Jordanians are almost always bilingual in the two languages.

TIME. Greenwich Mean Time plus two hours. Eastern Standard Time plus 7 hours.

WEIGHTS AND MEASURES. Metric system.

ELECTRIC CURRENT. 220 A.C. volts, 50 cycles. Wall plugs are the round, two-prong European type (adapters for American products are available locally). Transformers are required for American products, but not for British ones.

BUSINESS HOURS. Government offices are open daily, except Friday, from 8 A.M. to 2 P.M. Banks are open to the public from 9:30 A.M. to 1:30 P.M. During Ramadan, the hours ae 9 A.M. to 1:30 P.M. Business offices follow the same hours, but some close on Sunday. Shops and other businesses are open from 9 A.M. to ½ or 1:30 P.M. and from 3 to 6:30 or 7 P.M.

MAIL AND TELEGRAMS. In Amman the Central Post Office is located on Prince Muhammad Street in the center of town, and there are branches conveniently located throughout the city. You may buy stamps between 8 A.M. and 8 P.M. at the main Post Office. The branch at the Jordan Inter-continental Hotel is open until 6 P.M.

Air mail postage to the U.S., Canada, Australia and South America is 125 fils for letters, 75 fils for postcards; to Europe, Africa, and Asia 75 fils for letters and 65 fils for postcards. International airmail to or from the U.S. takes about five to seven days. Airmail letters to all Arab countries and Pakistan are 40 fils, 25 fils for postcards.

You may send telegrams and cables and purchase stamps from leading hotels or post offices in Amman. The cost of cable to the U.S. is 108 fils per word. There is no nightletter rate.

You may send a package from Jordan after filling out a customs declaration and clearing it with the local Customs Office. Packages should be left open for custom officials to check their contents. For ordinary tourist gifts, ask the shop where you buy to mail your purchases for you.

 TELEPHONE. Amman and the main towns in Jordan are connected by automatic dial system. Telephones occasionally go out of service, and one should be prepared to encounter considerable delay in getting through to the party one is calling. Basically, the system is overloaded.

Jordan is connected by Telestar to Europe and the U.S. Calls can be made to most Arab countries, but the waiting time will vary considerably depending on the destination. Phone calls *cannot* be made from Jordan to Israel.

Long distance calls to the U.S. cost JD4.320 for the first three minutes and JD1.440 for each additional minute.

For telephone information, dial 122. English-speaking operators are available to assist you. For domestic calls and Middle East dial 10, and for overseas calls dial 17.

Anyone planning to live in Jordan should be aware that telephones are difficult to obtain in some quarters of the city where demand outpaces supply. The basic rate is JD18 per year for 5,000 phone calls.

 PHOTOGRAPHY. Jordan is a pleasure for photographers. The weird shapes and color-rich rocks of Petra and Wadi Rum, the drama of the Jordan Valley, the sunset at Jerash, the panorama from Kerak are only a few of the delightful subjects.

Bring all your film with you and plan to have it developed when you return home. Film—color and black and white—is available, but American film is more expensive than in the U.S. For example, B/W Kodak (36 exposures) is 500 fils, and Kodachrome II is JD3.500 (with developing). Also, you cannot always be sure that the type of film you need will be available, especially that for some of the newest instant and self-developing cameras. European film is also on sale.

If you want to photograph *local color,* you should remember that what sometimes appears picturesque to strangers might be merely poverty to the local inhabitants. Avoid embarrassing Jordanians, especially women, or yourself; ask permission first. They are often delighted to oblige—and you might want to offer them a little token for their cooperation. Military installations, including bridges, may not be photographed.

Slides of important sites are on sale at leading hotels and gift shops and at sites of antiquity and museums. The quality of the color varies from one vendor to another.

Serious amateur photographers should carry a light meter; unless you are familiar with desert conditions, you will be likely to overexpose film. The sun is deceptively bright, especially at sites of antiquity, and there is an enormous amount of reflected light, especially during midday. When in doubt, use one stop below the normal setting.

For black and white film, you will be happy with the results of a yellow filter. Tri-X or other fast film is terrific for inside shots, but is often too fast for normal outside shots in the bright sun.

As for color, wonderful results can be had with low ASA film such as Kodachrome 25 because lighting conditions are ideal. Except that your photographs will have shadows, the best times of the day for picture-taking are early morning and late afternoon, when colors are deeper and antique stone is mellow.

Should you need passport-size photographs in a hurry, they can be made at any of the photo shops on or near King Feisal Street, most of which offer second-day service.

 HEALTH PRECAUTIONS. Water in Amman is usually safe to drink. If you have any doubts, ask for bottled water, which is available in hotels and restaurants. On trips to the desert and to small villages take along water or bottled soft drinks. You will find it handy to include a collapsible drinking cup in your hand luggage for such occasions.

Hotels serve both European and Jordanian dishes. Jordan has a wide variety of good fruits and vegetables. Eat what is in season. Peel the fruit and vegetables until your system has had time to adjust. More important, eat lightly. Tourists become ill from overeating—and overexerting themselves sightseeing—more frequently than from the food itself.

Should you feel any stomach illness coming on, *Lomotil* is the most immediately effective medicine if taken promptly. It is readily available from local pharmacies.

 HOW TO GET AROUND. By Middle Eastern standards, taxi drivers in Jordan are fairly tame. You might wonder, though, how their flowing headdress, known as a *kafiya,* does not get caught in the car mechanism. Then, too, as in all the Middle East, you may sometimes wish the automobile horn had never been invented.

Buses operate in Amman and between cities and villages throughout Jordan. An average bus ride in Amman costs 30 fils.

You need not be timid about trying the bus system. English is the second language in Jordan and widely spoken. Jordanians are extremely kind and hospitable to strangers and eager to help. If you are unsure, ask the bus driver or a passenger. You might also carry a piece of paper with your destination written in Arabic as an aid for such times when language does become a barrier.

Even though buses are easy and cheap, you will probably prefer to use taxis, which are reasonably priced, or the *taxi-service* system, which is efficient and inexpensive. *Service* (pronounced *servees*) are five-passenger cars, each passenger paying for one seat as on a bus. The *service* runs along set routes in town and to outlying areas. The cost is 35 to 50 fils per seat, no matter how far along the route you travel.

For inside Amman, most taxi-*service* leave from the main downtown square on King Faisal Street or adjacent side streets. If you plan an extended visit in Jordan, you will find it worthwhile to learn the bus and *taxi-service* system.

Taxis are all privately owned and operate within Amman and between cities, towns and villages. They can be recognized by their green license plates. Those with a white square on the front doors and a white light on the roof are *taxi-service*. The white square indicates, in Arabic, the route and destination. Cars with a yellow square on the front doors and a yellow light on the roof are regular taxis, and cost about 300 fils from one Jebel (or hill) to another. The name of the taxi firm is usually written in English as well as Arabic on the door of the taxi.

Intra-city *taxi-service* operate with set rates from fixed points in Amman, depending on the destination. All northbound *service* leave from Abdali Station, King Hussein Street, and Shab Sough Street (downtown behind the Gold Market). The southbound ones leave from Wahdat (near Amman New Camp).

Private taxi companies also offer seats-in-a-taxi to points inside Jordan as well as to the neighboring countries of Syria and Lebanon.

Sample *service* prices: *Southbound:* Madaba, .250 fils; Kerak, .600 fils; Wadi Musa (Petra), JD1. *Northbound:* Jerash, .350 fils; Ajlun, .500 fils; Irbid, .450 fils; Ramtha, .600 fils.

Northbound taxi companies, which also go to Damascus, are Hadad, Feras and Hilal. Southbound ones are Aqaba, Kabriti and Andalus (which also has a bus).

Car Rental: There are five car rental companies in Amman:

	Phone	**P.O. Box**
Avis, Jebel Amman	41350/44355	
Avis, Amman Airport	56347	305
Jordan Touring Company, Jebel Amman	44938	6951
National, Jebel Amman	39197	2020
Satellite, Abdali	25767	9180
Tyche, Jebel Amman	22195/25700	1300

Rates for Car Rentals range from JD2 per day for a small car to 3.500 for a large one, and 300 fils to 500 fils for each hour after 24 hours, plus 20 to 35 fils per kilometer. Weekly fees range from JD12 to 21 for rental only.

A car can be hired through hotels and travel agents. Or, you may hire a car and driver for the day from any taxi company. A taxi with driver for the day in Amman should be about JD5-6. Outside Amman the price depends on distance, but the following are sample prices:

From Amman to

Jerash	& return	half day	4.000
Jerash, Ajlun	& return	three-quarters day	6.500
Madaba, Mt. Nebo	& return	three-quarters day	3.500

Madaba, Kerak	& return	three-quarters day	8.000
Petra	& return	full day	12.000
Aqaba	& return	full day	15.000
Dead Sea	& return	half day	5.000
Desert Palaces	& return	half day	15.000
Azrak, Amra Palace	& return	half day	9.000
King Hussein (Allenby) Bridge	one way		4.000
Damascus	one way		7.500
Beirut	one way		12.000

By Train: There are no passenger trains in Jordan. Plans to rebuild the Hejaz Railway to Medina are being studied by a committee from the Ministries of Transportation of Jordan, Syria and Saudi Arabia.

The railway, built over an eight-year period by nearly 6,000 Turkish soldiers, started running in 1908. From Damascus to Medina the trip took three days, a vast and miraculous improvement in those days to Moslem pilgrims, who previously had to spend 40 to 50 days traveling in the fastest camel caravan.

The railway remained in full use for only six years, until 1914. With the outbreak of World War I and the Arab revolt against the Ottomans, it became an important military target and was repeatedly attacked. By 1917 most of the line was out of use, although the Ma'an (Jordan)–Damascus stretch continued to operate and is still running.

Reconstruction of the old line could cost $1 billion. Still-born efforts to revive the line have been made several times in the past 40 years—in 1935, 1938 and 1955. It was not until 1964, however, that actual work began. It resulted only in laying a stretch of new track from Ma'an to the Saudi border, still some distance from Medina.

The present plan is more ambitious. The intention is to build an entirely modern railway, replacing the old narrow-gauge track with the standard gauge now in use throughout Europe.

By Air: The only regularly scheduled internal air service in Jordan is Alia's flight to Aqaba four times weekly, at 8 A.M. on Mondays, Wednesdays, Saturdays and Sundays. It costs JD5 one way, JD10 round trip. Return flights are on the same days at 9:10 A.M. The jet flight takes 40 minutes.

Arab Wings, Alia's executive jet service, is available for local and long-distance flights. Alia is also planning to add helicopters.

MOTORING IN JORDAN

PRIVATE AUTOMOBILES. You may bring your automobile duty-free into Jordan for a maximum period of one year upon the presentation of a triptych issued by a recognized automobile club. If you sell the automobile in Jordan, the duty must be paid. You need a license for the vehicle. An international driver's license may be used on a short visit. Foreigners planning to live in Jordan must obtain a local driver's license.

Third-party automobile insurance is compulsory. Annual rates are JD13 for American cars and JD11 for non-American cars (subject to increase according to increase of limits of liabilities).

Comprehensive coverage is strongly recommended, and can be purchased locally at an annual cost of JD125-200 for American cars and JD60-150 for non-American cars (rates depend on type, value, horsepower and model of car).

ROAD CONDITIONS. Jordan has 7,000 miles of excellent roads, many of which have been added only in the past few years. The main highways run the length of the country, north-south, and its breadth, east-west. From these major arteries into and out of Amman other roads branch to give access to all the populated towns of the country.

With a few exceptions, most of the historic or otherwise interesting sights in Jordan can be reached over a paved road in an ordinary automobile or bus, on a half- or full-day tour. The main exception is a tour of the Umayyad desert palaces, which are accessible only by desert track and need a Land-Rover or similar high-built car with four-wheel drive.

Two highways lead from Amman to Aqaba, the King's Highway and the Desert Highway. A third road along the Dead Sea, when completed, will connect with a new road already finished through Wadi Araba to Aqaba.

Jordan's main highway connecting the East and West Banks runs from Amman to Jerusalem across the Jordan River at the King Hussein Bridge. It is open daily except Saturday from 7 A.M. to 1 P.M. *Service* from Amman is JD1.200 to the security point at the bridge; taxi fare is JD4. Another road via Salt crosses the river further north at the Prince Muhammad Bridge and continues to Nablus. It is open the same hours, but is not used by tourists.

There are no security regulations banning motoring in any part of Jordan, but there are several check points on major roads where you may be asked to show identification.

CAUTION should be used in driving in those parts of desert where there are no roads. It is absolutely foolhardy to strike off on one's own to remote areas of the desert; you could get lost. Now that the road across the desert to Azraq is surfaced, the trip, which once took all day, is an easy morning's excursion. The ease of such a journey could give the uninitiated a sense of false security. The desert is hostile terrain for the automobile, especially after rain and in the dead heat of summer. Hard desert tracks can suddenly turn into mud or soft sand into which car tires sink—and it takes several very strong people to pull them out. This is not meant to frighten anyone—travel in the desert is fabulous—but only to warn you to be careful and plan properly.

The Desert Police Patrol, who can be easily recognized by their splendid uniforms of khaki with red trim and red and white checked *kafiya,* are cooperative in arranging an escort for travel to remote areas of the desert where tourists are likely to lose their way. For your own protection, you are asked to check in at police posts stationed in the desert. You should comply with these requests.

GASOLINE AND SERVICE STATIONS. In town, gas and service stations are ample, but on the open road they are scarce. Be sure you have plenty of gas before starting, and for trips into the desert carry along an extra supply. Gasoline costs JD1.500 for 20 liter regular, JD2 for super.

Servicing is adequate on most Japanese, American and European cars. Low- and medium-priced cars give the best road service, as repairs are less likely to be needed and spare parts are more readily available.

AUTOMOBILE CLUB. Royal Automobile Club, Amman, phone 22467.

CITY MAPS AND WALKING. New, detailed maps of Amman are being made as we go to press, and should be available from the Tourist Office soon. Since Amman has very few name signs for streets in Arabic and even fewer in English, you should try to learn a few landmarks in town to enable you to find your way around quickly. Basically, Amman is built on seven hills, and each part or district is designated by the "Jebel" or hill where it is located. In the district where most of the hotels are situated—Jebel Amman—locations are designated by a series of roundabouts—*i.e.,* First Circle, Second Circle and Third Circle. The American Embassy and the Jordan Inter-Continental Hotel, two landmarks for American travelers, are located near the Third Circle on Jebel Amman.

TRANSPORTATION TO NEARBY COUNTRIES. Jordan Express Tourist Transport 64146 has daily bus service to Damascus. It leaves from Abdali Road at 8:00, 10:00 A.M.; 3:00, 5:00 P.M. in winter; 7:00, 9:00 A.M.; 3:00, 5:00 P.M. in summer. One way costs JD1.250.

PLANNING YOUR SIGHTSEEING. What to see in Jordan largely depends on the amount of time one has to spend. The country is compact and travel is easy. Many highlights can be seen in three days, but it takes at least a week to cover all the main attractions. Most places can be visited in a half-day from Amman; the others require a full day.

With a few exceptions, all historic or otherwise interesting sites can be reached by paved road in an ordinary automobile or bus.

On a long trip it is wise to start with a full gas tank and to carry a supply of drinking water. The Ministry of Tourism and Antiquities distributes free maps and literature.

For a three-to-four-day visit we suggest the following itinerary, which can be expanded to a week by adding other attractions or by dividing the first day into two half-days:

A city tour of Amman covering the Citadel, the Antiquities Museum, the

Roman Theater and folk museums will consume a morning. In the afternoon, a visit can be made to Jerash and, depending upon one's time and interest, it can be combined with a drive through the Debbin (Dibbeen) Park to Ajlun.

A second day will take in Madaba, Mt. Nebo and a drive through the Wadi Mujib to Kerak. To reduce travel time, one can return from Kerak by the desert road for an overnight in Amman. Other possibilities are to remain in Kerak or continue to Petra for overnight, though the latter makes for a long day. If this itinerary is chosen, it is essential to get an early start and to move along at a brisk pace.

Alternatively, one can drive to Petra via the desert road and return to Amman on the second or third day via Kerak and Madaba. We should also point out that since Madaba is so close to Amman, it can easily be visited on a short trip from the city and does not have to be part of a longer itinerary.

A third day can be spent in Petra. Many tours offered by U.S. operators unfortunately spend only a few hours in Petra. The minimum time needed to see the ancient city is two full days; anything less is cheating yourself of seeing properly one of the greatest sites in the world. Even three or four days is not too long for enthusiasts. Petra is spread over a large area, and simply cannot be covered in a hurry.

If you have the time, it is convenient to continue south from Petra to Aqaba, particularly if you would like to have a day or two on the beach. From Aqaba a short trip can be made into Wadi Rum, and for those with adequate time, a camping trip—with or without a camel caravan—can be arranged.

Another all-day excursion which can be made from Amman takes you to the Desert Castles east of the capital to Azraq. Several of these sites can be visited in a long half-day, but to make the complete circuit you will need a full day—and a vehicle with four-wheel drive.

These are the most important attractions in Jordan, but, as you will see in the following pages, there are many lesser-known places to visit. To include them would require a stay of two weeks.

Additional information and assistance in planning your tour is available from the Ministry of Tourism and Antiquities. Publications of the Ministry and such books as Lankester Harding's *Antiquities of Jordan* and Eugene Hoade's *East of the Jordan* (available at most bookshops) will also be useful. For those with academic or archeological interests, the annual reports of the Department of Antiquities are valuable.

EMERGENCY TELEPHONE NUMBERS

First Aid, Fire, Police	19
Ambulance (Government)	75111
Cablegram or Telegram	18
Civil Defense Rescue	24391/4
Fire Headquarters	22090
Jordan Electric Power Co.	36381/2
Municipal Water Service	37111/3

Police Headquarters	39141
Roving Patrol Rescue Police (English spoken)	
24-hour emergency	21111/37717

OTHER USEFUL NUMBERS

Airport Information (ALIA)	55205
American Center (USIS)	41520
British Council	36147
French Cultural Center	37009
Goethe Institute	41993

BY WAY OF BACKGROUND

Jordan in Arabic is *Al Urdan*. It is known officially as the Hashemite Kingdom of Jordan.

Located in the heart of the Middle East and the Arab world, it covers an area of approximately 37,300 square miles (about 35,100 square miles are on the East Bank, 2,165 square miles on the West Bank). The area is about the size of Indiana.

Jordan is bordered on the north by Syria, on the east by Iraq and Saudi Arabia, on the south by Saudi Arabia and the Gulf of Aqaba, its only sea outlet, which gives access to the Red Sea. On the west its boundary is the uneasy frontier with Israel established by the United Nations Armistice Agreement of 1949. In the subsequent war of 1967 the West Bank of the Jordan came under Israeli occupation.

Jordan's borders with Saudi Arabia were established in a series of agreements made by Great Britian in 1925. In an exchange of territory in 1965 Jordan's coastline on the Gulf of Aqaba was extended by about twelve miles. This border, which passes through almost rainless and unpopulated desert, established a zone where Jordan and Saudi Arabia would share revenues on an equal basis if oil were discovered in the area.

Physical Features

The country's major river is the famous Jordan, which starts from the melting snows of Mount Hermon in Syria and collects the waters of the Yarmuk and lesser streams on its journey south. After winding snakelike for 200 miles through the Jordan Valley, it reaches the Jericho oasis and empties into the Dead Sea, at 1306 feet below sea level, the lowest point on the earth's surface.

The Jordan Valley (El Ghor), together with the Dead Sea and Wadi Araba, forms one continuous depression through the country from north to south and is part of the Great Rift Valley of Africa and the Middle East. The depression is warm year-round, and with new irrigation it has enabled Jordan to develop a new agricultural base to its economy.

Rising out of the Jordan Valley to an average altitude of 3,000 and up to 5,400 feet are the hills of Biblical history. West of the Jordan, the hills of Judaea stretch from Samaria in the north to Beersheba in the south.

East of the river the mountains are divided into four districts by three steep gorges *(wadis)* with perennial streams. The four districts correspond roughly to the Kingdoms of the Old Testament: *Ajlun* (the Biblical land of Gilead) lies between the Yarmuk and Wadi Zerqa; *Balqa* (part of Moab and the lands of the Ammonites) is the area between Zerqa and Mujib; *Kerak* (the land of Moab) extends from Wadi Mujib to Wadi al Hasa, and *Ma'an* (the land of the Edomites and later of the Nabataeans) stretches from Wadi Hasa to the Gulf of Aqaba. Beyond the eastern highlands the ever-encroaching desert extends into Iraq on the east and Saudi Arabia on the south.

The Yarmuk River, the main tributary of the Jordan River, forms the border between Israel on the northwest, Syria on the northeast and Jordan on the south. The Zerqa River, the Jordan's second main tributary, rises and empties entirely inside the East Bank. It has been developed in recent years to provide irrigation for the lower eastern Jordan Valley.

Jordan's population is concentrated in the northern highlands of the country, where the major towns are located near the Jordan River system, and where rainfall is sufficient to support cultivation.

With 80 percent of its land as desert, needless to say arable land is the country's most valued resource. The East Ghor Canal, completed in 1966, has brought much of the Jordan Valley under irrigation. Additional projects in the Jordan Valley are aimed at further land reclamation, greater exploitation of water resources, and infrastructure development including construction of roads, bridges, dams and electrical plants to improve the quality of life for the farmers of the region and enable them to achieve maximum productivity from their efforts.

Jordan consists of a high plateau divided into ridges by valleys and gorges. Repeated earthquakes through the ages are evident throughout. In the north, toward the Syrian border, there are fields of broken lava and basaltic rock. The greater part of the country east of the Rift depression is desert, arid and sparsely populated. Most of the land is part of the great Syrian or north Arabian desert, consisting of salt flats and broad expanses of sand and dunes, particularly in the south.

The rolling hills and the low mountains support a meager and stunted vegetation most of the year, except in spring when these brown hillsides are carpeted with green grass and flowers. Toward the depression in the western part of the East Bank, there is a rise which evolves into the Jordanian highlands, a steppe of high limestone plateaus and an area of *wadis* which are dry except in the short winter rainy season.

Wheat, barley and other cereals, corn, tobacco, peanuts, fruit and vegetables are the chief crops in this area. The market furnished by the neighboring oil-producing countries has stimulated the cultivation of cash crops, including tomatoes, citrus fruit and potatoes. Government-sponsored agricultural extension work to prevent soil erosion and flash-flooding has also stimulated agricultural production. The development of dams and outlets for tributary streams from the plateau is significantly increasing the region's agricultural potential.

The People

The population, which numbers about 2.8 million, is preponderantly Arab in origin and Sunni Moslem in religion. The main schism in Islam occurred early in its history over the question of the rightful succession to the Prophet Muhammad. The orthodox group is called *Sunni* and the dissenting one *Shiite*.

About 7 percent of Jordanians are Christians. The country also has many distinctive ethnic groups such as Circassians, who are Sunni Moslems from the Caucasus.

According to the latest available figures, Jordan reckons its population as 2,200,000 East Bank; 600,000 West Bank.

The majority of the population lives in or near the capitals of Jordan's five main administrative districts: Amman, 1,180,000 (including the country's capital); Irbid, about 582,000; Balqa, 134,000; Kerak, 111,300, and Ma'an, 53,000. Population growth exceeds 3 percent annually, and half the population is under 15 years of age.

About one-third of the population are residents of what was formerly Transjordan; another 40 percent are Palestinian refugees from the wars of 1948 and 1967. About 11 percent of the population are nomadic or seminomadic tribes, *i.e.,* bedouin.

The original Jordanians are members of several hundred tribes who have lived in the area for centuries. Some came from Hejaz, the home of the Prophet Muhammad, and were soldiers and followers of the Arab armies who carried the banner of Islam out of Arabia in the 7th and 8th centuries. Others wandered into the land across the River Jordan from Palestine or from the south from Egypt or Yemen. Still others were pushed into the area by wars from the north or the south, or tracked across the Syrian desert from the Mesopotamia Valley in the east. Some have come from Hauran and Damascus in Syria and from Lebanon.

Those who trace their origins to antiquity do so through legends and poetry, the Arab's greatest body of literature. With the great movement of tribes, land ownership changed hands many times.

The Bedouin

To be a bedouin or to come from bedouin stock is a matter of pride for many Jordanians. The bedouin virtues and values are an important part of the Jordanian character—the traditional freedom of the desert, a sense of honor, pride in noble blood, bravery, generosity, hospitality, protection of the weak, emphasis on the importance of the family. Although some of the bedouin of Jordan are still nomads, most are in the transitional stage toward becoming settled villagers.

There are an estimated 40,000 bedouin in Jordan. Their camps are found mainly east of the Desert Highway in an area approximately 248 miles long and 155 miles wide. Settlements of semi-nomads are located near the Qaal Jafr and Azraq oases. The former is the site of a government-sponsored agricultural project. A similar settlement has been established near Al Hasa, the center of the phosphate industry, and several villages along the desert highway between Amman and Aqaba.

The following are among the main bedouin tribes:

—Beni Attiya, who wandered gradually into Transjordan from the Hejaz.

—al Majalli, who came to the Kerak district about 1759 to take refuge after a quarrel within the tribe.

—al Huweitat, who inhabit southern Jordan and claim descent from the Prophet through his daughter Fatima. They are thought to be descendants of the Nabataeans.

—al Isa, who claim to be an offshoot of a large tribe near the Euphrates.

—Beni Khalid, who claim relationship with a tribe of southern Iraq and who moved into Jordan about 100 years ago.

—al Sirhan, an ancient tribe said to originate in the Hauran (Syria), where they had established a semi-autonomous state which was overthrown by tribes pushing northward from the Hejaz. The easternmost desert of Jordan on the border of Iraq is known as Wadi Sirhan.

A description of the bedouin way of life will be found in the chapter on the Jordanian Way of Life.

The Circassians

The non-Arab Sunni Moslem minority known as Circassians (or *Sharakisah* in Arabic) settled in Jordan in the late 19th century. They trace their origins to two Indo-European Moslem tribes, the warrior Iassi and the Kossogs of the Caucasus, and are said to be akin to the Mameluks, who ruled Egypt from the 13th century to the Ottoman period.

In the wake of the Russian conquest of the Caucasus from the 10th to the 19th century there was a southward migration of Caucasian tribes. In the late 19th century, under Turkish Sultan Abdel Hamid as the traditional protector of all Moslems, a large number of Circassian refugees were settled on land in Turkey, Syria and Jordan. The first Circassian community reached Amman in 1878; others settled in Jerash, Naur and Wadi Seer.

In Jordan the Circassian tribes are known as the *Adigah*. They number about 25,000, and consist of several groups: the Kabardian tribes in Amman and Jerash; the Bzadugh and the Abzakh in Naur and Wadi-Seer. Another group, the Chechens, or Shishans, are politically and socially identified with the Circassians in Jordan but speak an entirely different language. Chechen settlements are found in Suweilih, Ruseifa, Zerqa, Sukhne and Azraq. The community numbers about 5,000.

The two seats allotted to the Circassians in the Jordanian Parliament are always occupied by a member of each community With no common tribal language between them, the two communities use Arabic to communicate.

The Circassians are credited with helping to recreate Amman, which was all but abandoned when they arrived in the late 19th century. They helped also to establish the first government and police force in Jordan, introduced a system of agriculture and helped to act as a settling influence on the surrounding area.

The Circassians today are predominantly agricultural and urban landlords, high government officials and top ranking army and air force officers. Said al Mufti, the best known of the community, was prime minister and a prominent member of the senate. A Chechen has been the Imam of the Zerqa mosque; another, the mayor of Zerqa.

Although the traditional tribal hierarchy is fading, it is still an important factor in marriage. On the other hand, as the Circassians change from an agrarian to an urbanized and culturally Arabized community, their intermarriage with Arab Jordanians, too, has increased.

The community's social and cultural life centers in the Circassian Charitable Association located in Amman. The Circassians have produced many of Jordan's best athletes.

Other Minorities

In addition to the Circassians there is also a small community of Turcomans, and another of Bahais who came from Iran in 1910 to settle on land purchased in 1879 by Abdul Baha Abbas, head of the Bahai faith.

Two small tribes, the Layathna of Wadi Musa and the al-Bdul in the hills around Petra, are Moslem. Because they have retained some Jewish customs, some scholars suggest they may be the descendents of the early Hebrew tribes.

Jordan's Christian population is divided into tribal groupings also. Many are descendants of the early Christian converts in the area and of the Greeks, Romans and Crusaders who ruled it. Some trace their origins to Egypt, Syria, Lebanon and, of course, to Nazareth, Bethlehem, Jerusalem and the West Bank towns, which have been predominantly Christian for centuries. The Christian denominations include Greek Orthodox, Catholic and Protestant. There is a small community of Armenians.

Also not to be overlooked is the country's fast-growing American, European and other foreign communities. The largest single group of Americans are those married to Jordanians—an estimated 300. After the war in Lebanon many American and British companies moved their regional headquarters to Amman because of its central location and easy access, comfort and relatively low cost of living, prevalence of spoken English and of trained or trainable personnel.

The Palestinians of Jordan—Refugees and Citizens

As noted earlier, about 40 percent of Jordan's population are Palestinians who came during and after the wars of 1948 and 1967. Some live in the ten refugee camps on the East Bank administered by UNRWA, the United Nations Relief and Works Agency for Palestine Refugees in the Near East. Four camps were set up in 1949 and six emergency camps were created after the 1967 war.

It is difficult to come by an exact count of the Palestinians in Jordan. The number of refugees who fled from the West Bank to the East Bank in the months following the war of 1967 is as controversial as the number of refugees following the war in 1948.

Uprooted from their homes and villages in 1948, and from their wretched camps of tents and mud and tin shacks in 1967, the refugees have twice exploded onto Jordan's economy and forced rapid urbanization, particularly in the Amman area.

From the outset, no distinctions were made in official Jordanian statistics between the settled population and the newcomers. Jordan gave all the refugees immediate citizenship. It has also offered the Palestinians greater opportunities for participating in political and economic life than has any other Arab state. They have been granted the same political rights as other citizens; they may purchase or rent homes or farms outside the camps and may engage in business and all forms of employment. Palestinians today hold dominant positions in industry, commerce, finance, civil services, educational and health services and other sectors of the economy.

The direct cost of providing basic services for the refugees is borne by UNRWA, various international aid programs, governments and welfare agencies. However, Jordan, although its budget did not label specific allocations, each time has increased its expenditure for the Ministries of Education, Health and Social Affairs, Labor, Information, and Development and Reconstruction to extend these services and benefits to them.

Although Jordan accepted the 1974 resolution of the Rabat

Conference that the Palestine Liberation Organization represents the Palestinians, all West Bankers have continued to be Jordanian citizens, and the West Bank members of the Jordanian Parliament have continued to receive their salaries without interruption since 1967. With the changed political realities following Egyptian President Sadat's peace initiative in November 1977, the future of the West Bank is anything but clear. Jordan adheres to U.N. Resolution 242 as the basis of any peace negotiations.

Government

Jordan is a constitutional monarchy with a bicameral legislature. It is headed by King Hussein, who succeeded to the throne in 1952. The King's younger brother Prince Hassan was named Crown Prince in 1965. The official religion of Jordan is Islam.

Legislative power is vested in the National Assembly and the King. The National Assembly consists of two houses, the Senate and the House of Representatives. The latter has 60 members elected by direct secret ballot of all citizens over 18 years of age. Thirty of the members come from the East Bank and 30 from the West Bank. Members are elected for a four-year term of office.

The Senate consists of 30 members who are appointed by the King upon recommendation of the Cabinet. Senators must not be related to the King, must be over 40 years of age, and are chosen from present and former prime ministers, other ministers and past ambassadors, and from the members of the civil and *shari'a* courts (Islamic law courts). They may be retired army generals or former members of the House of Representatives. Senators are appointed for four years and may be reappointed.

The King approves laws and promulgates them. He is empowered to declare war, conclude peace and sign treaties, which must be approved by the National Assembly. He orders the holding of elections, convenes and adjourns the House, and appoints the prime minister and the speaker of the Senate.

The prime minister selects his cabinet; he and the cabinet are responsible to the Parliament.

The Council of Ministers, consisting of the prime minister, president of the council and his ministers, conducts all affairs of state both internal and external.

The Constitution provides that the cabinet be responsible to Parliament. The King is empowered to dissolve Parliament and delay calling elections for a period of 12 months.

The Constitution provides that there be no discrimination on account of race, religion or language among Jordanian citizens and that there be equal opportunities in work and education. It provides for individual freedom, a free press, for schools to be established freely provided they follow a recognized curriculum and educational policy, and free and compulsory elementary education.

Administratively, the East Bank is divided into five major districts, known as *Muhafezate* (governorates) or *liwa:* Amman, Balqa, Irbid, Kerak and Ma'an. The West Bank is divided into the three governorates of al-Quds (Jerusalem), Nablus and al Khalil (Hebron). Each governorate is centered around a major town which is the political and economic hub of the surrounding area.

Great Britain recognized Transjordan as a sovereign independent state by a treaty signed in London on March 22, 1946. Emir Abdallah, King Hussein's grandfather, assumed the title of King on May 25, 1946. In June 1946, upon ratification of the Anglo-Jordanian treaty, the name of the territory was changed to the Hashemite Kingdom of Transjordan. Following the armistice in 1949 Central Palestine, as the West Bank was known, joined Transjordan in 1950.

Economy

Jordan's gross national product has grown from about JD199 million in 1971 to over JD567 million in 1977, and this would appear to be only the beginning.

Although only about 10 percent of Jordan's land can be cultivated, agriculture is one of the most important sectors of the economy, accounting for 10 percent of the gross domestic product but employing over half of the population. In the development of agriculture, Jordan has put its greatest emphasis on expanding the irrigation facilities in the Jordan Valley. The Jordan Valley Development project, begun in 1958, has brought 30,000 acres under cultivation and will have a total of 90,000 acres available when all stages are completed.

At the time of the 1967 war an estimated 80 percent of the fruit-growing area, 45 percent of the vegetable area and 25 percent of the cereal area were on the West Bank. Jordan's development of the East Bank of the Jordan Valley over the past decade has, however, altered the relative significance of these percentages. (A description of the Jordan Valley development is available in a later chapter.)

Agriculture is carried on in three regions.

The Jordan Valley, known as Al Ghor, is part of the Dead Sea Basin. It will have 100,000 acres available for cultivation when current projects are completed. The entire area is below sea level and watered by irrigation. It lies between the Yarmuk River in the north, the Jordan River on the west, the Dead Sea in the south and the Eastern Highlands. Because of its climate two crops are produced annually, and it has the potential for three. The region's early production capability, compared with other areas and neighboring countries, also gives it a commercial advantage. The Ghor produces a wide variety of fruits and vegetables, a large part of which are exported to the oil-producing countries of the Arabian Peninsula.

The Ghor region is divided into two main parts, the North Ghor with about 81,250 acres of cultivable land, and the South Ghor with 15,000 acres. The Dead Sea lies between. The main source of water in the North Ghor is the Yarmuk River and tributaries of the Jordan River. The annual discharge of water is approximately 660 million cubic meters. Water in the South Ghor comes from the Mujib and Hasa Valleys and a number of lesser streams and springs. The annual discharge is around 90 million cubic meters.

The Highland region, which is dependent on rainfall, grows mainly wheat, barley, beans and tobacco. Terracing and planting of some fruit trees has been started. For the most part land holdings are fragmented and small. Soil erosion and erratic rainfall are the major problems, but afforestation programs have been started to help combat the problem, and exploitation of springs and groundwater are helping to regulate water supplies.

The Highland region lies between the Yarmuk River and the Syrian border on the north, the Ghor and Wadi Araba in the west, Wadi Musa in the south, and the Badia region in the east and south. Average rainfall is 200-600 mm. in the north and middle parts; 200-300 mm. in the southern part of the region. The average annual rainfall in the Highlands represents 44 percent of the total annual rainfall in Jordan. Other sources of water are scattered springs and small amounts of groundwater throughout the highlands. Land partially irrigated by springs is around 15,000 acres, while areas under irrigation from groundwater are estimated to be about 3,250 acres.

The Badia or desert region is by far the largest in terms of area and is used mainly for grazing of sheep, goats and camel in the valleys and rain-fed areas. This region lies south and east of the Highland region and occupies 87 percent of Jordan east of the Jordan River.

Research has shown that underground water is available to irrigate 7,500 acres in the north, but only 4,250 acres are presently utilized. In the south, groundwater could irrigate an estimated 22,000 acres of which less than a thousand are presently utilized.

Tourism, which was Jordan's most important source of foreign exchange prior to the war of 1967, suffered a crushing blow with the loss of Jerusalem and other sites on the West Bank. In the past few years, however, it has made a comeback and has surpassed its pre-1967 level. Income from tourism after the Israeli occupation of the West Bank in 1967 dropped to JD4.6 million in 1968 as compared with JD11.3 million in 1966, which had been the peak year. But by 1974 it had reached JD17.3 million, an increase of 53 percent, and by 1976 receipts from tourism were JD68.86 million and the number of visitors was 1,063,294—compared to 617,000 in 1966.

New projects have included the completion of a new airport at Aqaba in 1971, a highway to the Saudi Arabian border, and many new hotels. A new international airport for Amman is under construction with West German aid at a cost of about JD30 million and is scheduled for completion by 1980. And a minimum of 5,000 beds will be added to the hotel plant in the next three years.

Industry, concentrated in Amman, Irbid and Zerqa, is recent and accounts for approximately 12 percent of the GDP. Its growth is limited to some extent by the country's lack of certain raw materials and a small home market. However, its real growth is as a manufacturing and distribution center for the Middle East. Industry is playing an increasingly important role in the economy and growing annually as a source of revenue. Jordan's five-year plan aims at an annual growth rate of 14 percent in the industrial sector.

Since 80 percent of manufacturing and mining has been concentrated in the East Bank before the war in 1967, the occupation of the West Bank had only a minor effect on this sector.

Phosphate rock, located at Wadi al Hasa, 90 miles south of Amman, is Jordan's most important mineral resource, with reserves estimated at about 3 billion tons. It is mined at Al Hasa and Ruseifa; most is exported. Another of the country's major minerals is potash, which is extracted from an area along the east bank of the Dead Sea.

Oil has not been discovered in any commercially feasible quantity in Jordan, although geologists believe that there is oil here and the government continues to encourage oil companies to explore for it. If oil is discovered in commercial quantities, the government will take a 65 percent share and the company 35 percent.

A large proportion of local demand for refined oil products is met by the Jordanian Refinery Company at Zerqa, with an output of about 828,000 tons per year. The refinery is supplied from Tapline, which runs through the country from Saudi Arabia to Lebanon.

Jordan may be the poor kid on the block when it comes to oil, but it is rich in minerals—more than two dozen of them, in addition to phosphate and potash, can be exploited commercially. The major one is copper—about 55 million tons—in the Wadi Araba, the site of mines exploited before King Solomon. A pilot plant for the region is to be built under the current Five-Year Plan. The manganese ore in the Dead Sea area is said to have a high copper content, and there are copper deposits near Aqaba. Among other known minerals are cobalt, iron ore and uranium.

The target of the current Five-Year Plan is to increase Jordan's income from mineral sales from JD45 million in 1975 to JD144 million in 1980, or an average annual increase of 26 percent. This sector will receive 30 percent of the planned investment for the country under the Plan and is slated to account for over 28 percent of the GDP by 1980.

Manufactured and processed goods include cement, batteries, cigarettes, matches and some processed food, and there has been significant expansion into new industries such as clothing, pharmaceuticals, marble, soaps, olive oil, toys and beer. Work is under way to establish large factories for the production of paper, ceramics, processed food, detergents, woolen cloth, steel tubes, and a vehicle assembly plant, among others.

Recently a footwear manufacturing company became the first wholly private Jordanian-American joint industrial venture. International Leather Products Co., Inc., is owned equally by Wolverine World Wide, Inc., and the Jordan Tanning Company. Its new 25,000-square-foot facility is capable of producing 250,000 pairs of shoes a year for the Middle East market and is expected to employ about 150 Jordanians. The Jordan Tanning Company, located in Amman, owns and operates one of the most modern cowhide tanneries in the Arab countries. Wolverine World Wide, headquartered in Rockford, Michigan, manufactures and markets Hush Puppies and a variety of other footwear. The joint venture company is licensed to produce and market footwear under the Hush Puppies and Wolverine labels.

In the 1976-80 development plan JD100 million has been earmarked for a phosphate fertilizer complex in Aqaba; JD140 million for potash extraction at the Dead Sea by the Arab Potash Company, which is already in operation; expansion of the cement factory at

Fuheis; establishment of another cement factory costing JD21.3 million; and a textile factory at Zerqa costing JD3 million. Combined government and private investment in the mining and manufacturing sector under the five year period of the plan is expected to reach over a billion dollars.

The Amman Stock Exchange, the first in Jordan and one of the few in the Arab World, opened for business in January 1978. All transactions in shares of listed Jordanian companies must now be conducted through licensed brokers on the floor of the Exchange. Private trades between shareholders outside the company are exempted.

Initially, trading on the Exchange will be restricted to the 62 Jordanian public shareholding companies with a paid-up capital of over $300,000. The annual trading volume, based on studies of these companies, is expected to reach $30 million in 1979.

Total assets of these companies amount to $434.7 million. Total number of shareholders are 170,367, who among them hold a total of 68,838,681 shares.

During the 1950s and 1960s the government placed great emphasis on the development of a modern transportation system. Now there are good all-weather roads from Amman to Aqaba, Azraq, Jerusalem, Damascus and Mafraq on the Iraqi frontier. Other roads that have been developed run from Yarmuk to the Dead Sea, Safi-Aqaba, Ma'an-Rum and Azraq to the Saudi border.

The railway consists of a 52-mile line between Amman and the Syrian border, a 93-mile line between Amman and Hasa, a 157-mile line between Hasa and Aqaba through Hittiya, and a 24-mile line between Ma'an and Ras Naqab.

Telephone lines in the cities are insufficient, and the Five Year Plan aims to modernize and expand the system. Telex services operate through four exchanges at Amman, Aqaba, Irbid and Zerqa. A new exchange is to be built in Amman at the cost of JD1 million to provide 700 and later 1,000 additional lines.

Jordan has long been dependent on foreign aid. Its budget deficits are largely financed with loans and grants from the oil-rich Arab Gulf states and the West. U.S. budgetary support in 1977 amounted to JD14 million. An additional JD19.3 million in budgetary assistance was provided in 1976 by other Arab countries, chiefly Saudi Arabia and the Gulf states. U.N. agencies, the Kuwait Fund, and a number of Western countries—notably Great Britain and West Germany—also provide assistance.

The 1976-80 plan calls for investment of JD765 million and an annual growth rate in GDP of 11.9 percent. This will mean an overall increase in the five years of 75.2 percent, from JD290 million to JD508 million. Jordan's goal is fiscal independence by 1980.

It should be noted that, meager as Jordan's resources may be, one of its most surprising aspects to a visitor is its vitality. The accomplishments of this young nation are amazing and have come as a result of the ingenuity, resourcefulness and sheer determination of its people and the leadership of King Hussein. They evoke profound admiration.

JORDAN—TEN MILLENNIA

A Brief History

The Hashemite Kingdom of Jordan is, politically, only 33 years old. Yet, as a land where people have lived, Jordan is as old as civilization itself. Indeed, here in the Jordan Valley the earliest evidence of man's communal life is found.

Archaeologists tell us that Jordan was occupied by settled communities, such as Beida and Jericho, as early as 7000 B.C. Virtually all migrations and conquering armies of ancient times had to cross this land bridge which connected Asia and Africa. Over the centuries many of their numbers settled in the Jordan Valley and the surrounding highlands.

Jordan first appears prominently in the Bible with the arrival of Abraham in the Land of Canaan. The event probably corresponds with the great migration of a northwestern Semitic tribe, the Amorites, who appeared in Jordan about 2000 B.C.

During the 17th century B.C. North Palestine, as it was later called, was conquered by the Biblical Horites, later to be pushed out by the Edomites (Gen. 36:20). The southern portion was taken over by the Hyksos (the Shepherd Kings), who introduced horse-drawn chariots and subsequently revolutionized the art of war. Culturally and politically, Palestine was part of the Hyksos Empire of Egypt until the Hyksos were expelled from Egypt in 1550 B.C.

Less than a century later, during the reign of Egyptian Queen Hatshepsut, Palestine and southern Syria again came under the control of Egypt. A revolt against the Egyptians was put down by Hatshepsut's successor, Thothmes III, and for another century Palestine remained under Egyptian rule. Most of what is known about the period comes from a cache of a hundred or more letters found at Tell al-Amarna in Upper Egypt. These letters, which had been sent from Palestine to Egypt in the 15th and 14th centuries B.C., revealed that Egypt's main interest in Palestine was to use it to defend Phoenicia and southern Syria against the Hittites advancing from the north. In the 13th century the Hittites were finally checked by Ramses II at Kadesh on the Orontes in Syria.

At about the same time the Phoenician coast was invaded by the "Sea People" from the Aegean, called the Philistines. Within 150 years after the settling of the coast the Philistines (from whom Palestine gets its name) had conquered all Palestine. Simultaneously, three other groups settled east of the Jordan: Edomites in the south, Moabites east of the Dead Sea, and Ammonites east of Gilead on the edge of the Syrian Desert.

According to the Bible, the Edomites were the descendants of Esau (Gen. 36:9) and the Moabites and Ammonites were descended from Lot (Gen. 19:37, 38). The Ammonites are described as having taken their land from the Zamzummim, a giant race, and established their capital at Rabbath Ammon, present-day Amman (Deut. 2:20).

Another prominent Biblical tribe, the Amorites, were located at Heshbon (Hisban), their capital, and their territory extended from the Dead Sea to the Lake of Galilee. Their king was Sihon, who defeated the King of Moab (Num. 21:26).

Another Amorite Kingdom, Bashan, had its capital at Edrei (Dera'a). Its King was Og, and its territory was situated north of the Ammonites, from Jabbok (Wadi Zerqa) to the Yarmuk (Deut. 3).

The period introduced the next important episode involving Jordan in Biblical history. In the late 14th or early 13th century B.C. the Israelites left Egypt, and after their long wandering in the wilderness moved north into the land of the Edomites. The Edomites refused them permission to pass through their land and forced them to detour northeast through the desert to reach the

Arnon River, the north boundary of Moab (Num. 21:21). The weakness of the local rulers made it easy for the newcomers to occupy the hill country of Transjordan.

Historians and archaeologists vary widely on the dates of the Philistine invasion, the settlement of the Edomites, Moabites and Ammonites, and the Exodus. Some authorities date the Exodus as early as the 15th century B.C. Many, however, call Ramses II the Pharaoh of the Oppression and his successor, Meremptah, the Pharaoh of the Exodus. This, then, would place the Exodus in the mid-13th century.

After defeating the Amorites and King Og of Bashan, Moses moved south to conquer Moab. He then alotted the newly won lands of Transjordan to the children of Reuben, Gad, and half the tribe of Manasseh.

After the death of Moses, Joshua with the twelve tribes crossed the Jordan (whose waters divided as did those of the Red Sea) and conquered Jericho. (Kathleen Kenyon in *Digging Up Jericho* dates the fall of Jericho to Joshua in the last quarter of the 14th century.)

By the success of his campaigns in the south and north, Joshua became master of the whole territory and divided the land among the tribes.

In the two centuries following Joshua's death, the Israelites were constantly at war with the Philistines. The slaying of Saul, who had been made king of all Israel in 1020 B.C., signaled Israel's defeat. The final blow came when the Philistines captured the Ark of the Covenant, symbol of unity in the Israelite tribes.

Under the leadership of David (c. 1000-961 B.C.), Israel's strength returned. After consolidating his position in Palestine, David crossed east over Jordan and conquered the three states of Edom, Moab and Ammon (2 Sam. 10). Later he seized part of Syria and established his control over the nomadic tribes as far east as the Euphrates River.

David was followed by Solomon (c. 961-922), whose reign was the high mark in Israel's political history and economic expansion. With the aid of the Phoenicians, Solomon developed trade between the Mediterranean, Red Sea and African coasts. By using the camel caravan he extended his trade in the Arabian Peninsula as far south as Sheba (Yemen). The copper mines of Edom were exploited and refineries constructed at Ezion-Geber (Tell al-Khalifa, near Aqaba).

Solomon's lavishness had been maintained by heavy taxes and conscription. Resentment over the burden led to revolt in the northern part of Israel after his death. (Eugene Hoade in *Guide to the Holy Land* places Solomon's death in 930 B.C.) Meanwhile Judah, the southern part, formed an alliance with Syria against north Israel. War broke out between the two groups, and in the struggle that followed north Israel lost Ammon, Moab and Edom. For the next two centuries the northern part was known as Israel, the southern part as Judah.

During the 9th century B.C., at the time of the great prophets Elijah and Elisha, a new capital was built at Samaria. Omri's son, Ahab, married the infamous Jezebel, a Phoenician princess. Under her influence worship of the pagan gods returned to Israel. As a result, Ahab was alternately hero and villain in the stories of the prophets.

Ahab was defeated about 850 B.C. by Mesha, King of Moab. The story is recorded on the famous "Moabite Stone" or Mesha Stele found at Dhiban. The Omrite dynasty ended amid torrents of blood and was followed by the dynasty of Jehu, which lasted until the mid-8th century.

Within a few years after Arpad in Syria had fallen to the Assyrian king Tiglath-Pileser III (745-727 B.C.), all Palestine and Jordan were in Assyrian hands, who "carried them away even the Reubenites, the Gadites and the half tribe of Manasseh." (1 Chron. 5:26). Lastly, Samaria fell to the Assyrians under Sargon II (721-705 B.C.), and Israel became extinct politically. Assyrian records of this period make reference to the Nabataeans, who occupied the territory south and east of Edom. These are the earliest historical mentions of the Nabataeans found to date.

In the following century Judah, the sole heir of the glories of David and Solomon, revived under the moral guidance of Isaiah and the kingship of Josiah, only to fall later to the armies of Nebuchadnezzar (2 Kings 24:1-4). Jerusalem was destroyed in 587 B.C. and the Jews were taken captive to Babylon. The Prophet Jeremiah, having foreseen these events, repeatedly warned his people.

After Cyrus came to power in Persia in 539 B.C. and extended his empire to Syria and Palestine, he allowed the Jews to return to Palestine and to rebuild the temple in Jerusalem.

During Alexander the Great's campaigns in the East, Palestine was merely a corridor to Egypt. His armies confined their attacks to the coastal cities which might have been used as bases for the Persian fleet.

After Alexander's death, his empire was divided among his generals. Palestine and parts of Syria and Phoenicia fell to Ptolemy, who established a dynasty in Egypt that lasted 300 years. The northern boundary of Palestine was set at Tripoli (Lebanon) on the

Nahr el-Kabir. Syria went to Seleucus, who disputed Ptolemy's claim to Palestine and Phoenicia. The dispute resulted in war five times within a century, and was only settled when Palestine passed into the hands of the Seleucids in 198 B.C.

Early in the following century the Seleucids under Antiochus invaded Egypt, and later attacked Jerusalem. They seized the city's wealth, forbade many religious practices of the Jews, and set up an alter to Zeus in the Temple of Jerusalem. This last act was resisted by a section of the population under the leadership of Judas Maccabaeus. Later, because of the corruption of the high priests and the weakness of the Seleucids, Judas' followers were able to establish a dynasty. They were granted the office of high priest and were in time recognized as secular rulers as well.

Upon the death of Antiochus Sidetes, the last great Seleucid king, John Hyrcanus I (135-104 B.C.) extended the boundaries of Judea and Samaria. His successors further enlarged the territory and expanded their rule over Transjordan and the coastal cities. Upon his death, however, his brothers, Aristobulus and Hyrcanus II, quarreled over the succession and appealed to Rome for assistance.

The Romans under Pompey took Damascus in 64 B.C. and Jerusalem in 63 B.C., ending the Seleucid Kingdom. Hyrcanus II was appointed high priest without the title of king. Pompey taxed the Jews and curtailed their domain. After Pompey's death, Antipater (governor of Idumaea, supporter of Hyrcanus II, and father of Herod the Great) was granted Roman citizenship in return for his services to Julius Caesar and awarded the title of Procurator of Judea. His sons were made governors of Jerusalem and Galilee.

In 40 B.C. Parthian troops unexpectedly occupied Palestine. They favored Antigonus as the legitimate heir in Judea, and installed him as king and high priest. Herod escaped to Rome.

In Rome, Herod was recognized as King of Judea by the Senate with the approval of Octavian and Mark Antony. He returned to Palestine in 39 B.C., and with the aid of Roman troops expelled the Parthians. Under Herod's long reign (37 B.C.–A.D. 4) Palestine enjoyed a period of peace and prosperity. Only in his last years did he become the vicious figure tradition has made so familiar.

On Herod's death, rule of the country was divided. A period of unrest followed, and finally erupted in A.D. 66. The following year the Roman army of Vespasian and his son, Titus, captured Galilee. Four years later Jerusalem fell and the Temple was destroyed. Palestine became the Province of Judea, administered by the Commander of the 10th Roman Legion.

At first, the Romans attempted to reconcile the Jews by a policy of leniency. When this failed, Hadrian (in Syria) issued an edict to the Jews that led to another outbreak in 132. Hadrian put down the revolt, turned Jerusalem into a Roman colony, built pagan temples on Mount Moriah and Mount Golgotha, and renamed the city Aelia Capitolina.

About the time of the Persian occupation in the 6th century B.C., the Nabataean Arabs became prominent in south Jordan. They established their capital at Petra, and for 600 years held the land formerly occupied by the Edomites. The location of their territory astride the southern and eastern trade routes from south Arabia and Egypt to Syria enabled them to demand high tariffs for protecting the caravans. Taking advantage of the frequent wars between the Seleucids and the Ptolemies, the Nabataeans extended their land north into Moab, west into the Negev, east to the Euphrates and south along the Red Sea.

At the time of the Natabaean expansion in the south, a confederation of ten cities situated on both sides of the Jordan came into being in the north. The Decapolis, as it was called, was patterned after Greek cities in language, culture and religion.

The original cities were probably Seythopolis (Beisan), Pella (Khirbet Fahil), Dion (Husn), Gadara (Um Qais), Hippos (Fiq), Gerasa (Jerash), Philadelphia (Amman), Kamatha (Qanawat), Raphana (Al Rafah), and Damascus. All except one were east of the Jordan. Apparently the cities were never a fixed group of ten; cities joined and withdrew. Among them were Arbila (Irbid), Capitolias (Beit Ras), Edrei (Deraa) and Bosra (in Syria). Pella, Dion and Gerasa are thought to have been founded by Greek soldiers. The others were older towns.

On the arrival of Pompey, the Romans formed the towns of the Decapolis into a military alliance for self-protection against the Jews, the Nabataeans and the desert tribes. Later the Emperor Trajan joined Perea, the district between Arnon and the Decapolis, with the latter to create the Province of Arabia (90 A.D.).

The capital of the new province, Arabia Petraea, was first at Petra and then at Bosra in Syria. The third legion (Cyrenaica) was posted in the north and the fourth (Martia) in the south of the country. Two great camps built to accommodate the latter, at Lajjun near Kerak and Adhruh near Petra, can still be seen. The great road from Bosra to Aqaba was begun by Trajan and finished under Hadrian.

Christianity gained a foothold in Palestine and Jordan between the second and third centuries and spread rapidly after the conversion of Constantine in the fourth century. Under the Byzantines the area enjoyed a period of peace and prosperity for 200 years. During the reign of Justinian (527-565) a large number of churches were built and pilgrimage was fostered. East of the Jordan approximately 20 places were episcopal sees in the Byzantine period, and many of them still have titular bishops.

The country's tranquility ended abruptly in A.D. 614, when the Persians, aided by the Jews who wanted to avenge their misfortunes, swept through the country, devastating it as they went.

Coming of Islam

Not long after the Persian conquest a new faith was born deep in the heart of Arabia under the leadership of the Prophet Muhammad. Fired with the zeal of Islam, the new converts marched out of the desert, and within less than a century after Muhammad's death in 632 had conquered the lands from the Atlantic on the west to the Indus River on the east. The empire they established was more extensive than Rome's at its zenith. More important, the religion of Islam and the culture of the Arabs left an indelible mark on the history of the lands they conquered, especially in North Africa and the Middle East.

The weakened state of the Byzantine Empire had enabled the Arab armies to move swiftly. The first battle between the Moslems and Byzantines took place in 629 at Mautah (near Kerak), where the Moslems were defeated and three of their leaders—Zaid ibn Harith, Jaafer ibn Abu Talib and Abdallah ibn Ruaha—were killed. They are buried in Mazar, where a mosque enshrines their tombs. The battle might be called the Arabs' Dunkirk, for it forced them to return to Medina, regroup and plan. They were at this time under the leadership of Khalid ibn Walid, who was to become one of history's greatest military geniuses.

The following year Muhammad himself led an expedition against the oasis of Tabuk. He made agreements with neighboring settlements granting the people security and the right to retain their property and religion on condition that they paid an annual tribute. These settlements were Ailah ('Aqaba), whose population was Christian; Maqna, south of Ailah, with a Jewish population; Adhruh and al-Jarba, north of it, also Christian. These were the only places outside of Arabia where Islam reached during the lifetime of the Prophet; all are in present-day Jordan.

In 633 A.D. the Arabs launched an invasion of Jordan and Syria, beginning their 100 years of conquest. The first engagement took place in the Wadi 'Araba, where Yazid defeated Sergius, the patriarch of Palestine. The country was soon overrun, and only some towns, such as Jerusalem and Caesarea, west of the Jordan, held out. The Emperor Heraclius with an army of 50,000 marched south to meet the Moslem troops at the juncture of the Yarmuk and Ruqqad, near the present al Yaqusah, on Aug. 20, 636. The Moslems won and the rest of the country surrendered, and by 640 all Palestine and Syria were under Moslem control. Mu'awiayah, the first caliph of the Umayyad dynasty, transferred the seat of the caliphate from Mecca to Damascus, where it remained until the Abbassids seized power and transferred the Caliphate to Baghdad in 750.

As long as the capital of the empire was in Damascus, Jordan, which lies on the route between Damascus and Arabia, continued to have some importance. The love of the Umayyad for the desert was another reason, as attested to by the ruins of many Umayyad palaces in the Jordan desert.

After the Abbassids transferred the capital to Baghdad, however, Jordan fell into decay. Jordan and Palestine remained part of the Arab Empire until 1099, when the Crusaders created the Latin Kingdom of Jerusalem.

The Crusaders

The Principality of Transjordan (Oultre-Jordain) was the most important fief of the kingdom, and its capital, Le Krak or La Pierre du Desert (ancient Kir Moab, present-day Kerak), was the center of all Crusader activity east of the Jordan. The principality extended from Wadi Zerqa Ma'in to the Gulf of Aqaba. Other fortresses were built at Shobak (Montreal), Wadi Musa (Le Vaux Moyse) and Jeziret Far'on (Isle de Graye). From these fortresses, and often in violation of truces, the Crusaders attacked Moslem caravans plying between Damascus, Mecca and Egypt. Qal'at el Rabad at Ajlun was built by one of Saladin's generals to protect the caravans against the Crusaders.

In 1187 Jerusalem fell to Saladin (Salah ed-Din) and Palestine was restored to the Arabs. In the early 13th century, Mongol tribes from central Asia seized Jerusalem and with the aid of Egypt under the Mameluks, marched on Syria. After a quarrel with the Mameluks, the Mongols withdrew, thus enabling the Mameluks, under Baybars and Qalawun, to capture the remaining Crusader relics in the

Levant. By the close of the century the Crusaders had vanished from the Holy Land.

The 14th century opened with another Mongol devastation, this time at the hands of Timur (Tamerlane). A century later all the Middle East fell to the Ottoman Turks, and for the next 400 years Palestine and Jordan were to be an Ottoman province.

The Turks' only concern with Jordan was to guard the pilgrim's road to Mecca. Its precise route changed several times through the centuries, but from the time of the Turks in the 16th century pilgrims took only one road from Damascus to Mecca through Jordan because the Turks built a series of fortified watering places which they kept garrisoned on the pilgrims' behalf. In Jordan the principal stations were Mafraq, Zerqa, Dab'a, Qatrana, Hasa, Aneiza, Ma'an, Aqaba and El Mudawwara. Today, the route of the railway and the Desert Highway almost parallel the old pilgrims' route, and ruins of the forts can still be seen.

At Mezerib in the north and at Ma'an in the south the caravans stopped for periods of a week to ten days to make final arrangements and to enable pilgrims from southern Lebanon and west of the Jordan to join.

At the opening of the 19th century, after Napoleon's unsuccessful campaign in Egypt, Palestine was drawn into the affairs of the European powers and became part of the "Eastern Question." Protection of religious shrines in the Holy Land became the pretext for European intervention in the area. Rivalries between the religious communities became so intense that their disputes were one of the immediate causes of the Crimean War.

In 1855, for the first time since the Crusades, a cross was carried through the streets of Jerusalem and Christians were allowed to visit the Dome of the Rock. The next fifty years saw the arrival of many missionary groups from Europe and America.

Also from the early 19th century, European explorers began to uncover the ancient sites so long lost to the western world, and their tales of adventure, such as Charles Doughty's *Travels in Arabia Deserta,* excited all Europe to follow in their path. Among the most famous was the Swiss explorer Burckhardt who discovered Petra in Jordan and Abu Simbel in Egypt.

During World War I Palestine and Jordan, as part of the Ottoman Empire, were garrisoned with Turkish troops. The Sherif of Mecca, Emir Hussein of the Hashemite family of Hejaz, sided with the allies. The Hashemites, the present ruling family of Jordan, trace their ancestry to the Prophet Muhammad, who was a member of the Hashem clan.

Modern Jordan

The history of modern Jordan begins with the drive to rid the country of the Turkish yoke. Indeed, the desire for independence from the Ottomans became the force that unified the Arabs from Syria to Arabia and from Egypt to Iraq.

In 1914 Hussein, the Sherif of Mecca, and great-grandfather of the present King Hussein of Jordan, assumed leadership of the Arab nationalist movement, and the Arab Revolt was under way by June of 1916. Hussein's son, Emir Faisal, with the aid of the British Colonel T.E. Lawrence—the legendary "Lawrence of Arabia"— took charge of the military campaign. The following year the Arab army captured Aqaba, and, almost four centuries to the year after the Ottoman conquest, together with the British troops, they took Jerusalem.

At the end of the war Transjordan and Palestine were placed under British Mandate by the League of Nations. By October 1920, however, Emir Abdullah, the second son of Emir Hussein, arrived in Ma'an in southern Jordan with the aim of liberating the land. In March of 1921 he entered Amman and established the Emirate of Trans-Jordan. He met with Winston Churchill in Jerusalem and secured British recognition of the Emirate. Britain remained as the mandatory power. Concurrently, the French established their mandate over Syria and Lebanon, and Emir Faisal was given the throne of Iraq.

On May 25, 1923, the British formally recognized the independent government of Trans-Jordan under Emir Abdullah. Five years later the Anglo-Jordanian Treaty was signed.

With a small number of British advisers headed by a British resident, Emir Abdullah ruled as an autocrat until 1939. In that year the power of the British resident was reduced, a cabinet responsible to the Emir was established, and a legislative assembly of twenty members was elected.

During World War II the Arab Legion aided the British in putting down an attempted pro-German coup in Iraq and fought against the Vichy French in Syria.

Following World War II, the British Mandate was ended and on May 25, 1946 the Emirate of Transjordan became a Kingdom with

Abdullah as King. (This is the date which is celebrated as Jordan's Independence Day.)

In 1947, the United Nations General Assembly recommended the partition of Palestine, and in the following year when the Mandate terminated and the British left, war broke out between Arabs and Jews over the establishment of the state of Israel.

Thousands of Arab refugees who fled the war zone were eventually accommodated in camps in the Jordan Valley and around Amman. Almost overnight Jordan's population doubled. An armistice was signed in 1949, and the following year, in April, 1950, Central Arab Palestine (the West Bank) voted to join Trans-Jordan. The two were united into one state called the Hashemite Kingdom of Jordan. From the outset Jordan with its meager resources accepted the refugees, giving them citizenship and allowing them to work and own land.

In 1951, King Abdullah was assassinated while he was attending prayer at the Al Aqsa Mosque in Jerusalem. Hussein, his grandson, who was later to become king, was with him. One of the assassin's bullets was deflected from Hussein by a small metal bar he was wearing on his chest. It was the first of many occasions in the tumultuous history of Jordan over the next quarter-century that Hussein came within a hair's breadth of death. His bravery in the face of danger and through the many crises he has faced has won him worldwide respect and admiration, even from his enemies.

Immediately following King Abdullah's death, his son Talal (Hussein's father) was proclaimed king, but due to ill health he reigned only a short while. Hussein became king in 1952 at the age of 17, while he was still a student at Sandhurst in England. In the interim a Regency Council was appointed by Parliament. Hussein formally ascended the throne in May 1953.

A list of the projects which were undertaken in the first ten years of his reign gives an idea of how basic were the problems of Jordan's development: the construction of the Amman-Aqaba desert highway, now one of the country's main roads; the establishment of the first labor law, the first cement factory, the first college of nursing; the formation of a phosphate mining company, a petroleum refining company, a potash company, an agricultural cooperative; the construction of a port at Aqaba, an irrigation project on the Yarmuk river, an automatic telephone exchange, and establishment of the University of Jordan and ALIA, the national airline.

All the while, Hussein had to prove his leadership over and over by thwarting attempts to unseat him both from within the country and from outside. In 1956, King Hussein dismissed Glubb Pasha, the British soldier who had headed the Arab Legion and had served as Chief of Staff of the Jordan Army. The following year the Anglo-Jordanian Treaty was terminated and the last British soldier left Jordan.

On the bright side was one of the most important archaeological events of modern times—the discovery of the Dead Sea Scrolls. These were copper rolls found by a shepherd in a cave on a desolate cliff high above the Dead Sea at Qumran.

King Hussein's first decade ended on a happy note with the birth of his first son, Prince Abdullah. The second ten years began with another important landmark, the visit of Pope Paul VI to the Holy Land in January 1964—the first visit by a pope in modern times.

The basic development of the country continued with the introduction of compulsory education, the launching of the first seven-year economic development program, and the opening of the country's first deluxe hotel by an international chain—the Jordan Inter-Continental Hotel.

The Central Bank of Jordan was inaugurated, reconstruction of the Hejaz Railway began, several dams were completed, television was introduced, and major reforestation projects were launched.

But once again Jordan suffered a sharp reversal. The June 1967 war with Israel resulted in the loss of the West Bank and Jerusalem and thus Jordan's two principal sources of income—agriculture and tourism. At the same time it received another wave of refugees, numbering more than 400,000. Once again Jordan was strained to its limits. In the following tense years, a confrontation with the Palestinian guerrilla movements became inevitable as they grew in strength and openly defied the government's authority. Many times throughout 1970 fighting broke out between the army and the guerrillas, until the final showdown in 1971 when the army launched a major offensive to drive the guerrillas out of the country. It was a costly, bloody struggle which alienated the king from his Arab neighbors for several years.

King Hussein's third decade took an upward turn with the granting of the vote to women in 1973 and an amnesty to all political prisoners and exiles. Restrictions were raised on travel to the West Bank.

Although no fighting took place on the Jordan border in the October War of 1973, Jordan sent troops and equipment to assist Syria. The following year a summit conference of the Arab heads of state in Rabat passed a resolution, which Jordan accepted, naming the Palestine Liberation Organization as the sole legitimate representative of the Palestinian people. Jordan moved to strengthen its ties with Syria through agreements to coordinate its economic, social and foreign policies and to launch major joint ventures as part of its economic and trade agreements.

Over the past five years, many of Jordan's economic projects begun in the 1960's and early 1970's began to bear fruit, particularly in the expansion of agriculture and the creation of an industrial base. In 1972, a conference which detailed a $555-million three-year development plan drew delegates from 26 countries and a wide variety of international organizations. In 1973, a $120 million-dollar project to irrigate the Jordan Valley and resettle 130,000 people there was announced. A new law to encourage investment was enacted; several more large hotels were opened; Alia launched Arab Wings, the Middle East's first business jet charter service, and Jordan World Airways, Alia's cargo subsidiary; the railroad line to Aqaba and several major roads were completed.

In 1976, a new $2.3 billion five-year development plan was launched: Yarmuk University in Irbid opened, plans were visualized to open training centers in Aqaba and in Kerak. In 1977, marking King Hussein's 25th Jubilee, the $35 million King Talal Dam was completed; several additional training schools, hospitals, housing projects were started around the country, Aqaba port was expanded, and Alia started direct airline service between Jordan and the U.S. for the first time.

Jordan, given a period of peace and stability, has impressive results to show. Its five year plan which will carry the country through 1980 has set even more ambitious goals than those already conquered.

Alia, The Royal Jordanian Airline

It might seem unusual in a book of this kind to include the history of an airline, but Alia, the Royal Jordanian Airlines, is so much a part of the history and development of modern Jordan that it deserves special mention.

In 1962 King Hussein, himself an accomplished pilot, asked Ali Ghandour, now Alia's chairman, to formulate plans for the new airline. Ghandour, an aeronautical engineer by training, had been with the Civil Aviation Department of Lebanon and a vice president of Lebanon International Airways.

There was a small airport in Amman; Jordan had been a signatory of the Civil Aviation Act of Chicago in 1944 and a member of the International Civil Aviation Organization in 1947; but one might say that aviation in Jordan—indeed, in the Middle East—was barely off the ground.

With the full backing of the King, Ghandour, a man of inexhaustible energy and great imagination, drew up a plan which was accepted immediately. On December 8, 1963, Alia was born, with instructions from the King to get the airline into operation within seven days!

"It's hard now to remember the sequence of events during that hectic, sleepless week," Ghandour says. "We had an airline on paper. The name, which is the same as that of the King's eldest daughter, Princess Alia, is a good one for an airline. In Arabic it means 'the high and exalted one.' "

Alia was given two former Royal Air Force Dart Heralds, and within a matter of days $460,000 in private capital was raised to buy a used Super DC-7. Qualified pilots were sought, offices rented, and technical workshops set up, and one week to the day—December 15, 1963—Alia was airborne. Within a week of the initial flight to Beirut, Alia's DC-7 was flying to Cairo and Kuwait. A month later a second DC-7 was purchased and Jeddah added.

One plane and a network covering three Arab countries have grown to a fleet of 17 jets, including 747s, which serve 32 cities on four continents—and, for the past four years, Alia has been operating at a profit.

But Alia had more than its share of difficulties—long, hard years of operating in the red and frequent crises, including two crippling wars. The months after the 1967 war with Israel were the worst. In one disastrous June week in 1967, a vital part of Jordan—Jerusalem, Bethlehem, Hebron, Jericho and the fertile Jordan Valley—was lost. The country's two major sources of income, tourism and agriculture, all but disappeared.

For Alia, it was a matter of survival and many doubted its ability to stay alive. The energy and determination behind the country's progress, despite all its setbacks, characterized Alia's response to the 1967 disaster. Perhaps more as a gesture of faith than anything else, the airline opened a new route to Athens at the end of 1967.

During this period Alia had trouble raising capital, which led the King to change the carrier's status from private venture to government-owned enterprise, enabling it to buy equipment and expand routes and offices. The most notable expansion was its non-stop service to the U.S.—it was the first regularly scheduled Arab carrier to connect the two destinations with regularly scheduled service, started in 1977.

Another part of Alia's success story is the related services and other activities it has developed. Arab Wings, an air taxi, was established in 1975 as a subsidiary to fill the demand for quick air transportation to different parts of the Middle East, particularly to remote spots lacking frequent service. Another subsidiary created the same year was Jordan World Airways, an all-cargo carrier. By 1979 Alia expects to have helicopter service to less accessible points in Jordan and neighboring countries.

On the ground, Alia has a catering service which prepares half a million meals a year; a duty-free shop at Amman International Airport; a training center, and even its own restaurant and night-club, *Flying Carpet,* one of Amman's leading nightspots.

Alia also plays a prominent role in the promotion and development of the country's tourism. Each of its sales offices abroad functions as a tourism office for the country. Within Jordan itself, Alia has been involved in strengthening and expanding the country's infrastructure and facilities, particularly in the construction of hotels. It holds financial and management interest in the Holiday Inns of Amman and Aqaba and is building its own hotel, *Flying Carpet* in Amman.

Ghandour's greatest dream is to have an Air University which would train personnel for all the Middle East. It's not an idle dream. The plan has the full backing of the King and the Civil Aviation Authorities in Jordan, and when last we checked, the groundwork was being laid.

CHRONOLOGY OF JORDANIAN AND BIBLICAL HISTORY

Historical   **Biblical**

Prehistory to Neolithic Period, c. 4000 B.C.   Genesis

    Traces of prehistoric man, artifacts older than 100,000 B.C.

Chalcolithic Period, c. 4000 - 3000 B.C.

    Canaanite settlement along coast, as well as in the interior.

Early Bronze Age, c. 3000 - 2000 B.C.

    Settlements at Beisan, Megiddo, Ai, and others. The Jordan Valley prosperous and densely populated. Palestine in close contact with Egypt.

Middle Bronze Age, c. 2000 - 1600 B.C.

    c. 1900 Abraham arrived in the Land of Canaan.   Abraham

    Joseph sold by brothers, taken to Egypt.   Joseph

Hyksos Empire   Hyksos (Shepherd Kings) established empire in Egypt lasting til 1550. Held Palestine til 1479 when defeated by Thothmes III at Megiddo. Palestine became part of Egypt for next 400 years.

    c. 1630 - Jacob to Egypt.   Jacob

Late Bronze Age, c. 1600 - 1200 B.C.

Egyptian Empire	15th - 14th centuries, Egypt controlled Palestine.	Exodus, Numbers, Deuteronomy
Hittite Invasion	1280 - Battle of Kadesh, Ramses II checked Hittites advancing from north.	
	Edomites in south Jordan; Moabites, east of the Dead Sea; and Ammonites, east of Gilead.	
Phœnician Empire	c. 1300 Philistine invasion. Settled coast, conquered all Palestine.	Moses and Exodus
	c. 1250 Joshua crossed Jordan, captured Jericho, and divided Palestine among the twelve tribes.	Joshua

Early Iron Age, c. 1200 - 950 B.C.

Judges, Samuel I,
Samuel II, Kings I

Samson killed c. 1100

Rulers   Prophets

Saul crowned King of all Israel c. 1020

c. 1000 B.C.

Saul slain and Philistines captured Ark c. 1004

	Rulers	Prophets
	Saul	Nathan
David's reign c. 1004 - 965	David	Gad
Solomon's reign c. 965 - 922 B.C. Expanded trade from Phœnicia in north to Sheba in south Arabia.	Solomon	Ahiyah

Late Iron Age, c. 950 - 549 B.C.

c. 900 B.C.

		Rulers	Prophets
	Israel (930-721 B.C.) Omrite Dynasty established. Ahab defeated by Mesha, King of Moab c. 850 B.C. Jehu Dynasty followed.	Omri Ahab/Jeho- shaphat Jehu	Jehul Elijah Elisha

c. 800 B.C.

		Rulers	Prophets
Assyrian Empire	883-626 B.C. Assyrian raids on coast intermittent with Egyptian raids. 721 B.C. Sargon II captured Samaria. Judah (930-587 B.C.)	Jeroboam II Zechariah Ahaz Hezekiah	Jonah Amos Hosea Isaiah

c. 700 B.C.

		Rulers	Prophets
Neo-Baby- lonian Invasion	605 - 562 B.C. Nebuchadnezzar's invasion of Phœnicia. 587 B.C. Babylon Captivity.	Manasseh Amon Josiah	Zephaniah Jeremiah Nahum

c. 600 B.C.

Historical	Biblical

Persian Period, 549 - 332 B.C.

Nabataeans prominent in south, established capital at Petra.   Zedekiah   Ezekiel

539 B.C. Jews allowed by Cyrus to return to Palestine.

Hellenistic Period, 332 - 63 B.C.

332 B.C. conquest of Alexander the Great. After his death Syria and Palestine were divided by Seleucid (north) and Ptolemy (south) until 198 B.C. when Palestine passed to Seleucids.

Revolt against Seleucids led by Judas Maccabaeus (166 - 160 B.C.), Jonathan (160 - 143 B.C.), and Simon (142 - 134 B.C.).

John Hyrcanus I (135 - 104 B.C.) extended boundaries of Judæa and Samaria.

Decapolis formed in north; Nabataean expansion in south.

Roman Period, 63 B.C. - A.D. 330

63 B.C. Roman conquest by Pompey. Hyrcanus II appointed High Priest.

40 B.C. Parthians occupied Palestine. Antigonus made King and High Priest. Herod escaped to Rome, recognized as King of Judæa by Roman Senate.

39 B.C. Herod returned to Palestine, expelled Parthians, and reigned until A.D. 4.   Birth of Christ

A.D. 26-36 - Pontius Pilate   John the Baptist
A.D. 30   Preaching of Jesus
   Roman Emperor, Caligula   Death of Jesus
A.D. 40   Conversion of Paul
   Roman Emperor, Claudius   James beheaded, Peter
   Agrippa I (41-44), ruler in Palestine   imprisoned, Paul's 1st,
   and Jordan   2nd journey
   A.D. 50   Paul's 3rd journey,
   Roman Emperor, Nero   Paul captured in
      Cæsarea, taken to
      Rome

A.D. 66 First Jewish revolt

A.D. 70 'Romans under Titus destroy Jerusalem

A.D. 106 Nabataeans defeated. Peræa and Petra joined into Roman Province of Arabia

Music is a vital part of Jordanian life, whether it be the kind played at a wedding or festival, or imported Scottish airs on the Army's bagpipes.

Shopping in the open air, whether it be in a market such as the one in Zerka (below), or at a potter's in Amman, is accompanied by bargaining in time-honored fashion.

Jordan is an archeologist's paradise, abounding in finds such as this votive block in Petra. Believed to be from the 1st century A.D., it is probably the goddess Uzzah, as indicated by the Nabataean inscription on the base.

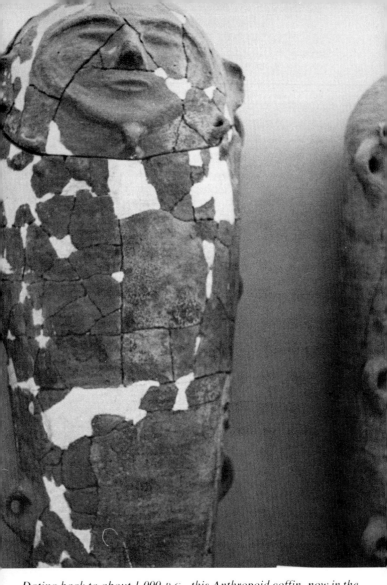

Dating back to about 1,000 B.C., this Anthropoid coffin, now in the Amman Antiquities Museum, was found by workmen leveling the ground of the present Royal Palace.

A.D. 132 Second Jewish revolt, put down by Hadrian.

Christianity took root.

Byzantine Period, A.D. 330 - 634

Christianity spread rapidly after Constantine conversion.

Reign of Justinian (A.D. 527 - 565)

A.D. 614 Persian invasion.

Arab Empire, 634 - 1099

By A.D. 635 all Palestine and Syria under Arab control. Umayyad Dynasty (634-750) established in Damascus, afterwards Caliphate transferred to Baghdad.

Crusader Period, 1099 - 1268

1098-99 First Crusade, Kingdom of Jerusalem established.

1187 - Jerusalem fell to Saladin.

Mameluk Period, 1263 - 1516

1263 Mameluk Sultan Baybers of Egypt captured Crusader strongholds at Kerak and Ajlun. Egyptian Mameluks held coast intermittently for next 250 years.

1400 Mongol invasion under Tamerlane.

Turkish Period, 1516 - 1917

1516 Turks conquered Jordan and Palestine. Its history insignificant for 300 years.

1855 Palestine drawn into affairs of Europe over rights in the Holy Land. European and American missionaries begin to arrive.

1908 Completion of Hejaz Railroad from Damascus to Medina.

1916 Arab Revolt against the Turks.

1917 Arabs capture Aqaba; Jerusalem taken by Allies.

Modern Jordan 1920–

1920 British Mandate over Palestine and Jordan; Emir Abdullah arrives in Ma'an.

1921 Abdullah reaches Amman, meets Churchill in Jerusalem and secures recognition of Emirate.

1923 Emirate of Trans-Jordan established under Abdullah.

1928 Anglo-Jordanian Treaty signed. British resident appointed.

1929 First Legislative Council established.

1939 Legislative Council transformed into a regular cabinet. Arab Legion fights with Allies in World War II.

1946 Mandate ends. Independence achieved (this date is celebrated as Jordan Independence Day, May 25). Abdullah becomes King of Transjordan.

1947 U.N. General Assembly recommends the partition of Palestine.

1948 British Mandate of Palestine terminated. Hostilities break out between Jews and Arabs.

1950 Transjordan and Central Palestine combined into the Hashemite Kingdom of Jordan.

1951 King Abdullah assassinated, July 20.

1952 Hussein proclaimed king.

1953 Hussein ascends the throne.

1955 Jordan joins U.N.

1956 Glubb Pasha dismissed as head of Arab Legion.

1957 Termination of Anglo-Jordanian Treaty.

1965 Prince Hassan proclaimed Crown Prince.

1967 War between Israel and Egypt, Syria, Jordan in June. U.N. Resolution 242 calls on Israeli withdrawal from occupied Arab territories.

1972 King Hussein's father Talal dies.

1973 War between Israel and Egypt and Syria in October. U.N. adapts Resolution 338 calling for implementation of Resolution 242.

1974 Arab Summit Conference in Rabat in October names PLO as sole representative of Palestinians.

1977 King Hussein's Silver Jubilee.

THE JORDANIAN WAY OF LIFE

Customs and Culture

Local residents of Amman are accustomed to foreign visitors and are helpful to them. In smaller towns and villages the people are courteous, but they appear more curious and are certainly more conservative.

Jordanians of all stations are formal in their greetings to friends and strangers. If you respect their customs and formality and are polite and smiling in manner, your attitude will be reciprocated.

Jordan is predominantly Moslem, and whether you are in Amman or in a village, you will hear the call to prayer five times a day from a minaret and will see many Jordanians stop their work to pray. Moslems are not self-conscious about praying in public, and often you will see a person on a side street, in front of a shop, in a field, or almost anywhere saying his prayers.

Strict Moslems do not drink alcoholic beverages at any time, nor eat foods prepared with wine. Even modern Moslems who are not so strict about alcohol abstain from eating pork.

During the Moslem month of fasting, known as Ramadan, Moslems do not eat from sunrise to sunset, nor do they smoke or drink. Out of respect, the visitor should refrain from drinking or smoking in public except in places that obviously cater to tourists. Many restaurants do not serve food during Ramadan before the hour of breaking the fast. Many places also will not serve beer or liquor during Ramadan or on several of the religious holidays.

Women Traveling Alone

Jordan is a male-dominated society, and you will be aware of it from the moment you arrive. However, women can and do travel alone with ease and safety in Jordan. The author has traveled alone from one end of the country to the other and never encountered anything but the most pleasant and courteous treatment.

Unless you are a seasoned traveler, your first trip to Jordan will be more fun and less costly if you join a group—even a small group of three or four. If you do not like to travel with others, however, you need not hesitate to strike out alone. Jordanians have become accustomed to foreign women traveling on their own. It is only fair to add, that your behavior should be circumspect and your dress modest. For example, bareback dresses and shorts absolutely must not be worn on the street.

Coffeehouses and sidewalk cafés in certain areas of town are frequented by men only. While no one is likely to ask you to leave, you will probably not feel comfortable, since all eyes will be fixed upon you. Also, at traditional dinners and weddings the men may be separated from the women to enjoy separate music and entertainment. You should follow the directions of your host or hostess.

Dress

While traditional Arab dress is seen less in towns than in the countryside, the male headdress—a checkered cloth of red or black and white—is seen throughout the country, even on men wearing western garb. The woman's traditional costume is a long dress with cross-stitch and other designs usually representative of a particular area of the country.

By contrast, Jordanians of the younger generation wear slacks and jeans or stylish European fashions. You can see almost all styles and wear almost all, too, except shorts. Even teenagers do not wear shorts anywhere in Jordan. As a visitor you should not, either.

A Jordanian Welcome

Jordanians are good-natured, friendly and accommodating to visitors, but they are more reserved than Americans. Highly educated Jordanians are quite sophisticated.

Throughout the Mediterranean world there is an unconcern for time which to westerners, and especially Americans, is frustrating and sometimes irritating. Yet it is precisely the Jordanians' relaxed manner that accounts for much of their charm. They are patient and gracious, and you should try to be likewise. Relax. You will enjoy your visit many times more if you adjust to the system rather than fight it.

Jordan is a country enriched by many cultures—Arab, Circassian, Armenian, Kurdish and European—all with their own customs and food. Entertaining in the home is still the traditional way of Arab hospitality. You will always be offered coffee or tea in a home, no matter how short your visit. Women are famous for their cooking and take great pride in the preparation and presentation of food.

Feasts are the time to exchange family visits and to give gifts. For a visitor, candy or flowers are customary—Arabs consider it necessary to reciprocate, so you should be careful not to embarrass someone with an expensive gift.

If at any time you encounter a problem, you should report it immediately to the Tourism Authority or to any policeman. Jordan is making a sincere effort to provide comfort and service to her visitors. Your criticism is welcomed, and the authorities work diligently to correct complaints.

Cuisine

Jordanians usually eat a light breakfast, the main meal at lunch, and a light supper. Restaurants and hotel dining rooms serve lunch from 1 to 3 P.M. and dinner after 8 P.M. You will have your greatest treat if you are invited to a Jordanian house for a meal.

Most hotels serve European as well as Jordanian dishes, which are similar to Lebanese and Syrian ones. Those which are traditionally Jordanian are described below:

Mensef: Roast lamb stuffed with rice, highly spiced with cinnamon, sprinkled with pine nuts and almonds, and served with *makheedh* (beaten yogurt combined with the fat of mutton). A mensaf is not just a dish, it's a feast and a ritual—the traditional feast of the Bedouin when a lamb is slaughtered for a guest or a special occasion. For such a ceremony, the whole lamb is served atop a huge tray of rice, and the honored guest is often presented with the eye of the lamb. (But don't fear, this won't happen to you in a restaurant!) If you want to try eating it with your hand the Bedouin way, remember to use only your right hand.

Musakhan: Chicken, previously steamed in a sauce of olive oil, onions and sumak, is baked on specially prepared bread and covered with a layer of onions marinated in oil and sumak. This is a specialty of Tulkarem (on the West Bank) and was borrowed by Ramallah and Jericho. Several restaurants in Amman specialize in it. The dish is very rich, highly seasoned, and one of the most delicious in the Middle East.

Maqlouba (literally, "upside down"): A stewlike dish of vegetables, usually cauliflower or eggplant, and meat served on rice. Leban (yogurt) is sometimes added on top. This is a specialty of Jerusalem.

Daud Pasha: Arab stew of meatballs, whole onions and pine nuts cooked with tomatoes, and served with rice.

Kidreh bil-Furn (Pot-in-Oven): Cubed meat, rice, chickpeas and spices are placed in an earthen jar and baked in the oven. This is a specialty of Hebron.

Kubbeh: A dish found in all the Arab countries of the Middle East, but the Jordanians give it a slightly different flavor and preparation. It is cracked wheat and ground meat with spices blended to a meatloaf consistency, shaped into large egg-shaped pieces, and stuffed with ground meat which has been sauteed with onions. The "egg" is fried in deep oil to give it a lightly crisp outer surface. It can be eaten hot or cold.

Bateenjan Battiri: A miniature light-purple eggplant (grown in Bittir, south of Jerusalem) is stuffed with meat and rice and cooked in tomato sauce.

Fattet el-Hummos: Bed of Arab bread chips covered with chickpeas and their juice and topped with yogurt, garlic and roasted pine nuts.

Salata bi-Tahini: Finely chopped tossed salad seasoned with the paste of sesame oil.

Fatayir Zalatimo: A pastry to be eaten at Zalatimo's in the Old City of Jerusalem. Mr. Zalatimo called it *mutabaq* rather than *fatayir*. It is a paper-thin dough folded corners-in and filled with cheese or walnuts. The pastry is baked in a brick oven situated in the original wall of ancient Jerusalem. The pastry is made prior to 10 A.M. and should be eaten in the morning. It is served with powdered sugar and syrup and is very rich.

Kanafa: A sweet cake filled with white cheese and served with hot, clear syrup. Often eaten for breakfast as well as dessert. This is the specialty of Nablus.

Khubiz: To Arabs perhaps more than most people, bread is the staff of life. They call it *khubiz* or *eish* (meaning "life"), and there is no meal, even one with a main dish of rice or potatoes, that is not accompanied by a generous serving of it. Lunch for a laborer, for instance, often consists of a loaf of *khubiz,* a tomato, some olives and a piece of cheese. It fills the stomach and, Arabs insist, nurtures the soul.

Looked upon as a gift from God, assuring that no man will go hungry, it is treated with reverence. A piece of bread fallen on the ground is picked up, kissed and replaced on the table. Leftover pieces of bread are not thrown away but put upon a window sill or building ledge for whatever hungry soul may pass. Old or dried bread is used in several dishes.

The shape of the bread is always as round as the eternal circle, sometimes thick and dense, sometimes hollow inside, and sometimes even paper thin . . . but always round and flat. It's made usually with white flour, yeast, water and salt, and preparing it, too, is a ritual.

Qahwa: Coffee, too, is a tradition and a ritual. The true Arab or Bedouin coffee is bitter, rather thin and heavily flavored with cardamom seed. It is poured from a metal pot with a long spout into tiny cups with no handles. The server (for this type, always a male) shows his skill by raising and lowering the pot in quick motions as he pours. He will continue refilling your cup as often as you hand it to him until you make the proper gesture to stop—a quick side-to-side roll of the hand. In traditional circles a guest takes three cups (each holds only a swallow) before giving the sign. You may stop after the first cup without offending anyone.

The other type of coffee is called Turkish and is thick with as much sugar as one likes. Jordanians tend to drink it very sweet, so if you want it medium or lightly sweetened ask for *sukar aleel* or *areeha.*

Coffee always completes a meal, but it is also offered at a meeting in an office or a visit in a home, as a gesture of welcome.

Wine: Red, rose and white wines from Latroun can be purchased at restaurants and groceries. Price ranges from 500-700 fils a bottle. *Cremisan,* another local wine (red and white), comes from Bethlehem and is priced at about 625 fils per bottle.

Beer: The local brewery bottles Amstel. The price in restaurants is 550 fils for a large, 300 for a small one.

A new book on Arabic cooking by the American Women's Club of Amman was released recently and contains recipes for most of the dishes mentioned above. It is available from members of the club for JD2, and is entitled *Sahtain Cookbook.*

The following series of articles by authorities on different aspects of Jordanian life and traditions are reprinted from Jordan, *a magazine published by the Ministry of Information and circulated as ALIA's inflight magazine. We have taken the liberty, with the permission of* Jordan's *publishers, to edit the articles when appropriate. In most cases the alterations were a matter of length or technical detail.*

CLASSICAL MUSIC

Adapted from an article by Afif Alvarez Bulos, *a Lebanese scholar, who studied in London and received his Ph.D. at Harvard University. An authority on the music of the Middle East, he has lectured on Arab music throughout Great Britain and the United States, and has made several recordings. Presently he is a lecturer at Beirut University College.*

When Westerners visit the Middle East for the first time their senses are assailed by new impressions. Perhaps most different of all is the music of the Arabs, which can be heard day and night from every taxi radio, transistor, television set, and record player in town.

Those unfamiliar with the music usually have the impression that the singer—man or woman—is mourning. "Wailing" is a description often used by the uninitiated; and they also quickly note the repetition in Arab songs—going over and over the same words, with the same tune, at the same tempo. Undulating, with an up-and-down quavering of the voice, the tune seems never to end, to have no beginning and no pauses.

Arab music is mainly vocal, often unaccompanied, and strongly influenced by simple folk songs. Uninitiated listeners can be put off by the unfamiliar sound of the Arabic language as used in a song they do not understand. If they were to hear purely instrumental renditions of these melodies, without human voices, probably the sound would not seem so foreign to them; generally speaking, voices change the effect. Unfortunately for the Western neophyte, little Arab music is written for instruments alone.

Usually only well-established singers give solo recitals, and these performances are invariably sold out soon after the high-priced tickets go on sale. The great Egyptian singer Um Kulthum, who died a few years ago, gave two recitals in her later years at the annual Festival of Baalbek, the impressive Roman ruin in the mountains outside Beirut. For as far as the eye could see, people were packed tightly into the huge amphitheater and even lined the very rims of the ancient battlements and ruins. Everyone wanted to get as close as possible to the great lady of Middle Eastern music and to listen to the legendary velvet voice.

Um Kulthum sang with unimpaired voice for over fifty years. And, it is safe to say, her popularity throughout the Middle East and North Africa exceeded by some considerable degree that of such singers as Bing Crosby or Frank Sinatra in the Western world.

Feyrouz, the pride of Lebanon, is a tremendously popular woman singer; Sabah is another, also from Lebanon. The emphasis on these women singers is not meant to indicate that only Arab women sing in public or that only Arab women sing well. There are also scores of fine Arab men singers.

Arab audiences express enthusiasm by clapping, rhythmically and endlessly, and listeners continually give out with loud, appreciative ooh's and aah's.

There was a time, in the tenth century, when a different state of affairs existed concerning performance decorum. In Damascus, for instance, vocal and instrumental concerts were held at the house of a singer called Azza al-Maila, and there the behavior of the audience was impeccable. No one talked or shouted appreciation while the artist was performing. If anyone was tempted to chat with his neighbor, an attendant with a long stick would reach out for the offender's knuckles and administer a disciplinary rap. Today's audiences are not so quiet or respectful of the artist's efforts.

After the foreign visitor has listened for a time to that endless repetition of the same phrases, he may begin to think about going home early. Why is there so much repetition? The answer lies partly in the psychology of the Arabs, who love to hear the same phrase over and over again.(Have you ever seen two friends meet unexpectedly? In Arabic countries such encounters generate a stream of "Ahlan, Ahlan wa Sahlan, Ahlan, Ahlan!")

Um Kulthum, when she felt her audience enjoyed a certain passage, would repeat it over and over again, sometimes eight times in a row. Now, it must be pointed out that there is also repetition in Western music; just think of Bach. But there it is more artfully disguised by rhythmic and harmonic variations. Arab music is much more "exposed."

If our visiting concertgoer stays throughout, he will find that the performance begins with *taqasim* (improvisations) on the *oud,* a sort of lute, or on the *qanun,* a mini-harpsichord. He may find this portion quite pleasant. In the orchestral prelude, if there is one, all the instruments, including violins, play in unison. Then the singer improvises on the *ya-leil* theme, in which the only words, sung over and over, are "O night!" From the rendition of the cadenza an experienced listener can gauge the skill and beauty of voice of the singer.

Finally the singer embarks on the body of the song, which may be in the form of a long ode *(qasida),* a *muwashah,* or a simple lyric *(dawr),* with the full orchestra playing the accompaniment. This is where the Western ear must prepare itself for a disciplined period of acute listening to the interweaving notes, to try to follow the tune. The orchestra plays the same notes.

Westerners often ask, "What is it that gives Arab music its distinctive flavor? Is it merely the strange language used, or is there also a musical difference?"

First of all, Arab tunes are not built on the Western major and minor scales but on more ancient forms known as modes. In Arabic these are called *maqams,* and some of them contain intervals of a quarter-tone. In conventional Western music, of course, the smallest interval is the half-tone; so one can see the reason for the slurring, slithery quality Arab music has for Western ears.

Furthermore, the absence of harmony in Arab music, which develops along horizontal lines, adds to its strangeness for Westerners. In Western music, which is developed vertically, the melody is seldom sounded alone; instead, a harmonic arrangement gives depth and color to the melodic line.

In Arab music, such combinations as duets, trios, or quartets do not exist. All the instruments of the orchestra accompanying the singer play the same melody in unison. Hence, the ear steeped in harmonized music goes into shock at first.

The past twenty years have witnessed considerable European influence on Arab music, both classical and popular. Now, one does hear harmony, and instruments such as the piano and accordion are added to the traditional instruments of the classic Arab orchestra. Many old Arab songs have even been rearranged as rhumbas, sambas, tangos, and so on. Feyrouz is one of the outstanding singers of this genre.

Feyrouz's name has also been linked with the revival of Arab folksongs in Lebanon, Syria, and Jordan. The warmth of her voice and the utter simplicity of her singing have not only endeared her to the Arab public; she is one of the reasons foreigners are now being wooed by Arab music. Sabah is a more traditional singer, and her songs are much less influenced by Western-inspired innovation.

Arab folksongs for the most part tend to be love songs, songs of yearning or nostalgia, songs praising one's beloved, or songs complaining of the beloved's coldness and indifference. But some songs are lively and lend themselves to dance, such as the *dabke.* A village wedding in traditional style is the ideal occasion for hearing the variety of dance songs with their subtly changing rhythms that stir the body to movement. To the Western ear they are in a minor key, seemingly with sad overtones; but to the ear attuned to their special qualities each one has a message.

Now, what instruments play in the *takht,* as the Arab orchestra is called?

First is the *oud,* known from pre-Islamic times, and from which the lute descended. Then there are the *kanun (qanun),* a trapezoidal stringed instrument mentioned in *The Thousand and One Nights* and similar to the harpsichord, with 24 cords; the *buzuq;* the *nay,* a vertical flute that can be traced back to 3000 B.C.; and percussion instruments such as the *riq,* the *daff* and the *tablah.* Percussion instruments are an absolute must in Arab music because of its pronounced rhythmic structure. Throughout the song a regular, strong pulse beats constantly. In the Western waltz there are three beats to the bar, with the accent falling on the first beat. A similar arrangement occurs in Arab music, except that the bar is much more complicated. The *nawakht* (rhythmical mode), for instance, contains seven beats to every bar, with accents falling on the first and fourth beats; the second and fifth beats are the weakest.

The melodic line of an Arab song has a distinctive pattern, and its cadences fall differently from those of Western music. The melody is, however, structured in a manner similar to the melodies of European composers of the eighteenth century. The author has often been struck with the similarity between some of Bach's melodies and the classical Arab songs that have descended to us from Moorish Spain. If the foreigner approaches Arab music with Bach or Vivaldi in mind, some of its apparent strangeness fades away.

FOLK MUSIC AND DANCE

Adapted from a script for the Hashemite Broadcasting Service by Maaz Shukayr, *former director of programs, English and Arabic Services.*

In Jordan each man's work, station in life, pastime or celebration has its traditional accompaniment in song. Day laborers swing to a work song; construction gangs heave on pulleys or work cement to the strongly accented beats that belong to the building trades. There is a plowing song, a seeding song and a harvest song. The harvest song is slower in tempo than, say, the lilting themes which the shepherd out in the desert with his flock uses to while away the hours. The tattoo that a taxi driver beats on the roof of his car to accompany the tune he is humming has the urgency of the crowded city streets, an urban tempo, different from his country cousin's.

The average Jordanian loves to listen to his country's music—on the lips of a folksinger, on the radio, over television. He probably knows every note; but each new verse with an added up-to-date variation, every fresh anecdote delights him. The traditional tunes are used over and over for current events, much like calypso in the Caribbean, bringing a new story in a familiar musical package.

Many Jordanian folksongs have for centuries celebrated the happy events marking village life. The folksinger gives rein to joy over the birth of a baby boy, expresses the mixed pride and nervousness of a first day at school, and of course becomes lyrical over betrothals and weddings. A Jordanian wedding is a festivity in which the whole village joins, dancing and feasting, and in fact people from all the neighboring villages will participate, coming on foot or by donkey if the family has not yet achieved the status of a car. The main festivity is making and listening to music, always with dancing.

Both classical and folk music in Jordan are constructed on the seventeen-note scale, so different in effect from the Western chromatic scale. Also, extremely complex rhythms are characteristic, one underlying beat counterpointed by rippling, undulating airs that leap and frolic extemporaneously at times. At the end of each couplet, the singer utters a long drawn out "Ooooooooof," lasting from 15 to 75 seconds, during which the audience claps and cheers and asks for a particular verse or theme for the next go-round. The Arab tradition is that the music acts as a background for the lyrics, whose content and poetic style occupy the center of attention. Often the poetry is of great beauty, particularly in dealing with love themes, wonders of nature, patriotic feelings and loyalty to one's king.

It doesn't take much for a Jordanian to make music—his own beating foot and a short reed flute will set a group to dancing. There are two reed flutes: one five-holed, the *qasaba,* and the other seven-holed, the *nay.* These are very popular—easily carried, ever-handy, and capable of producing the quarter-tones and three-quarter tones peculiar to Arab music.

The other oldest and most omnipresent musical instrument in Jordan is the *rababa*—a one-string violin with a square body and straight neck, still widely used by the Bedouins. Its body is stretched goatskin, and the bow elicits a weird keening sound, liquid or scratching according to the skill of the player. The wail of the *rababa* from a black goatskin tent at night is a true echo of centuries of Bedouin nomadic life. Any time one sees a Bedouin family striking camp, hoisting the whole tent and contents on to the backs of camels, the last thing that is carefully hitched on is the *rababa.*

Besides the reed and stringed instruments, the basic dancemaker is, of course, the percussion family. There is the *daff* or *riqq,* the circular tambourine, the most commonly seen and heard invitation to the dance. But also very popular is the *durbakkah,* a long drum with a skin drumhead. The hollow thump of these instruments is the inevitable background to the dancing of the *debkah,* a folk dance that seems to spring spontaneously into life whenever there are talk, coffee and more than five or six men gathered together. Properly, as in Jordan, it is a man's dance, with the participants lined up side by side, one elbow akimbo, following the intricate forward and backward steps, slides, jumps and stamps of a leader, who keeps a handkerchief twirling in one upraised hand throughout the dance.

More sophisticated musical instruments are found in the cities and towns—like the *oud,* a fat relative of the western mandolin, perhaps. It is a deeply ovate stringed instrument with a bent back and five double strings plucked with a quill of eagle's feather, and is usually quite a work of the wood mosaicist's art in its melon-shaped, inlaid belly. In the hands of a skilled performer the *oud* has a plangent, plaintive tone, and takes part in the intricate interweaving melodic strands that make true Arab music.

Ascending in scale of sophistication, the *qanoon* presents a real challenge to a music maker. It is an Oriental harp with 78 strings mounted on a trapezoidal box, played with two metal plectra worn on the two index fingers. It approximates a lute, and should be listened to for itself, with a good voice accompaniment.

A *rababa* and a *riqq* suffice to keep *debkah* dancers swaying and weaving for hours at a time, but one of the plucked instruments is used for a faster staccato dance with outspread arms called the *tayyara*—which translates literally as "airplane"—in which the dancer suits the movement of his body and arms to the name of the dance. The *dal'ona* is a very popular village dance, always performed at weddings, christenings and other happy occasions. A curious dance is the *arja,* meaning "lame"—a name derived from the rather off-beat hesitating and syncopated step, not unlike the movement of a lame man. Occasionally among the Bedouin comes the *sahja,* in which a young woman responds to the clapping of the men in a sort of symbolic duel: the girl carries a sword, emblem of her untouchability; the men act out the lyrics of the chanter, pursuing her. This mixing of the young men and women of the desert must be an occasion for surreptitious courting, for there is not a great deal of coeducational play among Bedouin.

Perhaps one of the most exciting dances in Jordan is the sword dance of Circassian origin performed in honor of a *mukhtar,* or head of a tribe, or coming to its peak of intensity for King Hussein himself. This dance becomes a test of steel nerves for the honoree. It involves a series of ever faster and faster lunges and retreats, swords swirling and slashing, as the dancers hail their lord. They work their way closer and closer to the king, who stands arrow-straight, and the swords flick about his head, with each newcomer protesting his allegiance, stamping and shouting in a frenzy of devotional zeal, *"Yah, Sayidneh, Yah, Hussein!"*

THE BEDOUIN

There are about 40,000 Bedouin in Jordan who manage to live as their ancestors have lived for hundreds of years. It is a rugged life, but safe and comforting in its sure design.

Bedouin (Arabic *bedu,* literally "inhabitants of the desert") are still found throughout most of the Arab world. Today's heaviest concentration of the true Bedouin is in eastern Jordan and the surrounding desert areas of Syria, Iraq, Saudi Arabia and the Naqab (Negev). In southern Jordan alone they number an estimated 70,000, although some 40 percent of these are settled and no longer roam the desert.

The Bedouin of the sands and lonely waterholes can be seen camped in the desert that flanks the north-south highway which runs through Jordan. They travel in groups, with dozens of camels or large flocks of sheep and goats, and pitch their goat-hair tents one next to the other, sometimes two or three, sometimes a score or more if it is a large tribe.

The Bedouin are strictly organized, with major subdivisions that, in turn, encompass a number of smaller groups. Occupationally, they are divided into three classes—camel herders, sheep herders and goat herders. Of the three, the camel herders are the real aristocrats of the desert, the *Aaiil* (thoroughbreds), and the ones whose way of life has the most romantic appeal to foreign visitors. The three major camel herding and breeding tribes in Jordan are the Beni Sakhr, the Huweitat and the Sirhan; among them they possess about 10,000 tents, 20,000 camels and 1,000 horses.

Despite popular belief, the Bedouin does not wander aimlessly about. He knows exactly where he's going, knows where to drive his flocks and set up his tents, knows where to find water and forage for his herds. Some Bedouin families have followed, more or less, the same migratory route year after year for generations. To the Western eye, the desert often appears much the same in whatever direction one looks. The Bedouin, however, has another eye; with some inner sense he can go back again and again to the same spot in the wide sands.

To read about the Bedouin is one thing; to know them is another. Many visitors to Jordan who sought the adventure of the desert have experienced the hospitality of the Bedouin, the repeated smiling greeting: *"Ahlan wa Sahlan"*—"Welcome, twice welcome." To a Bedouin hospitality is second only to honor, and the guest enters the tent as he would his own home.

There he will be seated on the softest, richest carpet and will be served freshly brewed coffee and special delicacies reserved for guests and festive occasions. Members of the family scurry about, seeking ways to make the guest feel more welcome.

The lucky guest is the one who is feted with a Bedouin *mensef*, the traditional feast of the desert. In his autobiography King Hussein describes a visit to a Bedouin tribe:

> When I visit one of our tribes, I sit in the tent with the other guests around me. The tent can be 50 yards long with carpets spread their length, and silken cushions to recline against. Members of the tribe gather before the tent and begin their traditional dances—usually the

debke—with the songs that go with the dancing. Since I am the honored guest, my name occurs frequently in the improvised songs, and when that happens, they shoot off their rifles as a salute.

After we all sit down and coffee is passed, the sheikh makes his welcoming speech, composing it as he goes along. After him appears the tribal poet who recites his verse of welcome and loyalty.

Then comes the *mensef*. This consists of a huge tray piled high with rice surmounted by a whole lamb, and all of it flavored with yogurt sauce *(jameed)*. A group of about eight or ten guests stand around each tray and, sometimes with the help of our host, pluck away at the lamb and roll the rice skillfully into a small ball and pop it in our mouths.

Always, of course, with the right hand.

In the Arab world, the left hand is never used to touch food.

Often believed, but now something of a myth, is the tradition that the honored guest is offered the eye of the sheep to eat.

The nomadic life of the desert is, of course, very hard. There are few modern conveniences out there in the blazing summer sun or the freezing winter nights. The wealthy sheikh's tent may be opulent, but any air conditioning he may enjoy is by God's grace. Much of the cooking is done over open fires fed by logs, twigs and charcoal, although in recent years small kerosene stoves have been making an appearance in the more affluent tents. The women, as in many other societies, do most of the work, though in the Bedouin home they are not often seen by visitors, especially if the visitor is a male. And they work hard, these women—cooking, washing, carrying water, tending to all the needs of their menfolk, and sewing and weaving besides.

Many of the textiles in and out of the tent, the floor coverings and the tent itself, are made or woven by the women, and they begin from scratch. The animal, whether camel, sheep or goat, is sheared, the wool washed and spun, sometimes dyed, then hand woven. It is in their dresses that the Bedouin women's fine artistry and talent are most evident. Robes of magnificence, they are usually black, dark blue or dark red; embroidered or woven into them are rich, brilliant designs in intricate geometric or flowered patterns. To the knowledgeable eye the design reveals what part of Jordan the woman comes from, what tribe, and even sometimes the wealth of her husband.

Some of these beautiful dresses are displayed in Jordan's Folklore and Costume Museums beneath the Roman Ampitheater in Amman. And recently some have found their way into the cocktail wardrobes of a number of Western women with a taste for the dramatically different in dress.

The male Bedouin's life is equally rugged. He is, in every sense of the word, the "provider" and "protector" of the family. He spends his days in the harsh desert, caring for his herds of camel, sheep or goats, to provide food, milk, wool and leather for his family's needs. Surplus products are sold at market and the money used to buy whatever the desert cannot provide—coffee, sugar, flour, household utensils . . . and jewelry for his wife.

But Bedouin life is often relaxed, too, and in the long, unhurried hours of the desert world there is always time for leisure and recreation. Camel and horse racing, falconry, *debke* and sword dancing are among the more vigorous pasttimes. In the evenings there are the quieter social hours, sitting around the brazier, brewing and drinking thick, sweet, cardamom-flavored coffee. This is a time for talk, about daily work, about the past accomplishments and future hopes of the tribe. There is also recitation of poetry, song, the soft, plaintive of the *rababa*.

To understand the Bedouin one must look beyond his costume and tent, his camel and nomadic existence, to the strict desert code of honor, loyalty, hospitality and courage which rules his life. In the desert, civil law is unknown. Bedouin have their own legal structure, their own code of ethics and laws that govern every aspect of behavior. Each tribe polices, governs and defends the rights of its members. Each member, in turn, carries a communal responsibility for the infraction of any law by any other member of the tribe. The code also protects the rights of any guest, even a foreigner, who happens to be visiting the tribe.

If, for instance, a tribe member commits a crime, he implicates and dishonors not only his own family but often the entire tribe. This is particularly serious when the crime is of a *muhlikat* type— premeditated murder, rape and other sex offenses, treason—where the punishment is death.

Thus desert society provides a large measure of law and order, and threats of anarchy or lawlessness are avoided. In actual fact, compared to large Western cities, the desert is extraordinarily safe. A woman need not fear attack; rape is practically unheard of among the Bedouin, who look upon it as a shameful act beneath the honor and dignity of a man. To the Bedouin, there are only three kinds of man—the brave, the hospitable and the wise. And all must be, first and foremost, honorable. It is his honor above all else that the Bedouin will defend—with his life, if necessary.

Bedouin are people of great strength and conviction, fiercely independent, and bound, out of choice and integrity, to the pattern of life that time and experience in the harsh desert have determined for them. If the word "free" can be applied to any people, it can be applied to the Bedouin. And they remain free—free to follow their own customs, laws and traditions—thanks to the Jordanian Government. The Government provides an alternative life for the Bedouin, offering him the comfort of a house instead of a tent, schools for his children, a settled agricultural life instead of desert wandering. But nothing is forced upon him. Sometimes he may accept the house, but will often pitch his tent next to it—wanting, no doubt, the best of two worlds.

In turn, the Bedouin has expressed his gratitude by being the most fiercely loyal subject in The Hashemite Kingdom of Jordan, and has stood staunchly by the King. Bedouin honor would not permit less.

THE CAMEL: THE BEDOUIN'S BEST FRIEND

He spits constantly, smells to high heaven, makes rude noises, is arrogant; he is foolish-looking with his bulbous belly and knobby-kneed, spindly legs; he is clumsy, stupid, lazy, gloomy, cantankerous even with himself, downright mean and hardhearted to his best friends, who feed and water him. And he gives you a bumpy, swaying, bucking ride that leaves you sore for a long time.

But don't tell a Bedouin this. He sees the camel differently. The Bedouin believes the camel is a lordly beast sent just to help him. And, in fact, he does.

The Bedouin finds the camel good for meat to eat, a producer of milk to drink and hair to make clothes and tents. His dried dung is excellent as a heating fuel. He drinks little water out in the desert, where water is scarce; he can go for days on a handful of acacia leaves or plain dry straw, can carry tremendous loads without stopping or sleeping or drinking or eating for far greater distances than any human being can; and he is a personnel carrier of inestimable value, even if he does leave you aching and begging for relief.

The Bedouin will tell you that the farther out in the desert you go, the prettier a camel becomes. And most Jordanians know that, despite the invention and development of the Land-Rover, the desert buggy, heavy-duty four-wheel-drive trucks, helicopters, light planes that land and take off short, or any other modern contraption, the camel is necessary for life in the desert. Without him, it is likely that there would be no Bedouin.

While some people call the camel "God's bad joke," the Bedouin calls him *Ata Allah,* which means "God's gift."

Jordan probably has about a million camels, and they are everywhere. They plod along with men or freight on their backs on some of the streets of Amman, are tethered outside mosques in cities and towns, wander about the valley of Petra and among the magnificent ruins of Jerash, form desert caravans for moving goods just as they have for thousands of years, wander freely in the desert, snort and bump each other at hundreds of waterholes, carry cargoes of fruits and vegetables to markets in the Jordan Valley, pull farm plows and platforms that skid across the ground like wheelless wagons, and walk slowly round and round to operate water pumps.

And camels provide the main transportation for several hundred elite troopers of Jordan's Desert Patrol. Out in the far desert the camel is used to chase down smugglers from neighboring states trying to reach Jordan's thriving markets with contraband goods. On those somewhat rare occasions when a Bedouin breaks a law, Desert Patrolmen track down the culprit by camelback.

The camel is a native of North America. His ancestors first appeared about 40 million years ago, and soon developed into several branches. One branch migrated to South America and eventually evolved into the modern vicuña, guanaco, llama and alpaca. Other branches crossed from North America into eastern Asia by the ancient Alaskan land bridge over the Bering Sea—a reverse movement of man's journey from eastern Asia across the same bridge to populate North and South America.

Over the centuries some camels developed two humps; these are called Bactrian camels. They are quite large—often eight or nine feet high, huge-bodied, heavily haired, and can tolerate intense cold. They are now found mostly in Siberia and China.

Another camel family branch developed only one hump; these are called dromedaries. Once having crossed from North America they did not stop in Siberia or China, but kept going until they reached the hot sands first of Araby and then of Africa.

The Jordanian dromedary, not as thick-bodied as the Bactrian, reaches seven to nine feet in height through the shoulders. The hump takes him up another foot. He weighs up to 1,400 or 1,600 pounds, and his feet look and act like floppy pillows—just what a beast or man needs to walk on hot and shifting sands.

Camels have two rows of eyelashes—just the thing to keep out blowing desert sands and to cut down the glare of the sun. His ears, mouth and eyes can close as tightly as a Bank of England vault, important when the desert environment gets rough with whistling winds and shifting sand. Camels can and do eat anything they come upon, including cacti and other desert plants with even sharper spines and barbs. The camel simply nibbles away with his pliable, tough lips, and down go the razor-sharp plants. On such nourishment the camel can go for several days without eating again.

The secret of a camel's digestive ability is his four stomachs—four distinct areas in his body through which food passes. By the time the camel has expelled his waste, it is totally dry and tightly packed, excellent to use as fuel in the Bedouin's open fire.

In the Jordanian desert, when the temperature hits 110 to 120 degrees, a dromedary can move smartly along on a big drink of water every four or five days. He can go much, much longer, but that is rarely necessary because many waterholes are maintained out in the wastelands. When a camel does stop for a drink he takes in gallons of water, and he sucks it up with a loud swish.

A camel makes total use of the water he drinks. Little evaporates or is passed off. The body throws off heat through the skin without sweating, thereby leaving the water inside. Heat from the sun is reflected and does not enter the body. And fat is stored in the hump to be used when other nourishment is not available. The camel is visible proof of Charles Darwin's theory that for animals, including man, to survive, they must adjust to their environment—he is possibly better adjusted to his environment than any other living thing, plant or animal.

Man makes many uses of the camel, but the two main ones are for his own transportation and to carry his baggage. Getting 700 or 800 pounds of freight on a camel's back is no great problem. Camels are lazy and spend much time on the ground, squatting on their legs, which are folded beneath them. Bedouin have only to strap the freight over the top of the hump, make it secure, thump the animal on the rear and the shoulders to get him up, and then take off across the desert.

For a person to mount a camel—well, that's something else again. So is staying on a swaying camel running all-out across rough terrain. And getting off is no small task, either.

How to Ride a Camel

You must mount a camel when he is squatting on the ground. You cannot throw a leg over him as he stands, as you would with a horse; he is too tall for that. The way to get on a camel is to come up on the squatting animal from the left and rear. Quickly reach for and grip tightly the saddle pommel with the left hand. This is the signal for the camel to get up, and from now on you have to act fast.

Get your right leg across the animal quickly, even if you have to brace yourself by putting your left knee in the saddle itself. A camel gets his hindquarters up first, and fast, by straightening out the hind legs. His front legs are still folded on the ground, and this means he is in a diving position. You've got to be in that saddle, holding on and leaning backward as far as you can, or you will pitch headfirst over the camel's head.

As soon as the two back legs are straight, the camel starts raising his front end. He pushes up with those spindly, unlikely-looking legs, and unless you are holding on tight and ready to shift from leaning backward to sharply leaning forward, you are going to get tossed off. The rider is on an even keel only when all four legs are straight.

As soon as those legs are straight the camel takes off. He doesn't have any idea where he is going, but he is going. And he usually moves off fast. You must turn him about and get him heading in the direction you want to go, stay in the swaying and pitching saddle, and try to look as dignified as possible—which isn't easy.

Some camels are guided entirely with long, pencil-thin sticks, or whops. If a Bedouin wants his animal to turn right, he strokes the camel's head or neck on the left side and more or less shoves the head toward the right. Some camels need the pressure of the stick plus a length of rope running from a bridle to the hand of the rider. This rope, or leather strap, can be used to guide the animal. Some other camels need a more standard bridle and rein controlled by the rider.

Most riders sit in the saddle with one leg hooked over the pommel. Some straddle the animal bareback and clamp their knees to his sides. A camel rocks almost violently from side to side, for the simple reason that he extends both his right front and right rear legs forward at the same time, then his two left legs. The ride would be much better if he worked on the diagonal, but the camel doesn't know or care about that, and he would rather you got off anyway.

Procedures for getting off a camel vary from simply jumping off to stopping the animal, then hanging on while he goes through the getting-up process in reverse. Down goes the animal to bended front knees, which pitches you forward precipitously; then he buckles his hind legs, down goes the rear end, and off you go if you don't hang on.

If you have managed to stay on throughout, it is now possible to step off the animal with some degree of dignity.

A warning note must now be sounded. Don't, after your first or second or third camel ride, try to run. Take it easy. Unless you are limber, strong-legged and young, you are going to be unsteady. Your knees might even buckle.

And, unless you have recently been regularly riding a horse, playing tennis, walking a couple of miles, jogging, or at least doing a dozen deep knee-bends daily, you are going to be sore. Oh, so sore.

ARABIAN HORSES: JORDAN'S BLOODED ARISTOCRATS

By Thomas C. Weaver

The author, a longtime resident of Aleppo and Beirut, has ridden, trained and shown horses for many years. His first Arab horse was the pride of his ten-year-old life in Ohio, and he has always owned one or more Arab horses ever since. He has been President of Aleppo College, where he was the authority on the buying, training and showing of Arab horses; in Beirut he was Chairman of the Committee on Horse Shows for the Lebanese Federation of Equestrian Sports.

Although unanimity has never for a moment, alas, characterized the views of Arabian horse fanciers throughout the world, in Jordan today the visiting horseman of whatever persuasion will find animals very much to his taste. Roughly, one might identify two basic points of view as the Bedouin and the European. While all agree that the Arabian horse is distinguished by superior beauty, intelligence and endurance, and further that he is generally recognized as the dominant blood source of all horses of quality, most particularly the English thoroughbred, there is a considerable difference of emphasis in the criteria of evaluation.

The Bedouin places endurance at the top of his list, and the breeder adopting this point of view uses in his stud only those animals that have adequately demonstrated this quality and the capacity to transmit it. The European fancier, on the other hand, puts beauty first, and prefers for his purposes only those animals of exceptional appearance, each one a picture of classical equine perfection. Unsurprisingly, these differing views are clearly reflected in the schooling and use of the horse, the Bedouin breeder concerning himself largely with racing, the European with dressage, saddle classes, and model events.

In Jordan today there are between ten and fifteen thousand horses. The largest private collection is owned by Sherif Nasser bin Jamil (the uncle of King Hussein), a very knowledgeable and devoted horseman who represents the Bedouin view par excellence.

From birth, desert methods are applied to his foals. At six months the colts are placed, several together, in small paddocks where they move about enough to begin development of shoulder muscles. Four or five months later they are transferred to much larger rectangular paddocks. Here gazelles await them, and in the cool of early morning and evening these new companions regularly race each other the length of the paddock, quickly arousing the competitive instincts of the colts, who most enthusiastically join in the fun. Thus the motor of the future race horse—his quarters and hocks—is built up day by day, so that when he is saddled at the age of 18 to 20 months his basic muscling is complete.

At Sherif Nasser's stud I saw two aged matrons, 31 and 34 years old, each with a fine new foal at her side. His horses are all in fine condition, due in part to Jordan's excellent dry climate, with deliciously cool mornings and evenings even in midsummer, and also to the owner's first-rate care, a felicitous combination of modern medicine and traditional Bedouin knowledge and skill. An example of Bedouin practice is to be found in the prudent consideration shown aged mares and their foals: a mare of 15 or more is expected to nurse only three months, and the foal's subsequent milk requirements are provided by a camel.

On this visit to Sherif Nasser's horses, I came away with an extra sense of pleasure deriving from the informal, democratic family atmosphere of the stables, reflecting the manners of the aristocratic Bedouin of the desert: the warmly gracious hospitality, the ready humor, the dignity, the easy relationships of staff, owner and guests.

Sherif Nasser showed me horses of all age groups and of different types—the mountain horse, for example, with his large open nostrils and small hoofs, and the desert horse with his long, relatively closed nostrils and larger hoofs. All of them were beautifully "dry," without an ounce of superfluous flesh, and they all tended to show what in Arabic is called *arih* or streamlining, stemming from a good length of back plus generous depth. In a word, they appeared to combine the speed and strength of the "drinkers of the wind."

Sherif Nasser's stable includes precious mares of ancient lineage long owned by members of his family—Sherif Hussein, King Abdullah, King Feisal I, and other royal figures. These mares are blood treasures comparable to the most precious heirlooms handed down through the successive generations of an old family. One of them, now a sound and cheerful 31 years, is a fine old desert animal of the Hamadani Simri strain, taken into Syria and Iraq by King Feisal I. She is appropriately named Um Dahab—Mother of Gold.

Among the horses one finds example after example of the Bedouin taste and view in the dry, strong, fast animals. I was reminded of a frequent experience from my years as an amateur trainer of a large stable of Arabians: whenever the genuine Bedouin connoisseur came to call, a man from a recognized horse-breeding tribe, he was invariably attracted to just this kind of horse— the doer. He expressed his appreciation in glances rather than words, lest an articulated compliment bring misfortune.

When I asked Sherif Nasser about his hopes for the future, quite apart from his regular involvement with racing in Amman, Beirut, Egypt and Greece, he replied promptly and precisely: first, to improve the quality of the horse; second, to encourage a new generation of owners and breeders; and third, to guide a new generation of racing jockeys.

Throughout the summer there are five races every Sunday in Amman, three of which are reserved for the Bedouin horses, whose owners and breeders are to be seen camping nearby in their black tents. Although he is a sophisticated and widely experienced horseman, Sherif Nasser holds fast to Bedouin traditions as the basis of his extensive efforts, with which the future of the horse in Jordan is very closely bound.

Another rewarding visit involves a drive of about thirty minutes from Amman to the royal stud of King Hussein, located in a pleasant hollow surrounded by gentle, thickly-wooded hills where the air is so light and dry it fairly sparkles. The stables are of white stucco, with generous stalls surrounding a large patio with a mosaic fountain at the center—altogether a handsome setting that is both Arab and Spanish. Here one meets the European tradition of the Arabian horse, which is itself an ancient line of taste arising from the Golden Age of Islam when the Arabs ruled the Iberian Peninsula, among other places, and involving also the central role of the Arabian horse in the early European schools of equitation.

His Majesty's stud, albeit small when compared to a large racing stable, contains a number of beautiful animals which the most discriminating European specialist would find it hard to fault. Here one sees the dashing of the head, the large, widely spaced and expressive eyes, the long, lightly curved, beautifully planed neck, the rounded delineation of the jaw, the generous pointed ears—all the hallmarks of the classical style of beauty one sees in old prints and paintings. One does not expect quite the lean dryness of the desert horse. These horses show their superior blood miles away and remind one of the best specimens of the Arabians' most distinguished offshoot, the English thoroughbred. That the royal stud contains breeding stock with the capacity to dominate and transmit fine quality is evident in the foals and youngsters to be seen.

There is an attractive outdoor school for the use of the royal family and for basic training and dressage exercises. Show jumping today depends in a large degree on thorough basic dressage, for modern courses require not only scope and the ability to jump large obstacles but also great precision, which is itself dependent on the harmony of horse and rider that results in a powerful, submitted and balanced horse, trained to accept his rider's direction in order to do his very best over an exacting course. The higher levels of dressage are to be found in European national and international events and, ultimately, in the *haute école* of the Spanische Hofreitschule of Vienna.

The museum here is an excellent beginning of a collection of saddlery of historic interest.

One leaves Jordan with the hope that conditions will one day permit the expansion of all activities related to the horse: breeding, racing, polo, dressage, trekking and export. An extensive effort is needed to register each individual horse so as to reveal his origins clearly and precisely in line with the understandable and legitimate requirements of potential buyers. Climatic conditions are nearly perfect.

THE FACE OF JORDAN

AMMAN

A Modern Capital 3,000 Years Old

Amman, the capital of the Hashemite Kingdom of Jordan, is a modern city spread across seven steep hills. It was only a village when King Abdullah moved the seat of his newly formed government there in the 1920's. Now, broad streets lined with modern shops and buildings have replaced the simple little town, and hilltops abound with spacious villas, gardens, government ministries, school and hospitals. The city's growth has been spectacular in the past decade, jumping from a population of 300,000 to 750,000—and still growing.

Recent excavations reveal that Amman was inhabited in the Early Bronze Age. The Bible mentions "Rabbath of Ammon" as the capital of the Ammonites about 1200 B.C. Two hundred years later David stormed the town. It was here that he sent Uriah the Hittite to his certain death in order to take Uriah's beautiful wife, Bathsheba. The city gained a reputation for pride, wealth and wickedness, and the prophets Amos, Jeremiah and Ezekiel foretold its destruction.

After the Babylonian captivity the Bible speaks no more of Rabbath-Ammon. Only after the general Ptolemy Philadelphus II (285–247 B.C.) took the town from the Greeks and renamed it for himself can its history be taken up again.

After the Roman conquest of the East, Philadelphia joined the Decapolis and was later captured by Herod the Great. As part of the Roman Province of Arabia the city was rebuilt *a la romana,* and flourished because of its location along the caravan trail. Amman's great Roman theater, seating 5,000 people, is still used today.

In the early Byzantine period the city became the seat of the Christian Bishopric of Petra and Philadelphia. Then, after a brief period of prominence under the Umayyads during the eighth century, it sank into obscurity.

Today Amman is the seat of government and the hub of the country's cultural and commercial activity. Indeed, its present growth is due in part to enormous business expansion, particularly with foreign investment and as headquarters for international business firms. Amman is one of the cleanest cities in the Middle East, and street crime is almost unheard of, making it especially pleasant as a place for families to live.

Amman is now the center of a network of new roads which greatly facilitate travel. Northward, a new highway runs through the hills of Gilead to Jerash, called the Pompeii of the East, and continues to Irbid, the second largest city, or to Ramtha on the Syrian border. Westward, another highway swings down through the hills of Moab to the Dead Sea, across the Jordan River, and onward to Jericho and Jerusalem.

Southward, the network offers two roads—the King's Highway, the well-trod route of antiquity which goes to Madaba and Mt. Nebo, Kerak and Petra, or the new Desert Road, which leads directly to Aqaba. Eastward, a new road crosses the desert to Azraq, making what was once an all-day journey by jeep an easy two hours' drive by car.

Newcomers may find Amman confusing at first because at ground level it is hard to grasp the city's layout. The best place for an overall view of the city is the summit of a hill known as the Citadel, situated in the center of town. It is also the best place to start one's sightseeing. In the panorama the seven major hills *Jebel* plus several minor knolls and valleys can be spotted.

Beginning on the south side, where the promontory overlooks the Roman amphitheater, you face the oldest part of the city, with Jebel Ashrafiyah in the background, distinguished by the Abu Darwish

Mosque, a stately structure of white and black stone. Moving clockwise, the next hill is Jebel Nadif, and further to the south and southeast is Jebel Nazal.

On the west and north—areas of most interest to tourists—lie Jebel Amman and Jebel Hussein, with El Webdeh and the new residential district of Shmeisani between them. These areas are the most affluent parts of town where most of the hotels, embassies, restaurants, modern shops, attractive houses and apartments are located.

Between Jebel Hussein and Jebel al Taj on the east are sections known as Nuzha, Qusur and Wadi Hadadieh. There are the poorer and older sections of the town, some completely filled with communities of refugees and other displaced persons.

EXPLORING AMMAN

The important site of antiquity in Amman can be visited in a half-day. The main ones date from the Roman period. The city's museums and places of interest pertaining to the modern aspects of Jordan may be seen in another half or full day, depending upon one's interests. Entrance to all antiquity sites and most museums throughout Jordan is free of charge, although there is talk of instituting a nominal fee at more of them.

Ancient Amman lies in Wadi Amman, a ravine through which a stream known as Seil Amman flows from west to east. It is a tributary of the Zerqa River, the Jabbok of the Bible. In ancient times the city consisted of a lower and an upper section. The latter

Points of Interest

1) Alia Head Office	12) Ministry of Tourism and
2) Antiquities Museum	Antiquities
3) Roman Amphitheater and	13) Philadelphia Hotel
Folklore Museum	14) Royal Palace
4) British Embassy	15) U.S. Embassy
5) Citadel	16) University of Jordan
6) Flying Carpet	17) Holiday Inn
7) Ambassador Hotel	18) Zahran Palace
8) Gold Market	19) First Circle
9) Grand Palace Hotel	20) Second Circle
10) Hussein Mosque	21) Third Circle
11) Jordan Inter-Continental	22) Hussein Sports City

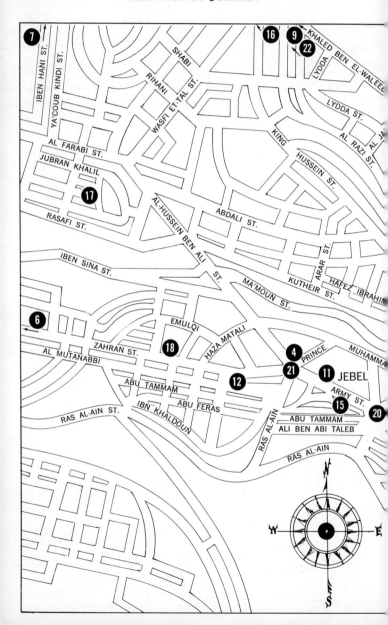

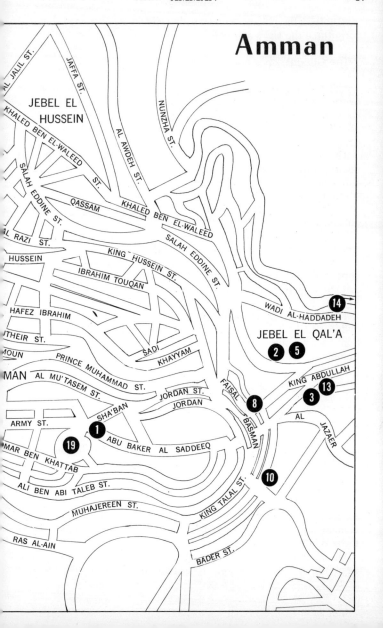

Amman

JEBEL EL HUSSEIN

JEBEL EL QAL'A

AL JALIL ST.

JAFFA ST.

KHALED BEN EL-WALEED ST.

NUNZHA ST.

SALAH EDDINE ST.

QASSAM ST.

KHALED BEN EL-WALEED

AL RAZI ST.

SALAH EDDINE ST.

HUSSEIN

KING HUSSEIN ST.

IBRAHIM TOUQAN

WADI AL-HADDADEH

HAFEZ IBRAHIM

UTHEIR ST.

SADI

KHAYYAM

MOUN

PRINCE MUHAMMAD ST.

MAN

AL MU'TASEM ST.

JORDAN ST.

FAISAL

KING ABDULLAH

JORDAN

BASMAN

ARMY ST.

SHA'BAN

AL

ABU BAKER AL SADDEEQ

JAZAER

MAR BEN KHATTAB

ALI BEN ABI TALEB ST.

MUHAJEREEN ST.

KING TALAL ST.

RAS AL-AIN

BADER ST.

was built on the hill now known as Jebel Qala'at, or the Citadel, and constituted the city's acropolis.

The Citadel

The hill is a strategically located, oblong-shaped plateau which overlooks the forum area of the lower city on the south. From very early times it was an important fortress. It is surrounded by valleys on all sides except the north, where an escarpment was cut to complete its isolation.

The upper section of the hill is in the shape of two rectangles of unequal dimensions. The first, which is oriented east-west, is about 2,700 feet long and about 180 feet wide. The second, oriented north-south, is about 1,200 feet long and 240 feet wide. The latter contains the ruins of a temple, a church, a Byzantine-Arab building and other ancient remnants.

The Romans rebuilt what was apparently an ancient fortress and surrounded it with massive walls which are among the finest of ancient fortifications to have survived to the present day. The walls consist of lower courses which incline inward in steps of heavy, well-jointed stonework overlaid by a wall of smooth square stones. The fortress' walls were fortified by towers at each corner.

The entrance to the Citadel leads into a spacious court, in the middle of which stand the ruins of a temple dedicated to Hercules, built during the reign of Marcus Aurelius (A.D. 161–180). A fragmentary inscription discovered in the debris around the temple indicated its date. It is situated close to the south wall of the acropolis. Only part of its podium and the bases of the entrance columns are still in place. Apparently the temple was once a magnificent monument towering above the lower city.

A joint British-Jordanian team headed by the well-known British archeologist Crystal Bennett carried out its third season of excavations at the Citadel in 1978. The aim is to establish a chronology of occupation of the site from earliest times.

Partial excavation near the temple shows that it was built on the site of a sacred rock which archeologists date to the Early Bronze Age, ca. 3000 B.C.

The Byzantine gate of the Citadel is still standing, and outside the Roman walls is a rock-carved cistern which supplied water to the fortress in times of siege.

On the north side of the Citadel lies *El-Qasr,* the castle, dating from the Umayyad period. It is built in the form of a square enclosing a cross, and its interior is decorated with stone carvings.

From the Citadel there is a good view of Raghdan, the Royal Palace offices across the way, used for official functions. The Palace is guarded by Circassian soldiers in colorful black and red uniforms.

The King's residence recently moved from Hashemiiya Palace on the road to the University to Basman Palace near Raghdan. It is not open to the public.

You should also take a drive around Amman to get oriented to the city. Another good panoramic view can be seen from the top of Jebel Ashrafiyah near the Abu Darivish Mosque.

The Amman Archaeological Museum

Hours: 8 A.M.–4 P.M. Closed Tuesdays. Phone 38795.

Exhibits in the museum are arranged chronologically, beginning at the right after you enter the front door and proceeding counterclockwise. A book describing the displays is available at the entrance.

Prehistoric Times (180,000 B.C. to the Neolithic Period): A skull discovered in Jerusalem revealed that man knew medicine and head surgery thousands of years ago.

Bronze Age (3000–1200 B.C.): The exhibits include pieces found in Jericho: copper lamps, coins, earrings and decorated pottery. A group of Early Bronze Age artifacts were found in a tomb alongside the Amman-Suweileh highway. Middle Bronze Age scarabs and pottery were found at the Citadel, and Late Bronze utensils come from a temple uncovered during the construction of Amman airport.

Iron Age (1200–500 B.C.): Exhibits of pottery, statues, implements, bronze and iron bracelets, gold ornaments, Egyptian scarabs and Assyrian seals. A group of pottery coffins imitating Egyptian ones were discovered in Jebel el-Qusur in 1968. (These will be found in a room on the north side of the main hall.) Most of the pottery of this period comes from Sahab, on the east side of Amman. Further excavations are planned here, since evidence shows the site was occupied in the Chalcolithic period.

Nabataean Objects: The Nabataeans are thought to have migrated into southern Jordan about the fifth century B.C. and established their capital at Petra. The objects here were found in Jebel Amman. (For the most part, objects found in the excavations at Petra are retained by the museum there.) The Amman museum's collection of Nabataean pottery is especially important as it contains excellent samples to show the fineness and decoration which made Nabataean pottery outstanding.

Hellenistic Age (330–64 B.C.): Pottery, glassware, jewelry and marble statues.

Roman Age (64 B.C.–A.D. 330): Marble statues representing gods and heroes, including a statue of Aphrodite found at Jawa, south of Amman; ornaments, glass and jewelry.

The museum also houses a collection of Byzantine, Moslem and Crusader items, and a display of the Dead Sea Scrolls.

The museum's collection has outgrown its space, and a great deal of the most recent finds are in storage. Through a joint project financed by the British and Jordanian governments a new museum will be built, and is scheduled for completion by 1980.

The Ancient Town

The ravine below the acropolis on the south is divided by the Seil Amman, a stream, into two long, narrow strips of land on which were built streets, public buildings and the forum. A colonnaded street ran along the north bank of the stream and at its eastern end there was a monumental gate, which probably led up to the temple on the hill.

The hills on both sides of the forum area have a sharp slope, causing a considerable amount of water to be carried down the hills to the forum, so that the stream overflows when the rains are heavy. The Romans solved the problem by covering the stream with a series of arches and vaults as well as installing a network of underground channels and conduits. Most of these have been damaged, either by natural causes or as a result of modern expansion, and some have completely disappeared.

It has been said that nowhere in the Roman Empire did the Roman legionnaires feel more at home than in Amman-Philadelphia. Like Rome, it was built on seven hills, and the city was embellished with fine paved streets, colonnaded plaza, baths, temples and theaters. Even the climate is similar to that of Rome.

Although the development of the town was restricted by the nature of the site, the traditional Roman city plan was used. Two great streets were the bases of the plan. The longest street, *decumanus maximus,* was a colonnaded street running along a northwest axis and ending at the foot of the acropolis. The *decumanus maximus* eventually led to a Roman road outside town that continued southward to Petra and Aila on the Gulf of Aqaba.

The *cardo,* a shorter street, ran from north to south and was lined with Corinthian columns. The two streets met at a right angle near the point where the Wadi Amman branches north.

Facing the Philadelphia Hotel today, in what is still the heart of the city, there is the large Roman theater built against the slope of a hill. It seats 5,000 spectators. Originally built in the second or third century A.D., it is still used for concerts and other outdoor events. The columns surrounding the forum have been partially reconstructed. The theater's orientation is said to be almost perfect, providing a minimum of sunlight in the spectators' eyes. Considerable restoration has already been done to the theater, and more is scheduled.

East of the hotel are the ruins of a small theater, commonly named the Odeum. To the west is the Nymphaeum, which has not been restored. No inscriptions have been found on the monuments, but the architecture suggests that they, too, were built in the second century A.D.

On either side of the large theater, inside the iron gates, are two museums.

Jordan Museum of Popular Traditions

Hours: 8 A.M.–5 P.M. daily. Phone 22316.
In the west wing of the Roman theater a museum has been created to display the rich variety of Jordan's traditional dress, jewelry and utensils.

If you do no other sightseeing in Amman, you should not miss a visit to this museum. The collection is fabulous, and it has been displayed with great taste and charm. A brochure describing the exhibits is available at the museum.

The museum is the creation of Saadiyeh Tell, widow of one of Jordan's most famous prime ministers, Wasfi Tell. Each item in the museum can be considered an heirloom. It is to Mrs. Tell's credit that she had the foresight to preserve this important national heritage and to present it in such an attractive way.

Upon entering the museum, the first hall has four standing figures on the right and two seated ones on the left. The seated lady nearest the door is from Nablus and is wearing a costume called Heaven (green) and Hell (red).

To the trained eye, the cut, color, and patterns of the embroidery on a woman's dress indicate her village or tribe, wealth and status—wife, widow, virgin. According to local tradition, the embroidery was carefully studied by young men seeking brides, for it was a good indication of a woman's skill and talent. Wherever you go in Jordan, you will see some women in embroidered native costume, but the really fine work is disappearing, and so is the beautiful old handworked silver jewelry, both of which are abundant in the museum.

In the group of standing figures (from right to left), the first wears a costume from Bethlehem made in the late 19th century. On her head she wears what looks like an inverted flowerpot, called a *shatweh*. It is a cut-off version of the medieval wimple cap or Camelot hat, which was in vogue at the time of the Crusaders. The cap is made of heavy padding and decorated with embroidery and gold and silver coins on the front. From the side of the cap seven strands of a silver necklace, known as the Seven Souls, are suspended and fall under the chin and across the chest. A waist-length jacket is worn over the dress. It is called a *taksireh,* but is often referred to as a Crusader's jacket. Both the dress and jacket are encrusted with silk and gilt cord embroidery in free-style motifs of flowers, leaves and birds—a feature which distinguishes it from the geometric cross-stitch designs which are found in most of the other dresses. Another distinguishing feature is the color—delicate pink, coral, blue and beige—in contrast to the predominantly bright red and blue of the cross-stitch.

The second figure is from Souf, a village near Ajlun. She wears a loosely fitted one-piece black dress with a narrow V-neckline. A soft black veil, caught to the sides of her turban, folds under the chin and fills in the neckline. This is bordered with blocks of color appliquéd on by a lace stitch called "daughter of the needle," which is also found on the hem and sleeves. Her whole figure is draped with chains, Koran holders, Turkish coins, and bobbles; tassels hang down her back and cascades of fringe and knots of beads and shells from her waist.

The third figure is from Beersheba. She looks tough, and is; the tribes of Beersheba are considered the toughest of the lot. The dress is voluminous and loaded with jewelry. A triangular face mask is suspended from her skullcap and spreads like wings across her cheeks, leaving only her eyes showing. The noseguard is covered with beads and shells, coins and embroidery. Around her waist a donkey belt is wound several times, ending in tassels and fringe, with seashells for good luck and the telling of fortunes. Little bells hang on swinging straps and move with her, so that she makes the sound of camel bells as she walks.

Resting at the side of the road, with her donkey's saddle bags hung on the wall behind her, is a woman from Salt. Her pipe is a good five feet long, painted all the way down to the small coal pot at its end. Her costume is called a *khalaga* and makes up in volume what it lacks in embroidery. Her dress is a triple length of strong black cotton, hiked up underneath by a waistline belt of two bands, to blouse over almost to the hem, where her only color is a zigzag embroidery.

Her top layer is shirred up midfront on a drawcord to keep the bulk of fabric from interfering with her walking. The sleeves are very long and are tied up behind her neck to carry bundles or baby. On her head is a turban, unique to Salt. It is a fat, squared, folded toque in heavy red silk, threaded with gold and silver, ending in fringes and tassels that bob about her face. The red silk, made in Damascus, is the trade mark of Salt.

More costumes, fabrics, utensils and a magnificent collection of Bedouin jewelry are displayed in several other rooms. Charming displays of hats and jewelry in four windows were recently added. Excellent labels describe each.

A showcase in the center of the jewelry room holds a huge ceremonial brass coffee pot given to the museum by the head of the Huweitat tribe. It carries the tribe's crest, the same emblem used to brand the tribe's camels and sheep. On the right side of the entrance door, there is a display of small mosaics from Madaba.

Folklore Museum

Hours: 8 A.M.–5P.M. daily except Tuesday. Phone 37196.

The east wing of the theater houses another folklore museum which is also attractively displayed. Its aim is to show traditional life—a Bedouin tent, a camel and rider in full regalia, cooking utensils, weaving, musical instruments, and a collection of old guns and swords.

Swafieh

While Ali Erar was digging in his garden one day on the western edge of Amman, he uncovered part of a beautiful mosaic floor, measuring about six by nine feet, in a good state of preservation and containing well-executed designs of birds, animals and human figures.

The mosaic, now covered by a protective metal hut, had been the floor of a church erected during the Byzantine era. The outside measurements are more than thirty feet by fifteen feet. Part of the floor was destroyed when the south wall of the church collapsed. It consists of a large rectangular field of figures surrounded by a border about two feet wide.

Outside the border there is a band of white mosaics with geometric designs and fragments of an inscription in Greek: "in the time of the holy Thomas, bishop . . . of the holy church, with zeal and labors . . ." Mention of a bishopric in the area, along with the designs and technique, which closely resemble those in Madaba, place this church in the sixth century A.D., a time when the area was part of the See of Madaba.

The discovery provided new insights into the art and life of early Christians. It is one of the most beautiful and best preserved mosaic floors in the area. There is a wide range of color and figures, and the intricate designs and details reveal a high quality of workmanship. There was an apparent attempt to portray ordinary activities rather than theological themes. This, scholars believe, reflects the early Christians' close integration of religion with everyday life.

The four corners of the border held faces representing the four seasons, similar to a design in a mosaic found in one of the Madaba churches. In the border on the north side were pairs of birds or animals facing each other. Vines extend from a colorful amphora in a symmetrical circular pattern to enclose the various figures. To the left of the amphora is a large animal with a remarkable blending of colors, and above it is a human figure leading a donkey. There are two other human figures represented, a camel girl leaning on a staff and a boy wearing shoes and holding a bow. Outside the border are two peasants facing a tree.

Swafieh is a bit difficult to find. It is nothing more than a cluster of houses on a small hill west of the highway about halfway between the sixth and seventh circles on Jebel Amman. There is a small road sign which is easy to miss.

Sports City

Hussein Sports City is a large complex on the outskirts of Amman on the road to the University. It is operated by the Al Hussein Youth and Sports Organization established in 1966.

The complex has a stadium, seating 25,000 spectators, which is used for soccer games, track and field meets, and various kinds of festivals. The oval-shaped building is circled by a sidewalk of hand-cut red stone; seats are made of white and rose stone. A covered pavillion along the west side shelters a special seating section which holds 2,500 people. A reserved section has a private entrance for King Hussein and his guests and a soundproof press room.

In addition to the main stadium, the complex contains two other soccer and track fields used for minor competition and training. There are three large swimming pools—a main pool for competition, a diving pool with five boards, and a smaller pool for training and for children. There is a spectator stand for 1,500 people. The poolside restaurant is one of Amman's most popular summer lunching spots.

The main tennis courts, which are used for international tournaments, have a seating section for 1,000 spectators. There are six practice courts and an adjoining section for badminton, six volleyball courts and six basketball courts, Jordan's second favorite sport after soccer. A separate clubhouse has a gymnasium, four squash courts, recreation hall, cafeteria, conference room, and dormitory for visiting teams.

The complex is dominated by the Palace of Culture, a dramatic structure designed to resemble a Bedouin tent. Its auditorium can seat up to 2,500 and is used for dramatic, musical, and social entertainment. It is also suitable for conferences and conventions.

Other facilities of the building include a small auditorium for art exhibitions and other cultural presentations, dressing rooms, press and radio rooms, and a restaurant area. It is centrally heated, air conditioned, and soundproofed.

Hussein Sports City also has its own public gardens where approximately 30,000 trees of different varieties have been planted. The National Martyrs Memorial to the Unknown Soldier includes a small military museum which contains mementos of the Hashemite family and Jordan's contemporary history. It is open to the public.

PRACTICAL INFORMATION FOR AMMAN

PERSONAL SERVICES. Beauty Shops: Amman appears to have a beauty shop on every corner. These shops are up to European standards and their prices are reasonable. Appointments may be made by phone, but most shops take customers without appointments. A wash and set will range from JD1–3; manicure, about 500 fils. Most leading American and European products for home permanent, rinse or tint are available locally.

Hanz, Jebel Amman, First Circle (Phone: 25279), is a long-established shop patronized by the Queen Mother and many of Amman's leading ladies.

Antoine, Jebel Amman, first circle (Phone: 25373), is another choice of Amman's social ladies.

Jordan Inter-Continental Beauty Salon is clean and quick. Wash and set costs JD2.

Raja, Jebel Webdeh, is another popular one, especially good at cutting hair, we are told. We've never tried him. JD1.500 for wash and set; JD1 for haircut.

Barbers: Leading hotels have barbers or will call one on request. A haircut costs from 500 fils for short hair, 600 fils and up for long hair, and JD1 for wash and cut.

Laundry and Dry Cleaning: Hotels have facilities for their clients. Most laundry and cleaning plants are small, hand-labor establishments. Laundry is good and speedy; dry cleaning is adequate. Cost for cleaning and pressing a man's suit is about 750 fils.

Shoe Repair: Most residential areas have tiny repair shops. Ask your hotel concierge to take care of emergency repairs; language might be a problem with tradesmen of this sort.

Watch Repair: Leading makes of Japanese, American and European watches are sold in Amman, and jewelers selling them will have repair service. Cost will be reasonable.

Pharmacies: There are always several pharmacies in every neighborhood, and they are well stocked with U.S. and European products. Pharmacies have a weekly rotating system so that at least one is open 24 hours. Its name and phone number is announced daily on the radio and in the local newspaper.

Baby Sitters: There is no organized service in Amman, but your hotel should be able to help you arrange for a sitter. Fee should be about 500 fils per hour.

NEWSPAPERS. In addition to the English-language daily *Jordan Times,* the *International Herald-Tribune* and British newspapers are available, usually a day late. Bookshops stock American and European periodicals including *Time, Newsweek,* and the *Economist,* and major Middle East ones—*Events, Middle East Digest, Middle East Economic Review, Monday Morning.* A new English-language women's magazine, *Perspective,* was started recently by a group of Jordanian women and is published in Amman. It includes local and international news and features of interest to women in the Arab World.

 ENTERTAINMENT. Most of the social life in Amman takes place in private homes and at clubs, but there are some activities available to visitors. To learn what is going on in Amman during your visit, consult the *Jordan Times,* the country's daily English-language newspaper. It carries a column listing special events. Notices are sometimes posted at leading hotels and travel agencies. A calendar of local activities also appears in *Perspective,* Jordan's monthly magazine for women.

Movie houses show American and English films as well as Arabic ones. Ask your hotel concierge to check the Arabic newspapers for showtime. Features change every week or so. Tickets are about 600 fils.

Cultural Activities. The Amman Amateur Theater, which draws its talent from British and American residents as well as Jordanians, is a new group that gives amateur performances throughout the year. The British Council also holds regular lectures and art exhibits, and has library facilities and educational and documentary films. There is a small membership fee.

The French Cultural Center, American Center, Goethe Institute, and Soviet Cultural Center sponsor programs of music and films, art shows and lectures. Most offer language classes and have libraries open to the public. American and British performers appear occasionally, under the sponsorship of the U.S. Information Service and the British Council.

 GALLERIES. The number of artists in Jordan has grown considerably during the past decade. There are over fifty painters and sculptors, both men and women, concentrated in the Amman area. Most are members of the recently organized Jordanian Artists Association, which serves as a cooperative body through which the artists receive governmental support in their activities. The Ministry of Culture has recently opened an exhibition center where the works of Jordanian artists are displayed on a rotating basis.

The only commercial gallery with a stock of paintings and prints by local artists is located in the Jordan Inter-Continental Hotel. The owner of the shop is very knowledgeable and can give you information on any of the artists whose work she shows. Prices range from JD20–60, although works by some of the better-known artists will cost more.

Despite a paucity of commercial art galleries, many exhibitions are held throughout the year in the various cultural centers, clubs and institutions of Amman. All are announced in the daily press and are open to the public.

Those interested in learning more about Jordan's art scene and perhaps getting to meet a few of the younger artists might pay a visit to the Royal Institute of Fine Arts, the government art school established several years ago. The man to see is Mohanna Durra, its director, who is one of the country's leading artists and an active force behind the development of contemporary art in Jordan.

 ARCHEOLOGY. In 1962 two American women living in Jordan formed Friends of Archaeology, a society to promote study and visits to archeological sites throughout the country, to enable members to partici-pate in archeological excavations, and to assist the Department of Antiq-uities. Within a year the organization's membership had grown to 200 with eleven nationalities represented, and it has continued to attract members through the years. Membership is JD3 per year, and applications may be obtained from the American Center or the British Council. Regular lectures in English by prominent archeologists and visiting scholars are held for members and are open to the public. Throughout the year field trips, usually led by a visiting archeologist, are arranged for members to places of archeological interest.

In addition, members have volunteered their services to the Department of Antiquities, participated in digs at locations throughout the country and assisted with the inventories of several museums. The Society publishes a booklet on visits to archeological sites in the Amman area.

If you have an interest in amateur archeology you might find membership in this group enjoyable and stimulating. Non-members may join an outing provided a member of the organization makes the arrangements. You may contact the Society through the director of the American School for Oriental Research in Amman, P.O. Box 2440, or through the Department of Antiquities.

 CLUBS. Social and service clubs in Amman offer activities and programs for residents. Foreigners who expect to live here for a time will find them an easy way to make new friends.

The *American Women of Amman Club* is open to all American women and wives of Americans. There is no membership fee. It meets on the second Monday of each month. Among other activities, it has put together a handbook, *Welcome to Amman,* which is helpful to newcomers; it contains general information, shopping maps and a telephone directory. It is on sale in Amman bookstores for JD1.250.

The *Home and Garden Club* is made up of Jordanites and foreigners living in Amman. It meets the first Monday of each month. Membership is JD2 per year.

Lions International meets twice a month at the Jordan Inter-Continental Hotel. *Rotary Club* holds weekly luncheon meetings each Tuesday at the Jordan Inter-Continental Hotel.

YWCA, Third Circle, Jebel Amman, offers cooking, exercise and language classes for a fee. It also has tennis courts available for both men and women members.

Haya Arts Center, a new Jordanian cultural club, is very active.

 SCHOOLS AND UNIVERSITIES. *American Community School* offers kindergarten through ninth grade in a two-semester school year, following the American system. All teachers have American degrees. The school years begins in early September and ends in early June.

International Community School offers kindergarten through sixth grade and follows the British system.

There is one English/Arabic-language kindergarten in Amman run by a British-trained teacher. It accepts children from three to five years.

There are many other schools, but instruction is in the Arabic language with English taught as a second language. A full description is available in the American Women's Club handbook.

The *University of Jordan*, established in 1962 with 167 students, has grown to an annual enrollment of over 7,000 students in seven faculties—Arts and Science, Economics and Commerce, Medicine and Nursing, Agriculture, Education, Engineering, Law and *Shari'a* (Moslem jurisprudence). The bachelor's degree is awarded in 29 fields of study and the master's degree in 15 fields of specialization. The faculty numbers about 300. Women students make up about 38% of the enrollment. All courses in the Humanities are taught in Arabic; those in Science are taught in English.

The campus, located north of Amman on the road to Jerash, is spread over 300 acres and has 26 buildings. The University expects to spend about $30 million through 1980 on further expansion. It derives its income from four sources. Two percent of all customs duties collected by the government and fees from certain commercial transactions are earmarked for the University; these make up about 45% of its budget. A second source is an annual government grant, which makes up about 27% of total revenues. Academic fees and tuition account for 13%. The balance of approximately 15% is obtained from aids and contributions from local private industry and individuals, foreign governments, foundations and international organizations.

The University is unusual in that it is a national institution created by the state but operated independently of any ministry of government.

The University of Yarmouk, created in 1976 in Irbid, is not connected with the University of Jordan. It opened on a 20-acre temporary campus with four buildings to house its School of Arts and Sciences. The new institution has 1,000 students and expects to have 20,000 by 1984.

When it has completed building at its permanent site it will have four faculties—Arts and Sciences, Medical Sciences, Engineering and Agriculture and Veterinary Medicine. There will be buildings for classrooms, dormitories, a library, civic and cultural centers, a sports complex, and a medical school with a training hospital of 500 beds, at an estimate cost of $150 million. The 2,500-acre campus is located on the Damascus road between Naimeh and Ramtha.

SPORTS. Sports Clubs: Amman has four clubs offering a variety of sports. They are open to international membership. Newcomers must be introduced by a member, and there may be a waiting list. Tourists cannot use the facilities except in the company of a member.

Al-Hussein Youth City (Sports City) is a large complex on the outskirts of Amman. It offers many sports facilities including tennis, squash, indoor and outdoor swimming, and a gymnasium. Membership is sometimes difficult to obtain and is restricted to families and single women; no single men.

The Orthodox Club is located about three miles outside the city. Sports activities include tennis, soccer and swimming.

The Royal Jordanian Automobile Club, 7th Circle, Jebel Amman, is on the

Wadi Seer Road near the American Community School. It has an archery range, a swimming pool and a tennis court. Membership is restricted. The Club also sponsors automobile rallies in Jordan several times a year.

The Royal Racing Club in Marka offers summer horse and camel racing. It also has bowling alleys for use by members.

All these clubs have restaurant facilities which are available for use by tourists, provided proper arrangements are made. Ask your hotel for assistance.

Archery: The Amman Archery Club is a part of the Royal Jordanian Automobile Club. It has practice ranges, and a limited supply of equipment is available.

Backgammon: Off King Feisal Street in an alley leading past an open-air coffee house you will find a group of Jordanian men hunched over upturned crates or boxes. Resting on the makeshift tables will be colorful highly polished mosaic boards with various geometric designs. From time to time a player at each table will roll a pair of dice and shout out the numbers. The other player will usually be smashing a handful of small discs on the board. There is much clatter. As the men play, they puff on their *nargileh,* or water pipes, or sip from small cups of coffee. They rarely look up from their game; they are just as serious about it as any poker or bridge player.

The game they play has been the single most popular game in the Middle East for thousands of years. To the Westerner it is known as backgammon. Jordanians call it "tric trac." Other Arabs call it *nard* or *towleh.* The ancient Arabs called a variation of the game *tabula.* Medieval Englishmen called it "tables." Romans called another variation "twelve-lined game." Westerners call still another variation "parcheesi."

Archeological digs have turned up a table made for a game very much like tric trac over 5,000 years ago in the ancient city of Ur in southern Iraq. The Iranians claim their ancient king, Nardashir, ordered that a game be developed which would balance luck—the thrown dice—and skill—the knowledge of which discs to move or not to move after each throw.

Camel racing and falconry are popular pasttimes in Jordan and throughout the Arab world, but nothing approaches the popularity of backgammon. It is played by men and women, young and old. It is played wherever a playing board can be set up—in homes, classrooms, restaurants, cafés, barber shops, police barracks and military guard booths. Quick games are played on business desks or shop counters during the noon break.

To understand tric-trac, think of it as it relates to the calendar. There are 30 discs, which stand for the days of the month. They are black and white, for night and day. Each playing board has four sections, which represent the seasons. There are 24 positions, representing the hours of the day and night. The 12 months of the year are found in each player's 12 positions. The object of the game is to see who can move his discs around the board—equal to completing the year—the fastest.

Bowling: The Bowling Club is situated at the Royal Racing Club near the airport. It has a four-lane bowling alley.

Camping: Jordan offers five totally different camping experiences: the desert in the Wadi Rum; the sea on the coast of Aqaba; the canyon at Petra; the mountains and hot springs at Zerka Ma'in; and the forest in Debbin National Park. Propane and kerosene stoves and lanterns for camping are available at reasonable prices in Amman, but other camping equipment is difficult to find. Camping trips of two or three days into the desert by camel caravan, can be organized by travel agencies in Amman.

Chess: The Chess Club, Wadi Seer Road, is open daily from 5 P.M. to late evening. Dues are JD1 per month, and visitors are welcome.

Fishing: A wide variety of colorful and exotic fish is found in the Gulf of Aqaba, where fishing is a year-round sport. A glass-bottom boat and fishing equipment can be rented through the hotels in Aqaba. Fresh-water fishing can be enjoyed at Wadi Zerka and Azraq. No Western-style tackle is available in Amman. A fishing license is required, and is available from the Royal Society for the Conservation of Wildlife, Fifth Circle, Jebel Amman.

Flying: The Royal Jordanian Air Academy at the Amman Airport offers instruction and the opportunity for flying.

Horseback Riding: Riding facilities are available by courtesy of the Jordan Army, which has a polo club. Stables are about a half-hour from Amman. Riding instruction is available. There is an hourly fee for riding. Some foreigners living in Amman have purchased Arabian horses. If you plan to ride, bring riding attire.

Horse Racing: Under the supervision of the Royal Racing Club, weekly horse races are held at Marka in Amman in spring and summer. Camel races are held intermittently at the same tracks. Yes, we said "camel races"; it's a-now-I've-seen-everything-experience. Riders bounce in their wooden saddles eight feet above the ground while their camels run with outstretched necks, feet flat to the ground. In a short run a good camel runs half as fast as a speedy Arabian horse, but in a long run a camel can overtake him.

Hunting: Wild boar, quail, desert sand grouse, partridge, pigeon, dove, duck, snipe and migratory birds are hunted in Jordan. The season begins in autumn and ends in spring. Jordan has hunting regulations, and you should inquire about these upon arrival. Shotgun shells may be purchased locally; guns are expensive. If you plan to bring firearms, inquire at the nearest Jordanian Embassy for the necessary papers. Good hunting requires excursions into fairly remote areas. These trips will require time and effort on your part. A hunting license is required, but first a gun license must be obtained. Full details are available from the Royal Society for the Conservation of Wildlife, Fifth Circle, Jebel Amman.

Scuba Diving and Snorkeling: Equipment and instruction are available in Aqaba. Spear-fishing is strictly prohibited. The newest addition to Aqaba is Aqua Marina, a diving club, which has its own boats and equipment. The club has a new building directly on the beach where rooms can be rented for JD5.500 double with shared bath. The facilities include a dive shop, restaurant, discotheque, chess and backgammon. The cost for diving instruction is JD3.500 per dive including equipment and transportation. The marina has about a dozen boats, and instruction is also available in sailing and water skiing. Information can be obtained by writing Aqua Marina, M.A.S.S., P.O. Box 6951, Amman. Phone: 44938; Aqaba, Phone: 3555. The company is headed by Simon Khoury, who was once water-ski champion of Lebanon. There are other scuba centers in Aqaba, either connected with or reached through your hotel.

Swimming: In Amman swimming pools are available to guests at the Jordan Inter-Continental Hotel and the Holiday Inn, and at the Hussein Sports City, the Orthodox Club and the Royal Jordanian Automobile Club to members only. In most cases single males are not accepted as members. Pools are open from the beginning of May until the end of September. Sports City has an indoor pool also.

The Dead Sea is less than an hour's drive from Amman. Swimming here is an experience you should not miss. The water contains so much salt you will float more than swim. The high salt content also makes it uncomfortable to stay in the water for more than a few minutes at a time.

The best area for swimming is the Gulf of Aqaba, five hours by car from Amman over a good highway, 30 minutes by plane. Air-conditioned hotel facilities are available, and the new Holiday Inn has a swimming pool. South of the town are crystal-clear seas washing miles of empty white sand beaches, and you can have both almost to yourself.

Tennis: Hussein Sports City, Automobile Club and Orthodox Club have tennis courts, but they are for members and their guests. There are also courts at the YWCA.

Water Skiing: At Aqaba, you may rent boats and ski. Cost: JD1 per person for a quarter-hour, including boat.

SHOPPING. The handicrafts of Jordan are interesting, varied and tempting. You can spend many hours wandering around the *souk,* or bazaar, stopping at shops along the way. Over a cup of coffee you will admire the wares, chat with the shopkeepers and be persuaded to buy through the innate skill of the merchants, for whom trade has been a tradition for centuries.

Modern shops are full of American and European products. If your favorite brand of a particular item is not available, you should be able to find a reasonable substitute. There are no stores resembling an American or British department store; rather, there are boutiques and specialty shops in the downtown shopping area and in neighborhoods through the city. In the *souk,* merchants selling similar wares are usually grouped together, as in the Gold Souk.

Fixed prices are becoming widespread, although merchants are still ready to bargain, especially in the Gold Souk and in souvenir shops. Then, too, if you buy a large quantity from any one shop you can expect to get a discount.

For shopping in town it is best to take a taxi or service to the center; parking is not permitted on the main streets of the downtown area.

Store hours: Generally 9 A.M. to 1 or 1:30 P.M. and 3 or 3:30 to 6:30 or 7 P.M. Many shops close on Fridays; others on Sundays.

HANDICRAFTS

The cross-culture of the Jordanians is visibly reflected in their handicrafts. Greek and Roman designs evolve into Byzantine and Crusader motifs and mingle with the arabesque. The products are readily available, but the history behind their creation and development is not always so discernible.

Silver Jewelry: Christian and Bedouin symbols prevail in this craft. The most characteristic is the Crusader's cross—five crosses grouped as one, symbolizing the five nations of the crusading armies. The Crusaders' cross is made in many sizes and often set with semiprecious stones. There is also the Jerusalem Cross, the St. James Cross, the Cappadocian and the Star of Bethlehem. They range in price from JD1.500–5.000. These crosses are also made as brooches, necklaces, earrings, bracelets and cuff links.

Jewelry still worn by Bedouin women—bracelets, earrings, necklaces and forehead ornaments—might include the Hand of Fatima (daughter of the Prophet Muhammad), worn as a good-luck charm. The hand is also symbolic to Christians (the hand of Mary) and to Jews (the hand of Esther). Actually, it is a pagan charm predating all three religions; it was found at Jericho in the pre-Hebraic period.

Often silver pieces are inset with blue stones to ward off the evil eye. Others are designed in traditional geometric and arabesque patterns.

The percentage of silver is stamped on all solid silver articles. It is approximately 90% sterling.

Carved Olivewood: The olivewood industry is comparatively new, but the products reflect centuries of tradition. Bethlehem is known for its skilled craftsmen who make rosaries, album and Bible covers, native-dressed figurines, bases, boxes, crucifixes, creches and the *masbaha,* which is a string of 33 or 99 beads, often carried by Moslem men. Each bead represents an attribute of Allah. Foreigners have dubbed them "worry beads." A small *masbaha* or a rosary of olivewood with a small glass bubble containing Jordan River water, certified by the Terra Santa, costs JD1 and up.

A popular gift for children is the caravan of three camels led by a donkey. The price is determined by size and carving, and ranges from JD1 to 10. Another popular item is a spoon-and-fork salad set, which costs JD1 to 3.

Mother-of-Pearl: Inlaid mother-of-pearl is a specialty of Bethlehem, where many establishments are engaged in the industry. The shell is imported from abroad, as it might have been in olden days. The mother-of-pearl is worked into intricate designs on crucifixes, picture frames, jewelry boxes, and covers for Bibles, prayer books and the Koran. The skill of the craftsman, rather than the material, determines the price. Mother-of-pearl rosaries cost JD1.500–2.000; crosses from 150 fils to JD1.500; jewelry boxes from JD2–25, more for the very large ones.

Cross-stitch Embroidery: This craft represents delicate skill and many traditions. (See under Jordan Museum of Popular Traditions earlier in this chapter for more information.) Most patterns and colors are copied from those on dresses of peasant women, whose home village or tribe may be identified by their dress. Both the handmade materials and the embroidery have undergone several stages of development and are excellent examples of the women's skills. In the past the towns best known for their handwork were Ramallah, Bethlehem and Jerusalem. Nowadays a great deal of it is being done by refugee ladies, especially widows, as a livelihood.

In the cross-stitch design three main origins are distinguishable. The Byzantine is geometric in form; the Persian uses plants, leaves, flowers and fruit, copied from rugs; and the third depicts the daily life of the country in the form of animals, birds and human figures.

The embroidery has two basic styles. One is the cross-stitch on silk, linen or handwoven cotton, using different colored threads, with red and black preferred. The second type is the freehand stitch in gold and silver thread on velvet, wool or silky textiles. The placing and size of designs are left to the imagination of the creator, but the designs themselves are traditional and stylized and bear names revealing their origin, such as the Star of Bethlehem, the Greek Key, the palm tree, the kohl bottle, and many others.

Several private groups such as the Arab Development Society and the Family Cooperative of Ramallah have adapted cross-stitch embroidery to useful products. Table linens, dolls, aprons, guest towels, belts, bookmarks, children's dresses, neckties, baby bibs, handbags and handkerchiefs are reasonably priced and make lovely gifts to take home. There is an Arab Development Society shop at the Jordan Inter-Continental Hotel with a nice selection of these gifts. Another shop is Jordan Craft Center, Second Circle, Jebel Amman. Almost all the souvenir and handicraft shops in Amman and elsewhere have at least a small selection.

Another popular item is a short coat or cape known as a Crusader's jacket, made of velvet and corded silk, usually in black, white, wine or blue and embroidered with gold or silver thread. The old ones are difficult to find and are now collector's items; the new ones are machine-made. Kaftans can be found machine stitched from JD2 to 10. The handmade ones cost as little as JD12 or as much as JD100, depending upon the amount and quality of the workmanship.

Palestine Pottery: The art of ceramics is one of the oldest crafts in the Middle East, although Jerusalem's pottery factory was for many years the only one to keep it alive. Now there are many in Hebron as well, and the products are readily available in gift and souvenir shops. The original factory, known as Palestine Pottery, was started in 1919 by two potters who were among those brought from Turkey to restore the 16th-century tiles in the Dome of the Rock in Jerusalem.

The tiles and pottery are painted with designs that follow the traditional Islamic art of geometric patterns, decorative Arabic script and representations of nature. Other pieces show designs of Christian significance, such as the cross, the fish, and scenes from the life of Christ. Another popular motif is a reproduction of the ancient mosaics found in the area. The most notable of these is a mosaic called the Tree of Life, found in the Hisham Palace in Jericho. Copies of ancient tiles in the great mosques of Iran and Turkey and the Dome of the Rock are also available. Prices are reasonable. Tiles, plates, small vases, beer mugs range from 500 fils to JD2.500, depending on size.

Hebron Glass: There are many places now producing glass in Hebron, but for years it was the tradition of one family, handed down for many generations. Ancient techniques are used to produce jugs, bowls, plates, vases, glasses and mugs that are charming for their primitive qualities—and very fragile. Chunky beads with symbols to ward off the evil eye are made into inexpensive necklaces and bracelets. The most popular color for the glass is deep blue, but it is also made in green, purple, amber and white. One of the most attractive items is a ceiling lamp made of different pieces of colored glass and costing about JD5. There is also a glass-blowing factory on the outskirts of Amman near the Jordan Television station.

Bedouin Rugs: Brightly colored rugs in traditional tribal designs are handwoven by the Bedouin today as they were in Biblical times. The best are made in Madaba, Shobak, Kerak and Tafileh, and are easily distinguished by their designs. There are also plain gray wool and multicolored ones. These rugs used to be very inexpensive, but no longer. A 9 x 4 rug costs from JD50 up, and they are becoming scarce.

To determine that a rug is a "genuine Bedouin," be sure the tassels are a continuation of the rug threads and not sewn on separately. If hemp and cotton are used and the colors are not fast, the rug is a fake. So, if you don't know rugs, know the merchant.

Aqaba Sand: Decorative patterns in different colors of sand in a bottle are popular souvenirs. Prices are 500 fils to JD1.

Coral: The bottom of the Gulf of Aqaba is one of the world's most beautiful underwater gardens; coral was fished here until laws were passed to prohibit it. There is still coral in the marketplace but it's expensive. A real coral *masbaha* costs JD80 and up. A substance that looks like black coral, and known as *usor* in Arabic, is made into inexpensive jewelry.

Candles: On Christian Street in the Old City of Jerusalem near the Church of the Holy Sepulchre are many candlemakers' shops. There are numerous types, but one in particular is unique to the Holy Land. It is shaped like flat, elongated bells, with a gold tracery design on one side and religious symbols on the other. It is decorative for any season and especially attractive at Christmas. Originally this candle was called *Al Kaff,* which means "the palm." Traditionally a bride held one of these candles in each hand and danced before the bridegroom on the evening of the wedding day.

Huge encrusted candles and bunches of votive tapers are also on sale. You may have candles (and rosaries) blessed in the Church of the Holy Sepulchre.

Fleece-lined Jackets and Slippers: Nothing could be warmer, and the slippers are wonderful for house or after-ski wear. Several shops in Amman specialize in sheepskin jackets. Prices start at JD15.

Gold: Amman is one of the best places in the world to buy gold, because it is sold by weight, and the price is based on the world-market rate. The price of an item will be the cost of the gold plus the workmanship. If you are planning to buy a valuable gold product you should know the current market rate of gold. You are then in a position to bargain for the finished product and to know if you are getting a fair price. The market in gold is closely supervised by the government, and all items must be marked for their gold content.

Some of the work is done in Jordan by hand. Shops sell rings, bracelets, chains, necklaces, earrings, pins, broaches, pendants, picture frames, charms, watches, clocks and many other small items.

About 50 shops make up the main gold market, Souk Ad-Dahhab, in the heart of downtown between King Feisal and Shab Sough Street and several tiny lanes in between.

Two shops not in the souk are jewelry shops in the Western sense. They are exclusive, elegant, and high priced, selling only high-quality jewelry, much of which is imported. *Marquise* is in a house between Second and Third Circles, Jebel Amman. The shop is half a block down and across the street from the Inter-Continental. Telephone: 41074. *Jabasini* is a half-block in the other direction, located directly on the Second Circle, Jebel Amman. Telephone: 22228.

Antiquities: According to the Director of Antiquities, it is prohibited to sell or buy antiquities older than 18th-century and to export them from the country. Items from the 18th and 19th centuries are available for purchase.

A small gallery in the lobby of the Inter-Continental Hotel has prints and paintings by Jordanian and other artists, as well as antique items and new objects of good workmanship. Phone: 41361, ext. 190.

The *Jordan Craft Center* on a narrow alley opening onto Zahran Street is a step from the Second Circle, Jebel Amman. A wall sign near the Babalu Restaurant points the way. This is a non-profit store that sells goods made by refugees and local craftsmen. There is some old silver jewelry and a good supply of kaftans. Phone: 44555.

Rabbath Ammon Oriental Bazaar on Jebel Hussein, located on Khaled Ibn Al Waleed Street, specializes in Crusader jackets and caps, scarfs, blouses, native costumes, gold and silver items, rugs, greeting cards and picture slides. Phone: 63636.

Jordan Souvenirs is in the center of Amman on Prince Mohammed Street near the General Post Office. Phone: 25645. It has one of the finest collections of old kaftans in Jordan. Many of these, which were made and used long ago, are virtually museum pieces. On some the embroidery is made up of thousands of stitches and knots. The dresses have been thoroughly cleaned before they are offered for sale. The shop has the same owners as *Amman Souvenirs*, Third Circle, Jebel Amman, and the gift shop at the airport.

The *Jordan Gift Store* in the lobby of the Inter-Continental Hotel has a very good selection and a great variety of handicrafts at reasonable prices. Phone: 41463.

MISCELLANEOUS

Art Supplies: Basic art supplies can be purchased at the *Art Supply Center,* Second Circle, Jebel Amman. It is operated by Samia Zaru, who is one of Jordan's well-known artists. The shop is in a house half a block on the right from the ALIA Public Relations Office, but you may not always find it open. Phone: 42741.

Bookshops: There are many small stores throughout the city. Stocks appeared to be limited to popular, fast-selling books. For books on Jordan and the Middle East try Amman Bookshop, Third Circle, Jebel Amman.

Clothing and Shoes: Selections of ready-to-wear clothing is improving all the time as many new stores open with the latest high-fashion styles. Some of the best, especially the smart boutiques, are situated on or near the First and Third Circles on Jebel Amman, near the Khalaf Circle on Jebel Webdeh and around the Feras Circle on Jebel Hussein. Less expensive clothes are found in stores on King Feisal Street and other nearby streets in the downtown area. Shoes with American lasts are not available on the local market.

Cosmetics and Toiletries: Most well-known brands of European and American cosmetics and toiletries are available at pharmacies and specialty stores throughout the city. Such shops are often in or near hotels, so if you forgot to pack something, you should have no difficulty finding it or an adequate substitute in Amman.

Florists: Flowers are seasonal and can be expensive. There are neighborhood shops, and your hotel can direct you to one nearby. It is appropriate to thank a host and hostess for a lunch or dinner invitation with flowers or a box of candy.

Food Products: A wide variety of fresh vegetables is available most of the year, but quality and price will depend on the season. Grocery stores carry imported canned goods, but prices will be double to triple the U.S. cost. Local fruit, especially citrus, is excellent.

Local fresh and imported frozen meat and poultry are available on the local market. The lamb and mutton are of better quality than the beef.

Liquor is readily available. Grocery stores sell wine, liquor and beer. Cost of liquor in a store begins at JD2 for Scotch, JD1.800 for gin, JD3.250 for bourbon.

Export of Local Items: Ask the store where you buy your gifts and souvenirs to ship your purchase to the U.S. or Europe. Generally, oriental stores in Jordan have a reputation for reliability in mailing or shipping parcels.

 HOTELS. Like other Middle East capitals, Amman has found itself short of hotel rooms in the midst of a business and travel boom. The problem should begin to ease soon with the opening of several hotels in different categories and extensions or renovations of some existing properties;

however, the situation will not really improve until 1980 and 1981 when several large projects should be completed.

Hotel rates and categories are established by the Ministry of Tourism. The government has been examining all hotels with a view to reclassifying them, and none too soon; many of them have been overrated, at least by international standards. For this reason we do not include the old categories here but rather describe those properties which we have examined in person and can recommend. They are listed in the order which we believe they would appeal to American travelers, depending on their budget.

Jordan Inter-Continental. Zahran St., 3rd Circle, Jebel Amman, P.O. Box 1827. Phone: 41361. Double, J.D.19.500.

Located across the street from the American Embassy on Jebel Amman with a commanding view of the city, the modern, glassy structure is mellowed by the warmth of its attractive interior design. The 250 guest rooms are large, comfortable and nicely furnished. Almost all are fitted with twin beds, and most have balconies; all have private bath, direct dial telephone, mini bars, and television on request.

Facilities include a swimming pool, rooftop restaurant, coffee shop, beauty salon, barber shop, newsstand, airline and car rental desks, bank, travel agency offices, telex, taxi service and several shops. Another nice feature: there's a laundry/dry cleaning shop which gives quick service. The bar off the main lobby has become a favorite meeting place for businessmen from around the world. There has been extensive remodeling of the restaurant facilities. The newest addition is a disco.

When the hotel was first built there was almost nothing else in the neighborhood; now the city has grown to such an extent that it is quite centrally located. It has been part of Pan Am's Inter-Continental chain since 1964. Another 150 rooms are planned; when they are completed, the older part will be completely refurbished. A shopping center is also to be added. American Express cards accepted.

Holiday Inn. Al Hussein Ben Ali St., Shmeisani, P.O. Box 6399. Phone: 65167. Double, J.D.19.

This brand-new inn is the first deluxe hotel to be built in the Jordanian capital since the Inter-Continental opened almost two decades ago, and the first of several planned international chain hotels. The Holiday Inn is a joint venture of the Nazzal family, well-known Jordanian innkeepers; Alia, and the Jordan government.

The 10-story tower has rooms on nine floors and a nightclub on the tenth. Each floor has four suites and four studios in addition to the standard room with two double beds. Each enjoys an unobstructed view of the city.

Facilities include five restaurants: a 24-hour coffee shop adjacent to the main dining room, Churchill Restaurant and bar; a steakhouse; the Oasis, a lounge patisserie; El Liwan for Jordanian cuisine; a French restaurant, and a ballroom which can seat 400 for dinner. A buffet lunch for J.D.3 on Fridays and Sundays is the hotel's specialty. Regina's Inner Circle is the discotheque. The Ambassador nightclub has a cabaret, dinner and dancing for J.D.6, and the bar becomes a piano bar after 9:30 P.M.

There is a swimming pool with cabanas.

The shopping arcade includes a curio shop, bank, newsstand, government press and telex center, and an Alia ticket office. The hotel plans to have its own courtesy bus to pick up passengers from the airport and town.

Grand Palace. University Street, Shmeisani, P.O. Box 6916; Telex 1292; Phone: 61121. Price: JD10 double.

The 160-room hotel is owned by the Sawalha family, which also has the Palace Hotels in Jerusalem and Bethlehem. The Grand Palace is located on the road to Hussein Sports City, a bit out of town. (Incidentally, there is another hotel named Grand. Be sure to ask for this by its full name, *Grand Palace*.) There are 12 single rooms, 4 suites and 6 triples; the rest are doubles. All have a private bath. There is a lobby lounge, meeting rooms, shops, hairdresser, barber shop, pharmacy, newsstand, bank, airline desk, travel agency and 24-hour taxi service. American Express cards accepted.

An extension of 300 rooms in a separate 22-story tower is now under construction and is scheduled to open in 1980. The new part is planned to be more deluxe than the present one, and will be managed by Sheraton Hotel Corporation. It will have a swimming pool, rooftop supper club, meeting facilities and shops.

Cameo, 5th Circle, Jebel Amman. Price: JD8 double.

This new 40-room hotel is located near the Ministry of Transportation in a pleasant residential area. All rooms are fitted with twin beds and have private bath, radio, direct dial phone, mini-bar, heat and air conditioning, and wall-to-wall carpeting. Facilities include a bar, restaurant, laundry, telex and television on request. American Express cards are accepted.

Philadelphia. Downtown Amman in front of the Roman theater, P.O. Box 10; Phone: 25191. Telex: NAZZAL 149050. Price: JD7.500.

Built in 1925, this was the city's leading hotel until the Inter-Continental opened. Now, frankly, it is old and has seen better times; but it has a fabulous location, and you can't beat the price. The hotel appears to be caught between those who want it demolished and those who do not. It occupies part of the site of ancient Amman, where excavations might uncover worthwhile antiquities. On the other hand, its location and long-standing tradition make it very desirable. Until Amman has overcome its hotel shortage, the Philadelphia will remain; but since demolition appears inevitable, there is understandably little incentive on the part of the Nazzal family, who own it, to make renovations.

Most of the 92 rooms are doubles, but there are a few singles and suites. Most rooms have private bath; all have phone and heat. Furnishings are simple. There are a bar, dining room and pool (on our last two visits the pool was not in use), and shops.

Manar. Shmeisani, P.O. Box 20730; Phone: 62187; Telex: 1624. Price: JD6 double.

A new hotel with 43 doubles and 20 singles plus a few suites, in two four-story buildings connected by a central building where the public rooms are located.

All rooms have private bath, phone, 24-hour room service, air conditioning, central heating and radio. Facilities include restaurant, bar, coffee shop and swimming pool. A wine and cheese cellar-bar is being added. There is a convenient bus stop near the hotel; taxi to the center of town costs 350 fils. The hotel is owned by Suchkhian and Amad, who also have the Holy Land Hotel in Jerusalem.

Ambassador. Shmeisani, P.O. Box 19014; Phone: 65161. Price: JD8.

A modern seven-story structure with 97 rooms, most of which are fitted with twin beds. Rooms are a comfortable size and simply furnished; all have private bathrooms (bathtubs are the small-tub-with-seat version, popular in Japan). The hotel is used a great deal by groups. Although it had been open less than a year, on our last visit we found maintenance to be poor. The nicest part of the hotel is its pleasant dining room and bar.

Hisham. 4th Circle, Jebel Amman, P.O. Box 5047; Phone: 42720. Price: JD8.

Located in a pleasant residential area next door to the Kuwaiti Embassy, the hotel has 23 rooms on three floors, in a family atmosphere. Rooms are unusually large, and all are fitted with twin beds plus a couch which can be made into another bed for two. All rooms have bath (six with shower only), phone, mini-bar, TV on request, 24-hour room service, heat/air conditioning. Facilities include a restaurant and outdoor terrace for dining. The hotel has its own bakery which also does catering. American Express and Diner's Club cards are accepted.

Shepherds. Al Khattab Street, Jebel Amman, P.O. Box 2020; Telex: 1410 Shepherd Jo. Phone: 39197. Price: JD8.

A modest hotel with 44 rooms on four floors, conveniently located to downtown. All rooms have private bath (some with shower only), phone and 24-hour room service. There is a bar/lounge, dining room, outside terrace for drinks and snacks. National Car Rental's office is in the hotel.

Omar Khayyam. Shmeisani. Price: JD12.500 double.

On our last inspection the 36-room hotel was not completely finished, and it would appear to be overpriced compared to other similar new ones.

Other medium-priced hotels: *Jordan Tower,* Shmeisani. 45 rooms; JD7.500 double. Recently refurnished.
Granada, Jebel Amman, First Circle. 30 rooms, JD6.
Firas Wing, Jebel Webdeh. 27 rooms, JD6.
Merry Land, King Hussein Street. 71 rooms, JD6.

Al Ghusein, Jebel Hussein. 21 rooms with kitchenette, JD6 double.

City Hotel, Prince Muhammad St. 27 rooms, JD6 double.

The **American School of Oriental Research** Phone: 44917, has rooms for seven people at its center in Shmeisani, at approximately J.D.3.50 per person including meals. Write to the director, Dr. James Sauer, P.O. Box 2470, Amman, Jordan.

At least 12 more hotels are under construction or planned for Amman, adding 1,000 more rooms to the capital by 1981. These include an Alia hotel, Flying Carpet; a 300-room hotel to be managed by Marriott, and several small, privately-financed hotels ranging from 25 to 169 rooms.

The Hotels and Resthouses Corporation, a government body, is responsible for building and operating facilities at the country's important tourist sites. Most of these have been constructed in the past decade and in many cases are the only ones available at the locales. Recently, a ten-year agreement was concluded with Grand Metropolitan Hotels, one of the major British hotel chains, to manage all 17 of the corporation's facilities. Under separate agreements, Grand Metropolitan is expected to be given the management contracts for the new 80-room hotel to be built at Petra, two new restaurants at Petra and Jerash, and a 300-room hotel being built in Amman and scheduled for completion in 1980.

 DINING OUT. The newness of Amman's big-city sophistication can be seen in the limited number of good restaurants. Some of the best ones are at hotels; others are in newly developing residential areas. Then, too, Jordanians prefer to entertain at home. Inviting someone to dine in one's home is the most basic expression of Arab hospitality.

Jordanians do not take lunch until 1 or 2 P.M. Restaurants begin serving lunch after 12 and will serve as late as 3 or 3:30 P.M. In the evening, dinner is served after 8 P.M., and by 10:30 P.M. most of the guests will have finished their meal and begun to leave.

Recently restaurants, like hotels, were classified with one- to five-star ratings. A typical meal at a five-star restaurant should cost JD2.500 and a three-star JD1.750, plus 10% service charge.

There are a few restaurants which serve good European dishes and even more that offer American snacks, but the best food is in restaurants which serve Jordanian specialties. Happily, Jordanians are better cooks than they are interior decorators. If you were to judge a restaurant by its decor, you might possibly stop cold at the door. There's a five-and-dime tackiness about even the best ones.

Restaurants are listed here by their locations.

Center of Town

Jabri, King Hussein Street, phone 24108, and **Jordan Restaurant,** Post Office Square, phone 38333, are run by the same family. Both offer Jordanian specialties at medium prices. The latter has mounds of *baklawi* and other sweets by the front door which can be purchased by the kilo to take out. (Sweetmeats are a popular gift to take on a visit to someone's house.)

Jerusalem Restaurant (known by its Arabic name, *Al Quds)* is similar to the two named above. It is located on King Hussein Street, phone 30168.

First Circle, Jebel Amman

Diplomat, facing the circle and diagonally across from ALIA's main office; phone 25592. Restaurant and sidewalk café with a large menu of sandwiches, snacks, steaks and desserts. Prices are moderate, food mediocre.

Second Circle, Jebel Amman

Babalu, half-block off the circle on a road leading to the First Circle, phone 41116. A mix of Jordanian specialties and international dishes. The decor is a little more attractive than most, except that it is so dark inside it may not be very inviting to unescorted women. Prices are moderate.

Istanbouli, on a side street down the hill between First and Second circles, one block from Mount Hotel, phone 38212. Considered by local residents to be one of the best for Jordanian food. It is situated in a house and has an informal atmosphere. Prices are moderate.

Third Circle, Jebel Amman

Jordan Inter-Continental, phone 41361. The hotel's rooftop dining room is popular for its businessman's buffet lunch. The coffee shop on the main floor is open 24 hours a day. By Jordanian standards, both are expensive.

Maatouk, facing Circle, a short walk from the Inter-Continental, phone 41337. The menu is in Arabic only, but waiters and the owners speak English. At the entrance there is a rotisserie for *shawarma,* roast lamb cut in slivers and served in loaves of Arabic or pita bread with onions, mint and sumak. Just inside the door are piles of sweets and meat- or cheese-filled pastries from which to choose. It's a sort of carry-out place with tables and a restaurant on the second floor. Don't be put off by the plastic tablecloths and tacky decor. The food is delicious and relatively inexpensive. Service is quick, so it's a good place for a fast meal.

New Orient Restaurant (also known as **Abu Ahmad** and **Oriental Restaurant**). Located on a side street one block below the Circle and one block from the Inter-Continental Hotel. Phone: 41879. The restaurant is in a house with a large outdoor garden where meals are served during warm weather. It specializes in Jordanian dishes, and is one of the few places which offers *musakhan,* chicken smothered in onions and sumak. Prices are moderate.

Nouroz. Facing the Circle. Phone: 42830. Snack bar and sidewalk café with a small menu of sandwiches and snacks, including hamburgers. Prices are moderate. **Riviera Snacks** and **Uncle Sam's** are two other snack shops nearby.

Omar Khayyam. Located on the top floor of an office and apartment building directly behind the Inter-Continental Hotel. Phone: 42910. One of the newest and best restaurants in the city. The menu includes a selection of Middle Eastern and international dishes. Prices are moderately expensive by Amman standards.

There are several bars and nightclubs—**Red Lion, Third Circle** and **Venus Club**—in the vicinity of the Second and Third Circles, but they are for men. Women, even if escorted, would not feel comfortable, though one would never know this before walking inside, since all tourist literature distributed by the government, ALIA and travel agents list them without explanation or qualification.

Two new nightspots that are popular with Amman's smart set are **The Key Club** and **The Cottage.** Both are located one block from the American Embassy, Third Circle.

University Road

Sports City Clubs. Phone: 39341. There are four restaurants in Hussein Sports complex. The main dining room offers a large menu of Jordanian and international dishes and is patronized by the country's leading government officials and businessmen and their families. The food is good; prices are reasonable.

El Bustan. Near the offices of the *Jordan Times.* This restaurant is especially popular in summer, when it moves to its outdoor garden.

Shmeisani

Flying Carpet. In a residential area within one block of four hotels—Ambassador, Manar, Tower and Omar Khayyam. Phone: 62181. The best and most popular restaurant-nightclub in the city, it is owned by ALIA. The restaurant is open for lunch as well as dinner. There is nightly entertainment by a group playing the latest hit tunes from around the world. The bar, where one can have a drink without having dinner, looks out over the nightclub and dance floor. By Amman standards, prices are expensive.

La Terrasse. On the second floor of an apartment building in a residential area. Phone: 62831. The menu is French; the food is excellent and ample. A couple can have a first course such as the pâté de maison, a main course of meat with four vegetables, coffee and wine for about $30, which by local standards is expensive. The restaurant is hard to find on one's own, but a taxi driver will know it. You should ask the taxi to come back for you or have the restaurant call one, since there will probably be none around by the time you have finished dinner.

Other places which have been recommended by Amman residents but which we have not had the opportunity to check include three Chinese restaurants, two in Jebel Amman and another in Jebel Hussein. Also: **Elite**, Jebel Webdeh, Phone: 22103. **Le Cesar**, Jebel Webdeh, Phone: 24421. **Le**

Privé, Jebel Amman, Phone: 44880. **Royal Automobile Club,** Wadi es Seer Road, Phone: 44261. **Orthodox Club,** Jebel Abdoun, Phone: 44491. The last two are private clubs; however, they accept individual nonmembers for dinner. Ask your hotel to make the arrangements. There are also a number of roast chicken take-out shops around town.

NORTH OF AMMAN

Jerash: 29 miles

A 45-minute drive over an excellent new highway through the lovely hills of Gilead takes one to Jerash, the best and most complete ruins of a provincial Roman city in the world. Jerash was buried under sand and rubble for centuries, until 1806, when the German traveler Seetzen discovered the site. Excavations were begun in 1925.

Five miles before reaching the site, the road crosses the Zerqa River, the Jabbok of the Bible. On the northwest you will see a lovely wooded area—this is one of the greenest parts of the country. The scenery is lovely throughout the drive.

Most authorities agree that Jerash (Gerasa) was founded by the soldiers of Alexander the Great about 332 B.C., although the site was occupied from Neolithic times. After the Roman conquest in 63 B.C., the city joined the Decapolis and established trade with the Nabataeans of Petra. Jesus may have passed through Jerash on a trip to Jerusalem, following the eastern highlands route through the Decapolis.

In A.D. 90, Jerash was absorbed into the Roman Province of Arabia. In the following two centuries the city reached the height of its prosperity. Afterward, the rise of Palmyra and a shift in trade routes caused its steady decline.

By the Byzantine period—from which most of its church ruins date—Jerash had deteriorated. The invasions of the Persians and later the Arabs in the seventh century added further to its decline. Finally, in the twelfth century, when the Crusaders attempted to take the city, it was practically demolished and later abandoned.

In 1878 under the Turks the east bank of the stream which flows through Jerash was settled by Circassians. Today the little town is a modern counterpoint to the ruins of the ancient city.

As one approaches Jerash from the south, one's first sight is the triple-arched gateway built in 129 A.D. to celebrate Emperor

Hadrian's visit to the city. On the west a road leads to Ajlun. Beyond the arch is the ancient Hippodrome.

A quick tour of the main ruins of Jerash takes a half-day. Those who are especially interested in Roman and Byzantine ruins should allow a full day. A government resthouse operated by the Jordan Hotels and Resthouses Corporation, is located at the entrance to the ruins, on a rise of ground which offers a good overview of the site. Refreshments and toilet facilities are available at the resthouse. There is an illuminated map and a plan of the town broken down into numbered walks for exploring a particular section. A member of the Jordan Tourist Police is on duty.

The present entrance to ancient Jerash is on the east side of the site. There is a guide in residence, but if you can carry along Harding's *The Antiquities of Jordan* you will find it is better than a guide.

On the south side of the site is the enormous oval-shaped Forum, encircled by 56 columns with Ionic capitals standing in their original position. Many have been restored. The Forum, which was used as a market and assembly place, is in a remarkable state of preservation. It is the only oval-shaped Roman forum ever uncovered.

On the hill above the forum is the Temple of Zeus built in the first century A.D. on the site of an earlier sanctuary. Next to it is the large Theater, where extensive restoration has been done. It contained 32 tiers of seats and accommodated 5,000 spectators. The theater is used today for plays and festivals.

From the highest level of this area there is a spectacular view, with ancient Jerash in the foreground and the modern town in the distance. It is also a good vantage point from which to take pictures of the Forum.

Beyond the Forum leading to the North Gate is the Street of Columns, the main thoroughfare of Jerash. Many of the columns were found in their original position; others have been restored. Their capitals are Corinthian. An aqueduct ran across the top of the columns, carrying fresh water to all parts of the city. Crossing the main street at right angles are two other streets, running east–west. At each crossroads was a tetrapylon, consisting of four piers, each supporting four columns, and probably surmounted by a statue.

On the west side of the Street of Columns about 180 yards beyond the South Tetrapylon is the Nymphaeum, a semicircular structure which was both a fountain and a temple of the nymphs. Its walls are elaborately carved. From the large urns held by the statues, water once cascaded over the face of the temple into a pool. The façade of the pool was decorated with lion's heads; the water passed through the lion's mouths into drains along the street below.

Immediately after the Nymphaeum, on the same side of the street, stands the Temple of Artemis. The temple, built in the second century A.D. for the patron goddess of Jerash, is the most imposing building on the site. From the massive Propylaeum a flight of stairs leads to a platform (now restored). Beyond, a second flight of stairs (also restored) running the width of the courtyard leads to the outer porch of the temple. This porch consists of the outer wall of the courtyard with a row of columns in front. Five doors lead from the outer porch into the courtyard, a rectangular enclosure lined with columns on all sides. The columns and the outer walls formed a kind of portico, lined with rooms or recesses.

In the middle of the courtyard stands the temple proper, originally approached by a flight of stairs. The *cella,* or holy part of the temple, was built on a platform and was surrounded on all sides by 45-foot columns with Corinthian capitals. Under the platform of the *cella* were vaults, one of which now houses a museum.

Facing the Temple of Artemis are the remains of the Viaduct Church, which was built over the forecourt of the Temple of Artemis.

Standing at the nave of the church, with a view of the Temple in the background and a panorama of the hills and valleys of Gilead in the foreground, you can easily envisage the spectacular sight the Temple must have been to travelers approaching Jerash in ancient days.

A few steps further along the Street of Columns on the right are the Baths, dating from the second Century A.D. The dome is the oldest known example built on pendentives.

Across the street from the Baths is the North Theatre, with a seating capacity of 1,200. Two hundred yards further along the same street is the North Gate, the north limit of the city.

Thirteen churches have been uncovered in Jerash, and authorities say that probably many more lie buried under the ground. All the known ones have been dated except one.

The Cathedral, dated A.D. 350, is the earliest known Christian building in Jerash. It lies south of the Nymphaeum, and consists of a central nave with north and south aisles. Most of the stones and architectural details were taken from the Temple of Dionysos. West of the Cathedral is the large Church of St. Theodore, built about

A.D. 496. Farther west are the ruins of three other churches. The plan of the middle church, dedicated to St. John, consists of a circle set in a square. The one on the north, dedicated to Saints Cosmos and Damianus, and the other on the south, dedicated to St. George, are of the usual basilica type, as is the Cathedral. The three churches had communicating doors and a common atrium, and were paved with mosaics.

The church west of the Temple of Artemis was originally a synagogue. It was converted into a church in A.D. 530.

The ruins of the other churches are not important enough to warrant description here. In general, one might say the churches in Jerash are some of the best examples of Byzantine architecture at its worst.

About a half-mile north of the city walls lies the principal cemetery of the ancient city. Nearby is a spring called *Birketain* ("two pools"), which supplied some of the city's water, and a small theater. According to an inscription on the latter, the licentious water festival of Maiumas was held here as late as the sixth century A.D.

Dr. Assem Bargouthi, professor of archeology at the University of Jordan, has headed three recent digs at Jerash that revealed a new residential area, exposing houses on a side street running off the Street of Columns. A minor drainage system connects each house with the drainage system of the main avenue.

Three types of water system also were uncovered. One consists of pieces of stone carved in a semicircular shape and fitted end to end, in the style of Roman aqueducts. Another type is lined with plaster and covered with slabs of stone. The third is constructed of round pottery pipes lined with plaster, resembling our present-day underground water pipes.

Further along the Street of Columns, excavations revealed a monumental structure 150 feet in length. Dr. Bargouthi believes that this could have had great public significance and may turn out to be the real forum of Jerash.

The team hopes to uncover more of the residential area in future excavations. Certainly there is much work to be done—an estimated 90 percent of ancient Jerash still lies buried.

The development plan for Jerash calls for upgrading the site, undertaking more excavations and restoration. A Sound and Light show is scheduled to be installed by next year. Walking trails with explanations posted at intervals are also to be added.

Peddlers of ancient coins and oil lamps are frequent visitors to sites of antiquity in Jordan, especially Jerash. Sometimes their wares are genuine, more often they are not; so let the buyer beware.

Ajlun: 41 miles (14 miles west of Jerash)

Ajlun is not often visited by foreign tourists, probably because they think it is difficult to reach, or because they are not aware of its attractions. It is only a short drive from Jerash, and in the past few years has been developed as a weekend resort with sports facilities, restaurant, and overnight sleeping accommodations at a Government Resthouse.

The approach to the town through the pine forest of the Debbin National Park is surrounded by beautiful natural scenery.

Ajlun's main attraction is a twelfth-century Arab castle, often mistaken for a Crusader fortification. Qala'at al Rabad was built as a defense against—not for—the Crusaders.

Qala'at al-Rabad is perched on top of a 4,068-foot mountain, with a spectacular view of the Jordan Valley and the Biblical land of Gilead. It is claimed that on a clear day one can see from Mt. Hermon in the north to the Dead Sea 90 miles away to the south.

The fortress is one of the best examples of Arab military architecture in Jordan. It was built in 1184 by Izzeddin Usama, one of the generals of Saladin, specifically to protect the caravan and pilgrimage route and to stem the advance of the Crusader armies spreading out from Jerusalem and Damascus.

The castle was destroyed in 1260 by the Mongols and rebuilt by the Mameluks, who took it over later in the same century. The Mameluks considered it too vulnerable, and reinforced it by doubling its walls and by constructing a second bastion outside the existing ones.

After you climb to the top, you will welcome a rest. Sit for a while and enjoy the view—a 360-degree sweep over half of ancient Palestine. To the west, verdant hills disappear into the haze over the Jordan River; nearby the Zerqa River rolls southward in a broad, green snakelike pattern. Eastward, Jerash's green shows up against the barren mountains of Gilead on the horizon; and far to the east, beyond the National Park's edge, the endless desert begins again.

Another point of interest in Ajlun is an old mosque built during the Middle Ages on the site of a church.

The Debbin National Park, reached by the old road to Jerash north of the Zerqa River, was opened in 1972. For a country which is

The Bedouin Corps, an important part of the Jordanian Army, is also the most colorful.

Only recently discovered, this Byzantine mosaic at Siyagha dates probably to the 6th century; its unearthing gives promise of more in the area.

At the rose-red city of Petra, lost to the world until the early 19th century, the tomb called the Treasury got its name from an old belief that pirates hid their gold here.

Imposing mosques, such as this one on Amman's Jebel Ashra Fiyeh, and simple mosques, in small towns and villages across the land, are centers of the Jordanian way of life.

80 percent desert, a national forest is a source of considerable pride, and Jordanians enjoy taking their families here to picnic and pass the day among the pines and oaks and, in the spring, to gather wildflowers. The Park stretches about 30 miles from Ajlun to the village of Debbin, and is part of the watershed whose rivers feed the Jordan River from the east. Snow run-off from the mountains of Gilead makes it one of the country's richest regions.

En route to Ajlun, there is the American Hospital of the Southern Baptist Church, which gives medical care to about 50 villages in the vicinity. Throughout the Ajlun area there are ancient sites which have only been partially investigated. Deir Abu Said is said to be the place of Absalom's death; Listib, the birthplace of the prophet Elijah. There are many old churches and ruins of ancient buildings in the vicinity.

Irbid: 53 miles (24 miles northwest of Jerash)

Irbid is one of Jordan's fastest growing industrial areas, and the administrative center of the country's most fertile region. A new university was open here last year on a temporary 20-acre campus. Planned for a capacity of 20,000 students by 1985, the University of Yarmuk has a School of Arts and Sciences and expects to add studies in medical sciences, engineering, agriculture and veterinary medicine.

The town is built on the site of an Early Bronze Age settlement. It is Beth Arbel of the Bible and Arbila of the Decapolis. Some authorities claim it is the burial place of Moses's mother and four of his sons.

South of Irbid is Tell al-Husn, another Early Bronze Age site, usually identified as Dion of the Decapolis.

Umm Qais: 95 miles (19 miles northwest of Irbid near the Syrian border)

Ancient Gadara, one of the important cities of the Decapolis, was the capital of the Roman district of Gadarites. The remains of three theaters, a temple, a colonnaded street and an aqueduct give an idea of the city's former grandeur. Situated at an altitude of 1,700 feet, it commands a magnificent view of the Sea of Galilee, the Yarmuk River Valley and the Golan Heights. Its strategic position must have been responsible for the development of the city, first mentioned in ancient records from about the third century B.C. as "an inexpung-

ible stronghold" during the wars between the Ptolemies of Egypt
and the Seleucides of Syria.

In 218 B.C., the Seleucid king Antiochus III, after a decisive
victory near Sidon, overran Galilee, crossed the Jordan River,
captured the city of Pella (Tabaqat Fahl in the Jordan Valley) and
laid siege to Gadara. The inhabitants did not resist, being apparently
eager to throw off the Egyptian yoke. Immediately after the fall of
Gadara, Philadelphia (Amman) was also conquered.

The penetration of Hellenism was feared by the Jews as a
challenge to their religious traditions, and led to a revolt during the
reign of Antiochus Epophanes (174–175 B.C.). Judas, son of the
priest Mathathias, defeated the Seleucids in 165 B.C. Under John
Hyrcanus in 100 B.C. Gadara was captured and destroyed after a six-
month siege.

The city recovered its independence in 65 B.C. when the Roman
general Pompey conquered the East. A new era began for Gadara
which continued until the Arab conquest. Under Pompey, the
Decapolis, a commonwealth of ten cities—most of them situated on
the East Bank of the Jordan—was created. Each city was a free city-
state *(polis)* and governed a large, intensively cultivated territory
with many small villages. Commercial activity increased the wealth
of the ten cities, and building was undertaken on a large scale. The
layout of each town was similar to those of Greek and Roman
cities—colonnaded streets, temples, theaters, public fountains,
agoras and stadiums. A Greek inscription found in the Gadara
forum tells us that wealthy citizens shared in paying the expenses of
public buildings.

One reason the Decapolis was created was to stop the Nabataean
advance to the north. The Nabataeans controlled most of Transjordan and the Negev; hence they controlled the trade and caravan
route. Under Aretas III (87–62 B.C.) the Nabataeans had pushed
their northern frontiers to Damascus.

During the time of Mark Antony part of the Nabataean territories
east of the Dead Sea were presented to Cleopatra. The Nabataean
king, Malichos I (47–30 B.C.), was allowed to rule his territories but
had to pay tribute to the queen. Apparently the Nabataean king was
averse to paying these taxes, causing Mark Antony to send Herod
against him. After many battles, Malichos was defeated near
Philadelphia in 31 B.C. Later Herod the Great was granted the cities
of Gadara and Hippos by Octavius after the latter's naval victory at
Actium. When Herod died in 4 B.C., Gadara recovered its independence.

According to the Bible (St. Matthew 8:28), Jesus visited the territory of Gadara and here exorcised two men possessed by devils. He ordered the demons to go out from the men and to enter into a herd of pigs. When news spread of this miracle, the whole town turned out to meet Jesus and "besought Him to remove Himself from their country." Hoade's *Guide to Jordan* maintains that the incident took place at Kursi on the east shore of the Sea of Galilee, rather than at Umm Qais.

In 68 A.D. the first Jewish revolt broke out. Vespasian captured the cities on the East Bank in order to destroy the Jewish colonies; he was welcomed in Gadara, apparently as a liberator.

When Trajan annexed the Nabataean kingdom into the Province of Arabia in 106 A.D., Gadara remained independent. Like many cities of the Decapolis, Gadara reached its golden age in the second century. It is from this period that most of its buildings date. In the fourth century it became an episcopal seat and flourished until the seventh century.

Apparently, Gadara was famous in ancient times for its hot springs. According to the Roman geographer Strabo, who lived in the time of Augustus, the pleasure-loving Romans came here "after having enjoyed the restorative effects of the hot springs of Amatha [el Hammi], retired for refreshments, enjoying the cooler heights of the city, and solacing their leisure with the plays performed in the theaters." This helps explain why three theaters were built in the city and why many poets and philosophers came from it. One of the natives of the city had written on his tomb, "I am from Gadara, fond of the muses."

In the second century A.D., Josephus described Gadara as a wealthy city, and wrote that "villas and small cities lay round about it." Gadara controlled a large area, extending to Lake Tiberias. After the Byzantine period it slowly declined, and by the Arab period was a small village.

Only limited excavations have been undertaken. Our earlier knowledge of the ruins is based mainly on the short account published by the archeologist Schumacher in 1880. In 1973, an archeological expedition began excavations under the German Evangelic School of Jerusalem. The group is continuing its work, and is undertaking restorations as well. The institute has a workshop near the University in Amman.

The city is approached from the east, where the acropolis is now covered with modern houses. On this side, a strong wall reinforced with towers once protected the city. Entering from the eastern gate, the visitor comes to the northern theater, badly damaged by earthquakes and vandalism. In front of the theater, there is an open area, most probably a forum. From here a colonnaded street, bordered by columns and shops, runs westward. It was paved with basalt slabs, and the marks of chariot wheels are visible.

The colonnaded street leads to the western gate. On the right a few feet before the gate are the ruins of a nymphaeum, and to the left the remains of a large basilica. A street running southward leads to the western theater. On the way, one can see the vaults which supported the basilica. A massive wall behind the basilica may have belonged to a temple.

The western theater is smaller than the northern one but is in better condition. Built of black basalt, the two-storied auditorium considered of 14 tiers on the first level and ten on the upper one. A horizontal gangway separates the two tiers; vaults support the seats, most of which are in good condition. The orchestra, now covered with stones, is more than a half-circle. At the lowest tier of the first story, near the central stairway, is a headless white marble statue, contrasting with the black basalt, representing a seated goddess holding a cornucopia in her left hand. The legs of her chair are adorned with lion heads, a symbol of Astarte. A similar goddess in a standing position is represented on the coins of Gadara.

From the western theater there is a sweeping view of the lake and the Golan Heights.

East of the city on the road to Tiberias, a large mausoleum was discovered in 1968 and excavated the following year. A large stairway of 18 steps leads to a rectangular courtyard, which was probably covered by a roof. Some columns crowned by Corinthian capitals are still standing in the middle of the court. Later on a smaller portico, semicircular in shape, was added. Four steps lead to the funeral chamber which was closed by a heavy, pivoted stone door. There are small chambers on three sides, six on each side arranged in two stories. This family mausoleum is one of the largest ever found in Jordan.

North of the mausoleum is a circular podium, 21 feet in diameter, perhaps belonging to another tomb. It is approached by a flight of steps, and scattered about in the surrounding fields are Ionic capitals which presumably once topped the columns. A third mausoleum, situated on the northern slopes near the Baths, is in ruins. In the Baths, mosaics in the floor and four basins can be seen. Greek inscriptions in the mosaic read "Health to Heraclides the founder and to the bathers." Heraclides is thought to have been a rich citizen of Gadara who financed the building of the Baths.

The East Ghor Canal, Jordan's most ambitious irrigation project, begins near Umm Qais and continues south through the Jordan Valley. A road south of Umm Qais and another west of Irbid lead to Pella, one of the major cities of the Decapolis and the city to which the earliest Christians fled from persecution in Jerusalem in the second century A.D. Pella can also be reached from Salt by a road along the Jordan Valley.

In January 1979 a joint project of Wooster College, the University of Sydney and the Department of Antiquities began a ten-year excavation to uncover the ruins of Pella, which are expected to be as extensive as those of Jerash by the time the work is finished. The site is important for its Early Bronze Age settlement as well as for the Roman one. The name of Pella comes from the birthplace of Alexander the Great in Greece. The site is known locally in Arabic as Tabaqat Fahil.

Ramtha: 64 miles; 35 miles north of Jerash

Ramtha is the northern frontier post where the visitor enters Jordan from Syria. Here papers and cars must be checked, customs passed, and visas obtained if necessary. The restaurant provides hot and cold food and drinks. Postcards and small souvenirs are on sale, and restroom facilities are available.

Four miles further is Dera'a in Syria, the Edrei of the Bible.

Umm el Jimal: 12 miles east of Mafraq, off the Baghdad Highway

Northeast of Amman, another good highway leads to Ruseifa (8 miles), situated in a lovely green valley. It is one of the main centers for the mining of phosphates, Jordan's main export.

Further along, the road passes through Zerqa (14 miles), which is the administrative center of the district by the same name. Once only a small Circassian village and headquarters of the Arab Legion, the town has grown into one of the main industrial centers of the country. Throughout the area there are many sites of antiquity which have been identified but never studied closely or excavated extensively. These date from Nabataean, Roman and Byzantine times, although several go back to the Chalcolithic period.

Approximately 9 miles north of Zerqa the highway divides, and a new road on the east leads to Azraq (see description later in this chapter) and the Umayyad Palace of Qasr el Hallabat.

Continuing north, the road comes to Mafraq (43 miles), the administrative center of the area. Its development started with the building of the oil pipeline from Iraq to Haifa in the 1930s. Mafraq is surrounded by a desert of black basalt (a volcanic lava stone) which stretches from the Jebel Druze in Syria south through eastern Jordan. Outside of Mafraq the area is sparsely populated today, but at one time it is believed to have supported a large population. One ancient center is Umm el Jimal, meaning "Mother of the Camel." Known as the black oasis, this curious place has extensive ruins of a Roman-Byzantine-Umayyad town built on an earlier Nabataean settlement, and constructed entirely of black and steel-gray basalt. From a distance it has the appearance of a bombed or burned-out city. As one writer has said, it would make a good setting for *Macbeth*. It is thought to have been a caravan staging post. The many open spaces within the town are assumed to have been for the accommodation of the caravans; hence its name.

Umm el Jimal is believed to have been founded in the early Roman period at a time when the area enjoyed considerable Nabataean influence. It flourished as a frontier city of the Roman and Byzantine Empires and continued to prosper in the Umayyad period. It was destroyed by earthquake at the end of the Umayyad period, and was not rebuilt because the region of the Hauran lost its preeminence when the seat of government shifted to Baghdad under the Abbassids.

The builders, using the hard rock as though it were wood—an architectural style known as corbeling—shaped the basalt into shingles and beams and constructed ceilings and roofs by laying the stone beams, six to nine feet long, on cantilevered supports protruding from the walls. They carved doors out of the basalt and balanced them on sockets in diamond-hard door jambs, and barred them shut with crossbars of basalt. They hollowed out drinking basins, still used today, and cut deep into the solid rock to make cisterns. Visitors will be able to appreciate the success of these methods. Numerous buildings are still standing two and three stories high, with some of their ceilings intact after 1500 years.

Perhaps even more impressive than the building skill of the first settlers was their excellent hydraulic engineering. Neither spring nor stream has ever been found in Umm el Jimal. Rainfall, minimal and sporadic, had to be collected and every drop stored to see the population of five to ten thousand through the long dry season.

They constructed a dam across the Wadi running west of the city to provide irrigation water for the surrounding fields, and a ground-level aquaduct many miles long to collect the runoff from the sloping terrain to the north. A number of branch channels were cut to direct the water into large open pools throughout the city as well as to smaller, roofed-over cisterns adjacent to nearly every house and public building. The supply of water thus created should have been ample for the people and their domestic animals, except perhaps in a succession of extremely dry winters.

The study of this ancient water system has inspired present-day engineers to consider the possibility of similar systems to support Jordan's growing population and to increase agriculture in village settlements.

The ruins of Umm el Jimal cover an area of about 200 acres and appear as one great tumbled mass. The houses follow the typical eastern style: a central courtyard with rooms around it and an external stairway leading to the upper stories.

A small temple inside the South Gate on the west side has been called the Nabataean temple because of a Nabataean carved lintel over the door. Otherwise, no Nabataean remains have been uncovered.

Numerous gravestones with Latin and Greek inscriptions have given archaeologists a catalogue of names of the inhabitants which indicates that the residents were local Arab nomads who settled in the region and who are believed to have built Umm el Jimal under the security of the Roman Empire.

Early in the second century A.D. the Romans appear to have taken over and may have called the site "Thantia;" there was a town by this name in the vicinity.

Nothing is known of the town during the early Christian period, but judging from the 15 churches on the site it must have been some kind of religious center. Furthermore, Christianity came here early; the church of Julianus, built in 345, is the earliest dated church east of the Jordan so far documented.

The city was enclosed by a wall with six gates, two each on the west, south and east sides. The walls were constructed about the second century A.D. and rebuilt in the fourth century. The only monumental gate is on the west side, but one gate on the south and one on the east are flanked by towers.

The Gate of Commodus (176-180 A.D.) on the west side consists of two towers projecting outside the city walls and connected by two arches. An inscription dates it to the joint reign of Marcus Aurelius and his son Commodus. The gate was named by H.C. Butler, who made the first detailed plan of Umm el Jimal in 1905.

The Praetorium (dated 371 A.D.) lies in a large open space between the two gates on the west side. It is the second grandest house in town, with a ceiling coming together to make a sort of dome, surrounded by a simple but well-defined moulding in a whiter stone. It consists of two buildings constructed along the north and west sides of an open court. The north building is rectangular. The door is in the middle of the south side and opens onto an atrium with four columns. The atrium is flanked by two large halls, while to the north are five rooms. There is evidence of another floor.

The Barracks, which dominate the town as one approaches, date from the fifth century. The building is located near the middle of the south wall, and is also known as the *Deir,* or monastery. The building is rectangular, with a chapel of three aisles on the east side. Around an open court are single and double rows of rooms. At the southwest corner is a six-story tower with a balcony on each side. The stonecutting is Roman, but by Byzantine times it is thought to have become a monastery. The inscription running round the tower has numerous crude crosses, and gives, in Greek, the names of the archangels Michael, Gabriel, Raphael and Uriel.

As in the houses, there is an outside staircase made of cantilevered corbels, and windows over which machicolations were hung for the purpose of pouring down hot oil or lead on attackers. The top floor of the tower has narrow slot windows with machicolations over the lower ones.

Churches

The number of churches is surpassed only by the number of cisterns. It seems strange that Christianity took such a grip on this town, although many other such improbable sites of early Christianity are found in the Syrian desert as well. As noted earlier, the church of Saint Julianus was built here in 345 A.D. It is located between the Gate of Commodus and the northwest corner of the city, and consists of ten transverse bays with a semicircular apse ending at the eastern end, as churches were then oriented. Everywhere amid the fallen stones large and small crosses, ornate and simple, are scratched in the surface.

Philip Hitti in his *History of Syria* says, "The one-nave church of Umm el Jimal illustrates the primitive type of Christian church . . . an elongated room, favored because of its simplicity and relation to the prevailing type of structure."

The other type of architecture used at Umm el Jimal is the basilica, which has a central nave and two later aisles, separated by arches which run parallel to the axis of the church and end in circular apses.

The Cathedral (dated 557 A.D.) is in the basilica style, and stands in the middle of the town, between the two gates on the west side.

The West Church, the best-preserved church, lies outside the north gate of the east wall. Four arches have survived and support a second story with high windows. There is a well-defined Jerusalem cross cut deep into an arch. The entrance is dignified and imposing with a high arched window over the door. Near it are the underground tombs, on which some names survive. These are large chambers entered by subterranean tunnels, with a series of arches supporting the main chamber's roof, and niches cut out all around them for the sarcophagi.

Other churches deserving mention are the *Numerianos Church,* situated north of the barracks in the open space; *Klondianos Church,* opposite the Gate of Commodus, and the *Double Church,* one basilica and one hall, situated between the two gates on the east side. Between the South Gate and the southwest corner there is a church called the Governorate.

In 1972 Dr. Bert DeVries, professor of history and archaeology at Calvin College in Grand Rapids, Michigan, began extensive work at Umm el Jimal with an aerial and ground survey to map out the entire city, its numerous buildings, defensive walls and water reservoirs. Two years later he and Dr. James Sauer, director of the American Center for Oriental Research, conducted a preliminary excavation to verify the periods of occupation of the city. This excavation, carried out in cooperation with the Department of Antiquities and the American Center for Oriental Research, yielded Roman, Byzantine and Umayyad pottery in successive strata of occupation. This pottery is the first systematically studied collection from the Southern Hauran region.

Dr. DeVries has also excavated some specific buildings at Umm el Jimal, including the Barracks, the Praetorium, a private house and the city wall, all located in the southern half of the city. In general, the dates of construction and occupation of these buildings proved to be later than previously thought.

The so-called Nabataean Temple was founded on Byzantine materials; the fifth century A.D. date for the Barracks was confirmed, and both the Praetorium and the private house contained good Byzantine and Umayyad occupation levels. Although pottery from these cultures was found mixed in with later materials, no

Roman or Nabataean occupation levels were found anywhere in the excavation.

Perhaps the most surprising result of this excavation is the discovery that Umm el Jimal was a significant Umayyad city, whereas previously it had been thought of only as a Nabataean, Roman and Byzantine city. Because several Umayyad occupation levels were found, a study of the pottery from these levels is expected to contribute significantly to refining the distinction between the early and late Umayyad periods.

Since September 1977, Dr. DeVries has been working with the Department of Antiquities on the consolidation of the buildings that were excavated. This phase of the project includes strengthening of walls to prevent further collapse; clearing debris and posting signs to make the buildings more accessible and understandable to visitors; and the writing of a booklet to be published by the Ministry of Tourism as a guide for visitors. With greater accessibility and more publicity, the Antiquities Department hopes to attract local and foreign visitors to the site.

Dr. DeVries is currently working on a book that will describe the results of his work at Umm el Jimal. After its completion, he plans to begin excavating the northern half of the city and to study the role of Umm el Jimal in the geographic region of the Hauran.

Nearby Sites

In 1944 Nelson Glueck examined other ancient sites in this region between the Iraq Petroleum Company pipeline and the Syrian border, *e.g.* Ba'ij, Sabha, Sabiyeh, and Umm el Quttein. These are all marked by basalt buildings similar to those of Umm el Jimal. They were occupied in Nabataean, Roman, Byzantine and medieval Arab times. Each has reservoirs hewn out of the solid rock, and each house had its own cistern. The district must have once had a population of thousands, compared with a few hundred of today.

Wadi Sirhan, which has an extensive supply of underground water, was the lifeline between the Nabataean kingdom in southern Syria and its territory in south Jordan. The Wadi extends from Azraq to within eight miles of Jauf, an oasis and former Nabataean outpost. Wadi Sirhan is 200 miles long and 18 miles wide, and today most of it lies in Saudi Arabia. This long, shallow depression acts as an extensive catchment basin for rain and rain run-offs. The line of the Desert Castles marks the line of the slope of the watershed eastward.

Although rains are infrequent in the Wadi Sirhan and the east desert of Jordan, at times heavy rain can fall for days. The water collects and may remain for months in low-lying lands.

SOUTH OF AMMAN

One of the most historic and scenic roads in the Middle East, the King's Highway runs from Amman to Aqaba through the ancient lands of Ammon, Moab and Edom. The road passes through Hesban, Madaba, the ancient cities of Dhibon, Kerak, Tafileh, Shobak and on to Petra. The route is spectacular when it winds through the gorges of Wadi Mujib and Wadi el Hasa. There are even parts of the ancient Roman road and column markers still visible in several places along the way.

Hisban: 12 miles on the King's Highway

On the road to Madaba west of the modern village of Hisban there is a large site occupied from 1200 B.C. to 1400 A.D., which is believed to be the Heshbon of the Bible. Old Testament references describe it as the capital of the Amorites, who had taken it from the Moabites (Num. 21:26; 32:37). Later Jeremiah assigned it to Ammon, and by Herod's time it was used as a buttress against the Nabataeans. Still later, Saladin occupied it, and in the 19th century a new village grew up in the vicinity.

In 1968 excavations were begun by Andrews University on the hillside covered with half-buried columns and foundation stones. A Byzantine church, Hellenistic and Persian walls and pottery, and a 500 B.C. ostracon inscribed with Egyptian, Babylonian and West-Semitic names was uncovered. A second season in 1971 produced Roman and Byzantine tombs from three different cemeteries, some with jewelry and gold, skeletons and an abundance of pottery.

In previous excavations the oldest material that had been found dated only to the seventh century B.C. In 1973, pottery and a small wall dating from the early Ammonite kingdom of the 12th-11th centuries B.C. were found. After a gap of 400 years, people lived here again during the sixth to seventh century B.C. Other aspects of the Ammonite era came to light on the western slope, where a strange complex of Iron Age walls were uncovered. The complex was built in six stages, partly over bedrock and partly over earlier rubble.

In the southwest cemetery nine more tombs were explored, and some yielded fine Byzantine glass, pottery vessels and evidence of burial customs and tomb construction.

For the first time, an investigation was made of the buildings which are visible above ground in the southwest village of Hisban. For years they had been called Turkish, but pottery identifies them as Mameluk. Also explored for the first time were the curious underground holes, each as big or bigger than a living room, that had been dug through the rock. They are interconnected with tunnels and ramps and an occasional hole made through the ceiling to the outside surface. They are thought to have been cisterns dug by the Romans or Byzantines.

In addition to the excavations, the Department of Antiquities and the Andrews University team made a detailed survey of the area within a six-mile radius. These included Wadi Hesban almost all the way to Tell er-Rama, ancient Livias in the Jordan Valley, from where, in ancient times, the road led to Jericho and Jerusalem. Hesban was part of a heavily populated region throughout history. Altogether about 103 sites were explored.

Madaba: 19 miles, on the King's Highway

Madaba, the city of mosaics, dates from the Middle Bronze Age, about 2000 B.C. It is mentioned in the Bible as Medeba, a border town of the Moabites at the time of the Exodus (Num. 21:30; Joshua 13:9).

In the mid-ninth century B.C. the Hebrews were driven out by the Moab king, Mesha. Madaba is mentioned on the famous Meshe stele, an inscribed stone left by King Mesha in praise of himself and his mighty conquests. Centuries later Madaba was promised to the Nabataeans in exchange for their helping John Hyrcanus I recover Jerusalem from the Seleucids at the end of the second century B.C.

After the death of Alexander the Great in 333 B.C. his generals held the area. With the peace which Roman rule brought to the area, Madaba became a typical provincial town like Jerash, and its trade helped it develop into one of the main cities of the region.

Under the Byzantines it became the seat of a bishopric; a Bishop Janios represented Madaba at the Council of Chalcedon in A.D. 451. During the Byzantine era Madaba reached its peak, and most of its famous mosaics date from this period.

In 614 it was destroyed by the Persians, and in 747 the town was badly damaged by earthquake and finally abandoned. And so it remained until the early 19th century, when 2,000 Christians from Kerak settled on the ancient site.

As the new settlers dug the foundations of their houses, many discovered ancient Byzantine mosaics. Today many of these are housed in the churches and homes of the town. The best example is in the modern Greek Orthodox Church of St. George. The mosaic, discovered in 1884, is a map picturing Palestine and Jerusalem, Egypt and the Nile at the time of Justinian. Most localities shown on the map were important cities or sites of events in the Old Testament. The map is designed in shadings of red, green, blue, brown, violet and yellow, and set on a background of white limestone. It depicts the countryside and its landmarks from the northern Jordan River Valley to the branches of the Nile, showing some Mediterranean coast with its cities, the Dead Sea and the mountains of Moab.

The most important part of the mosaic is a primitive, though clear, city plan of Jerusalem as it was in the sixth century. A street of columns, the walls and the gates of the city can be distinguished. One can also recognize principal buildings such as the Church of the Holy Sepulchre.

The sacred spring of Elisha is shown as a shrine with a red dome; a stream of water flows from it to Jericho, a many-towered city surrounded by palm trees—"a city of fragrance and palm," as in the Bible. The Greek name, "Neapolis," as in the West Bank town of Nablus, appears, and in the Nile fish are pictured as big as boats, while at the mouth of the Jordan, where the waters enter the Dead Sea, the fish turn away in agony.

The caretaker of the church will show visitors the mosaic by removing the plastic sheet which is used to protect this masterpiece, but which is clearly not enough of a protection. During the author's visit, several tourists tramped across the mosaic, oblivious to the damage they could cause.

More mosaics are housed in a little museum opposite the Police Station. Among them is a large one uncovered in 1960. It measures 18 feet by 21 feet and shows Achilles carrying a lyre, with Patroclus on his right and his favorite slave girl, Persis, on his left. Above the latter's head is Eros carrying a crown, and above Eros is a mythical creature, half-man, half-goat. Another mosaic, measuring 15 feet by 15 feet and filled with geometric designs, has exceptionally good color, and the workmanship rivals that of the mosaics of Ravenna.

There are dozens of small mosaics to be seen around town in

private houses, and others continue to turn up as foundations are dug for new buildings. Some of the houses are open to the public; at others the mosaics are shown by members of the family for a small fee.

Madaba is also a center of wool dying and weaving, where attractive and colorful rugs are turned out on hand looms. Madaba rugs are distinctive in style and derive from rugs woven by earlier Bedouin tribes. A good Madaba rug was once the mark of a wealthy sheikh's household.

The Madaba Rest House, half a block from St. George's Church, has a small gift shop. It serves refreshments and can provide information on the town.

Madaba can be reached from Amman by regular bus and taxi *service* which operate frequently.

Mount Nebo: 25 miles from Amman; 6 miles northwest of Madaba

The outer point of the Moab mountain is one of the alleged sites of the tomb of Moses. From here one sees a remarkable panorama across the Jordan Valley and the Dead Sea to the Judean Hills—the scene Moses saw (Num. 23:14). On a clear day the towers of the Mount of Olives in Jerusalem are visible.

For years the Franciscans have been excavating at Mt. Nebo, and on its topmost ridge, at Siyagha (which means "monastery" in Aramaic), they have uncovered the church and monasteries referred to by early pilgrims and travelers. Inside a Byzantine church (which dates from the late 6th century) is an unusually beautiful and almost perfectly preserved mosaic, 9 by 30 feet, which was discovered only a year ago. It has a large, richly colored pictorial area depicting rural scenes; a Greek inscription which dates the floor and names the artists and pious contributors.

According to M. Piccirillo, who excavated the site, the first Christian communities of the region wanted to perpetuate the memory of the last moments in Moses' life by building a sanctuary on top of Mount Nebo overlooking the Jordan Valley and the Dead Sea. The place may already have been identified by an earlier funeral monument. Etheria, a Roman pilgrim at the end of the fourth century, reported in her memoirs that she had visited a little church, the Memorial of Moses, built on the summit of the mountain and kept by Egyptian monks. In the next century another pilgrim recorded that he had seen the memorial in a large church. The

Franciscans' excavations from 1933–1937 and again in the 1960's confirmed these reports. In 1976 work was resumed, and, as Piccirillo notes, when the new discovery was made "the excavation, which was at first thought to be a routine job, became a scientific and artistic adventure that will remain an unforgettable experience for all the members of the expedition."

The mosaic is protected by a building. The custodian will show visitors this and other mosaics which have been uncovered.

Khirbet el-Mukhaiyat, about two miles southeast of Mt. Nebo, is the site of another sixth-century church with a beautifully preserved mosaic floor. The scenes depicted are anything but pious, and show the lingering influences of paganism—mythical sea beasts and other animals; lyrical dancing figures, and a complicated scene involving bulls, trees and a fine altar. Archaeologists believe that Mukhaiyat is the site of the ancient town of Nebo mentioned in the Bible (Num. 32:3, 38).

From Mount Nebo a new road runs southwest to the mineral springs of Zerka Ma'in, the Callirhoe of classical times, where Herod the Great, among others, came for the cure. It is still used today for the same purpose. In all, there are about 50 springs located along the canyon of Zerka Ma'in, forming small and large pools with temperatures ranging from warm to boiling; a hot waterfall spills into the largest of the pools. The waters of the Wadi empty into the Dead Sea.

On a nearby mountain top southwest of Madaba was Biblical Machaerus (present-day Mukawir), where Herod held court in a palace he built upon an ancient fortress. According to the historian Josephus, this is the place where Salome danced and John the Baptist was beheaded.

Throughout this area there are hundreds of ancient sites, far too many to enumerate. Most have been only partially excavated. Those visitors who have a keen interest in archeology or Biblical history might want to spend more time here or to return for several visits. Anyone planning to live in Jordan or to remain there for any length of time will find this a fabulous area for regular outings. One can easily spend a day at Madaba and the mountains of Moab and return to Amman in time for dinner.

Dhiban: 39 miles (27 miles south of Madaba)

Dhiban (Biblical Dibon), (Num. 21:26-30; 32:34), one-time capital of the Moabites, has now been excavated down to 3000 B.C.

levels. Here the Mesha stele, a carved stone which records the battles between the Moabites and the kings of Israel around 850 B.C., was found in 1868. The discovery was sensational for many reasons, not the least of which was the fact that at the time of its discovery it was the earliest example of Hebrew writing to be found in the region.

Approximately 10 miles beyond Dhiban the road reaches *Wadi Mujib,* the Arnon of the Bible (Num. 21:3-15; Deut. 2:24-36). The gorge is over two miles wide and drops approximately 3,600 feet; its river empties into the Dead Sea. In ancient times the gorge was the boundary between the Moabites on the south and the Amorites on the north.

All along the ancient route are magnificent views, famous sites and Biblical battlefields, Roman, Arab and Byzantine ruins, small villages, shepherds with their flocks and Bedouin with their tents. On the descent one can make out the old Roman road and the ruins of a Roman bridge. On the ascent one can see the Dead Sea in the distance. Where the present road and the Roman one meet, there is a fort dating from the Roman period which also has Nabataean ruins. It was used through the centuries as a station for pilgrims and is known as *Mahattat el Haj.*

The scenery throughout this route is among the most spectacular in all the Holy Land.

Kerak: 75 miles (55 miles south of Madaba)

Crak des Moabites, or Kir-Moab and Kir Hare-seth of the Bible (2 Kings 3:25; Is. 15:1), rises 3,400 feet above its surrounding plateau and the Dead Sea Valley and crowns a hilltop with enormous walls and battlements.

Kerak was a walled Crusader town, built for defense, not beauty. For 50 years it held out against attack from Moslem armies until finally in 1189 Saladin took it. Inside the walls today there is a predominantly Moslem town.

In the castle, masterful cross-vaulting leads into more and longer galleries, stables, chambers and lookouts. The total concept of the fortress gives one pause—the colossal task of building on this precipice, maintaining its defense and supplying the needs of thousands of men and animals staggers the imagination.

To those for whom the Crusaders hold a fascination, the exploration of their castles can be a haunting, melancholy experience. From Turkey to the Gulf of Aqaba, the Crusaders built a chain of hilltop strongholds, carefully planned to be approximately a day's journey apart, sometimes on the foundation and walls of earlier fortresses. Fire signals were sent at night from chateau to chateau, to tell the knights in Jerusalem the news from the See of the day before. Each castle had its distinction, but few matched Kerak for intrigue and chivalry, bravery and betrayal.

The mountaintop fortresses which the Crusaders built east of the Jordan were strategically located on a line between the Dead Sea and the King's Highway. To maintain themselves, the Crusaders cultivated and protected the lands in the nearby valleys, and from there extended their control eastward into the flatlands, where they grew wheat and other grains as the Romans had done before them. They also took revenues from the caravans which passed through the territories they controlled.

The main commercial caravans moved between Egypt and Syria via Sinai to Aila (Aqaba) before they turned north to Damascus or south to Arabia. This was the route which had also been used by the Biblical kings and later by the Greeks and the Romans. Further east, there was another lucrative route—the Hajj or pilgrimage track from Damascus to Mecca, with even bigger caravans.

The early kings of Jerusalem extended the Crusaders' domain as far south as the Gulf of Aqaba, where they put a small garrison on an offshore island to extort tolls from the trade coming by sea. From Aqaba the goods were transhipped over Sinai by caravan to Gaza or Egypt and thence to Europe. The Crusaders also had a garrison in Aqaba. Further north, to watch over the caravans in and out of Petra and to control their supply lines, they had built a fortress at Shobak.

In 1132 Baldwin I, King of Jerusalem, ordered the Lord of Transjordan, Payem the Butler, to build a fortress at Kerak to help strengthen his communication lines and defenses. Kerak was strategically situated halfway along the great stretch from Shobak to Jerusalem. From Kerak, Baldwin could receive warnings of an approaching enemy or respond to cries for help. From Kerak, the military route to Askalon—a favorite Egyptian attacking point— could be controlled. From here, the lines south could be kept open to Petra and Aqaba, and the caravans coming from Arabia could be made to pay tribute. Baldwin was right, and for him and his three successors, the money poured into the coffers of Jerusalem.

When Baldwin III died his son was not yet thirteen, and a leper. For a time Miles de Plancy, Lord of Trans-Jordan and Kerak, was regent for the young heir; but he was assassinated, leaving his wife, Stephanie, mistress of the Crak. Reynald, or Reginald de Chatillon, a knight who arrived in the Holy Land with the Second Crusade and who was anything but a flower of chivalry, upon hearing of the death of the regent, rushed to the widow Stephanie, one of the richest women in the Holy Land. He succeeded in winning her hand and with it her powerful domain.

By feudal law, the young heir had to be named Baldwin IV. As he reached 16, the Leper King grew worse and realized that he must die without an heir. With the affairs of the kingdom torn by infighting among the feudal nobles, he decided to sue for peace with the Moslems. He made a truce with Saladin, which granted safe passage to the caravans of both the Moslems and Christians through each other's lands.

After Baldwin's truce the caravan trade increased along the routes via Kerak. Reynald, unable to resist the temptation, broke the truce and his king's pledge and seized a rich caravan headed for Mecca. Saladin responded by capturing 1,500 pilgrims on their way to Jerusalem, and the long battle was on.

Although Saladin withdrew when Stephanie's fire signals brought help from Jerusalem, the Moslem warrior would come back.

According to legend, one of the chivalrous events of the Crusades took place at Kerak. During the wedding feast of Humphrey of Toron and Isabel, the sister of Baldwin, Saladin made a surprise attack on the castle. The Christian governor sent a gift of meat and wine to Saladin, informing him of the wedding. Saladin gracefully acknowledged the gift and sent a message asking which was the bridal suite so that his soldiers could avoid bombarding it.

Soon after the first incident, Reynald broke the truce again, whereupon Saladin crossed the Jordan with an enormous army. Reynald unfortunately persuaded King Guy of Jerusalem to attack, leading to a disastrous defeat for the Crusaders at the battle of the Horns of Hittin. When the slaughter ended, only King Guy and a few knights were left to surrender. Saladin received them in his tent and gave them water. But when he discovered Reynald among them, he upbraided him for his treachery, received a rude answer, and with one swing of his sword cut off Reynald's head.

That was July 3, 1187. King Guy and the other knights, with the True Cross, were sent to Damascus as prisoners. Stephanie held out at Kerak for another year, but finally Saladin cut off all supplies, threatened the local villagers against helping the Crusaders, and simply waited.

Saladin needed Kerak. For 50 years it had dominated the caravan routes to Arabia, Egypt and the pilgrimage route to Mecca.

Moreover, it had stuck like a bone in the Arab's throat. It had sent fire signals nightly to Jerusalem, keeping in touch with Crusader leaders; it had supplied its armies from the rich valleys at its feet; and it had made vassals of the local inhabitants.

More Crusades and many battles followed, but by the close of the 12th century the Christian knights had begun a slow retreat to the sea, and Moslem rule rolled in like a tide to replace them. Kerak became an administrative post of the Arabs, and in 1263 the Egyptian ruler Baybars is reported to have destroyed its Crusader church.

When the Turks conquered the Middle East, they used the castle for some time. The town prospered and grew to fill the area enclosed by the walls; but the castle itself was neglected.

Today many of its battlements have been shored up and its passages opened. There is an entrance gate where one registers and then enters the medieval world. There are remains of the reservoir where water had been stored, the chapel, and a little round enclosure where the only efforts toward decoration appear in rows of carvings around its dome.

The castle is open from sunup to sundown. There is an archeological museum within the castle walls. Guides are available through the Government Rest House next to the castle.

The Rest House, built from native stone to blend with the castle, sits on the crest of the mountain overlooking the valley and the Dead Sea. It has 13 twin-bedded rooms, each with a shower and toilet and warm water. The hostel's dining room has a terrace overlooking a magnificent view. Arabic food and international dishes are available; or the restaurant will pack picnic lunches.

The drive to Kerak from Amman takes about two hours, and you can see Kerak in its entirety in two to three hours. An excellent picnicking area is located by a spring in the valley below. Ask at the police post for directions.

There are many Christian families in Kerak with very old names that go back to and beyond the Crusaders to the Byzantine period, when Kerak was an important bishopric. On a hill below Kerak there is a village still called Franj—from "Franks."

Among the Moslems, too, some old Christian terms remain. For example, one of the tribes is called "Bawareesh"—probably from parish, since in Arabic "p" becomes "b." One of the families of this tribe is named Matraneh, which in Arabic means "bishop."

Below Kerak an interesting side trip can be taken down to the Dead Sea to the place where the Crusaders built a port—their nearest escape route to Jerusalem from Kerak. From here, a new road leads to Safi and the mining area for the Arab Potash Company. The area can also be reached by a new road through the Wadi Araba from Aqaba.

Continuing south on the King's Highway to Tafila there are two villages which are significant in the history of early Islam. It was on these plains that the first army of Islam suffered its first defeat against the Byzantines in 632. It was to be the Arabs' Dunkirk. Afterwards, the battered army returned to Arabia to regroup and plan. When they charged north again against the Byzantines a few years later, they did not stop until they took Damascus. Today, in the villages of Mauta and Mazar, there are two mosques which commemorate the Moslem leaders who were killed here in the first battle.

Khirbet el-Tannur is a Nabataean temple from the first century B.C. located in the vicinity on a mountain peak.

Qasr Tafila: 118 miles (40 miles south of Kerak)

After crossing Wadi Hasa, the road reaches Tafila, much of which is built from or into and around Crusader ruins. There is an enormous keep or donjon built in the early 12th century. A custodian has the key to this medieval relic and will also give you a tour of the other remaining Crusader and Mameluk structures, if requested. Tafila is set in a valley with abundant water and surrounded by olive groves.

Qasr Buseira, 9 miles south of Tafila, at the village of Buseira, is a huge pile of roughly fitted stones with an occasional arch or retaining wall still standing, on a cliff above Wadi Khanzira, a valley which extends to the Dead Sea. Buseira is thought to have been one of the main towns of the Edomite Kingdom.

The area which lies west of Tafila and Shobak is among the most important lands of ancient history. It was a mining and smelting center from the Bronze Age down through the Arab conquest. *Khirbet Nahas,* 21 miles south of the Dead Sea, is the site of copper mines which were in use during and after the reign of Solomon. The land was also part of the caravan route that led through the Wadi Araba to Aqaba. In Biblical times it was the land of the Edomites. Down through history control of this land ensured its owners great wealth. It was also the reason so many battles were fought here in ancient times. Just before reaching Shobak, the road crosses Wadi Fidan, which marks the north boundary of the Ma'an district that extends all the way to the Gulf of Aqaba. The main towns of the district are Ma'an, located on the Desert Highway, and Aqaba at the head of the Gulf.

Shobak: 154 miles (19 miles north of Petra) on the King's Highway; 117 on the Desert Highway

The ancient Crusader fortress of Montreal stands alone, crowning a mountain of rock overlooking the most barren, weather-worn, windswept and desolate land one can imagine. There is a good view of the fortress as one approaches from the south on a road that climbs up directly to the castle.

Mons Reglais, the Montreal Castle of Shobak, was the parent of the chain of Crusader castles built between the 11th and 13th centuries. It is situated about halfway between Kerak and Petra. Built by Baldwin I about 1115, it was besieged several times by Saladin and finally captured in 1189. The Mameluks restored it in the 14th century. Today, the castle is little more than a pile of stone except for its outside walls, a square keep and a donjon beautifully carved with Arabic inscriptions. It is built on a hill surrounded by a natural moat, and contains a rock-cut well shaft of 375 steps leading down to an underground water supply—one of the deepest well shafts ever dug by the Crusaders. As with all mountaintop Crusader castles, the view is magnificent.

From Shobak the road passes through rolling highlands on which there is snow as late as mid-March, and leads to Wadi Musa, a picturesque village near the entrance to Petra. Wadi Musa ("the springs of Moses") was apparently named in the belief that it was the site where Moses struck the rocks that brought forth water.

About one mile before the village there is a magnificent view of Wadi Musa in the foreground and the mountains of the Petra canyon in the background. It is an excellent spot to take photographs.

Petra: 160 miles

> Match me such marvel save in Eastern clime,
> A rose-red city half as old as time.—*Dean Burgon*

These words were written decades ago by a traveler who rode camel and horse over mountains, through valleys, across streams, into desert to reach a site hidden in the mountain fastness of southern Jordan. After its rediscovery in the early 19th century, ancient Petra, capital of the Nabataean Arabs, became a goal of adventurers, globe-trotters, explorers, historians and archeologists.

Over the century the way to Petra became easier and safer, but even as late as 1955 the trip from Amman was ten days by horse or a day of rough driving by car, available only to the few who could afford the time and cost of such a trip. Today, the new road from Amman to Petra has changed all this.

Those captivated by the romance of the East may regret the passing of an era when the remoteness of ancient Petra added to its fascination and lure. Now that the long trek is no longer necessary, one could afford to agree with them. Frankly, we enjoyed the comfortable car ride from Amman to the entrance of Petra. The fact that the drive on the Desert Highway takes only three hours need not lessen one's enthusiasm or detract from Petra's wondrousness in the slightest. Petra is still mysterious, formidable and magnificent.

Petra, which means "rock," was a fortress city set in a canyon whose only entrance was a long, narrow passage, the Siq. Inside the canyon the Nabataeans created a city by carving houses and temples out of the variegated rock of the canyon walls. The sunlight plays on the rock, changing its colors from hot yellow at high noon to red in the reflection of the setting sun, to purple in the afterglow of twilight. The changing light casts a mood over Petra—and all the hundreds of words written about it cannot adequately describe its effect.

The story of Petra prior to the Nabataeans is vague in our history books. It was probably the land of the Biblical Horites around 2000 B.C., and later the land of the Edomites, who controlled southern Jordan at the time of Moses and the Exodus. Petra is sometimes identified with Sela, the capital of the Edomites in the Bible (2 Kings 14:7; Is. 16:1). When the Crusaders occupied the site in the 12th century they called it Sel, recalling its Biblical name. Sela, too, means rock.

The Nabataeans, a Semitic tribe from North Arabia, settled in Petra probably around 800 B.C. By the 4th century B.C. they had occupied the territory astride the main trade route from Arabia to the Fertile Crescent and had become protectors of the caravans which passed through their lands. As payment for this protection, the Nabataeans were able to extract enormous tolls from the caravan traders.

In 312 B.C. the Seleucids, heirs of Alexander the Great's empire in Syria, attempted to dislodge the Nabataeans from their envious position. Instead, the Nabataeans routed their enemy in a night attack and ended conclusively any Seleucid designs on their territory.

For the two centuries that followed, the Nabataeans maintained their independence and carved out an empire which extended as far north as Damascus. With their wealth from the caravans and their expert engineering skills, the Nabataeans enlarged their rose-colored city and embellished it with high temples, houses and tombs.

After Pompey's conquest of Syria and Palestine in 63 B.C., the Romans gradually extended their control into south Jordan. The Nabataean domain remained autonomous but was dependent upon Rome. Finally, in A.D. 106, Nabataean power gave way and their lands, along with most of Palestine and Jordan, were incorporated into the Roman Province of Arabia.

Under the Romans Petra reached its height. Many buildings were added, including a rock-carved theater, baths, a colonnaded street, a forum and temple (the most complete free-standing building which can be seen there today). Other buildings were carved out of the living rock.

Eventually, when one of its main competitors, Palmyra (Tadmor) in Syria, started to emerge as an important caravan trade center, Petra's prominence began to dwindle. The end came when the Romans began to use ships to bring the merchandise from South Arabia north through the Red Sea, making caravans, already risky, too slow to be profitable. Some inhabitants, of course, stayed in Petra.

Early in the Christian era Petra became part of the Byzantine Empire, and a number of important buildings, alterations of earlier Nabataean ones, date from this period. Later, when the Moslem armies marched north from Arabia, Petra fell to the Arabs. But by this period the main trade routes of the East had shifted, and Petra's source of wealth had vanished. With time, Petra's glories were forgotten, and for hundreds of years even its location was lost to the world, until the early 19th century when the Swiss explorer John Burckhardt stumbled upon it by chance during a Middle Eastern expedition he had undertaken for an English learned society.

When Burckhardt was traveling from Damascus to Cairo by way of Aqaba, he heard stories from local Bedouin about a strange place with ancient ruins. From the descriptions he thought the site might be the lost city of Petra. Because of his expert knowledge of Arabic and Islam, Burckhardt could pass himself off as a Moslem and move about unexplored areas without being questioned. On the pretext of having vowed to make a sacrifice at the tomb of Aaron, Burckhardt was allowed by local tribes to proceed to Mt. Hor. En route he saw Petra, but unfortunately he could not linger for fear of arousing suspicion. Apparently, however, he made a few stops, for he later described some of the monuments in his writings.

The track into Petra leads down a hill past the ancient dam of the Nabataeans. In olden times the dam dispersed the dangerous floodwaters of the wadi (valley) into channels, and a canal sent a large part of it by a circuitous route outside the canyon walls. Later, the Romans developed a similar system using terra cotta pipes. Both the Nabataean channels and the Roman pipes are clearly visible.

After centuries of neglect the dam collapsed. In 1963, after a group of tourists were caught in a flash flood in the wadi, the dam was reconstructed to ensure the year-round safety of the Siq. In building the new dam, modern engineers followed the basic plan which the Nabataeans had used more than twenty centuries earlier.

Beyond the dam one enters the Siq. From here, the dreamlike world of Petra begins. The Siq, barely wide enough for a car, hides between sheer rocks towering 200 to 300 feet. In some places the walls are so close they appear to be meeting overhead. In ancient days the Siq was Petra's protection from surprise attack; only a few men were needed to hold the passage against invaders. In Roman times a stone-paved road led through the passage and into the main thoroughfare of the city.

Upon emerging from the path, you will be dazzled by the sight of an imposing tomb in classic Greek style carved out of rose-colored rock on the side of a cliff. This is the *Treasury*, or Khaznat Faron, one of the best preserved monuments in Petra. Its surface appears so smooth it would seem to be covered with a film of rose-colored powder. The Treasury gets its name from an old belief that pirates (perhaps Ali Baba and the Forty Thieves!) hid their stolen treasures here.

Beyond the Treasury the path turns to the right and leads past many of Petra's fine tombs and temples topped with the characteristic crow-step design, the hallmark of Nabataean architecture. Further along, the trail runs by a second-century Roman Theater carved from rock at the foot of Mt. Nejr. The theater once seated 3,000 spectators. Behind it a trail and steps lead to the High Place of Sacrifice, a mountaintop sanctuary in the center of Petra canyon.

East of the main road a cliffside is lined with more of Petra's beautiful tombs and temples—the largest cluster and among the most beautiful groups in the canyon at easy access. Further ahead on the original Roman road stand the remains of the Nymphaeum, the

Roman Triumphal Arch and a structure known as Kasr al-Bint. In front of this Roman temple, excavations of the Jordanian Department of Antiquities continue to probe Petra's hidden past. The entire center area is believed to be the old city—now under centuries of earth. It will take archeologists decades to uncover it.

Immediately beyond the temple and excavation area is the Nazzal hostel and camp, where adequate sleeping accommodation and good food are available for several nights' stay. Some rooms are in the hostel, others are in caves behind it. This camp is scheduled to be demolished in another year as part of the Petra Development Project.

In order to see the ruins of Petra, one must climb several cliffs and mountains within the canyon. The principal sites are the Monastery and the High Place of Sacrifice. Each is a half-day's excursion at a leisurely pace.

North of the hostel a footpath leads up the mountain to the *Monastery,* or Deir. Along the way one can marvel at the beautiful rock formation and the carvings on the side of the cliffs. Upon arrival at the top one is directly in front of the Monastery, one of the largest and most handsome temples in Petra.

The Monastery was carved about the third century A.D. as a temple to the glory of the Nabataean god Dhu-shara, chief diety of Petra. Crosses carved on the temple walls probably indicate that at some later date the temple was used as a church. The edifice measures 165 feet wide and 148 feet high, but its size is deceiving. Only when you see someone standing in the doorway does the enormous size of the façade become apparent.

The panoramic view from the hill beyond the Monastery is one of the most impressive in the Middle East. Some 4,000 feet below lie Wadi as-Siyagh and Wadi Araba, part of the Great Rift Valley extending from the Jordan Valley in the north to the eastern coast of Africa in the south. Sinai, the Negev and the Biblical lands of Canaan are on the horizon.

Three hundred meters to the southwest is Jebel Harun (Mt. Hor), site of the tomb of Aaron, the brother of Moses. An annual sacrifice is made on Mt. Hor by local Bedouin during Id al-Adha, the Moslem Feast of Sacrifice. In Moslem tradition the feast is held at the end of the pilgrimage to Mecca, and the sacrifice is symbolic of Abraham's offering of his son.

A trail southeast of the hostel along the Wadi Tarasa leads up the side of Mt. Nejr to the *High Place of Sacrifice.* Along the way more of Petra's stupendous rock formation, temples and tombs are in evidence. Especially important are the *Tomb of the Soldiers* and the inner chamber of the *Festival Hall.*

At the High Place the ancient altar, with drains for the blood of the sacrifice, is flanked by two obelisks of solid rock. These were probably meant to mark the limits of the sanctuary. The altar is said to be exactly east-west at the equinox. From the summit of Mt. Nejr, one of the highest peaks in Petra, the entire canyon and surrounding area are in view.

The descent from Mt. Nejr can be made by an ancient rock-cut stairway (restored by the Jordanian Department of Antiquities) on the reverse side of the mountain. The way is lined with houses, temples and tombs topped with the traditional Nabataean crowstep design. The path ends near the Roman Theater and the main road to Petra.

A third climb—not so steep—can be made east of the hostel by way of the old Roman road to a cliffside faced with many amazing structures. These include the dramatic *Corinthian Tomb,* the *Palace Tomb* (a three-story edifice thought to be a copy of a Roman palace) and the *Urn Tomb,* which has a paved and colonnaded courtyard extending over a two-story vault. A Greek inscription inside the Urn Tomb says that the building was used as a church in A.D. 447. The variegated rock on this cliffside is some of the best in Petra. For hearty climbers there are several paths and rock steps which lead to the very top of the cliff. It is worth the climb; the color of the rock is fantastic and the view of the canyon is magnificent.

A small museum of Petra, arranged by the Friends of Archeology and the Department of Antiquities, is located in a cave a few yards west of the hostel.

PRACTICAL INFORMATION FOR PETRA

 HOW TO GET THERE. On the Desert Highway from Amman to Ma'an you can drive to Petra in three hours. The old road via Madaba, Kerak and Shobak is an eight-hour drive.

A mile or so beyond Wadi Musa at Al-Ji Police Post, or the Visitors Center in front of the Government Rest House, you can hire a horse or donkey to ride the trail through the Siq into Petra. The horses are docile old souls, and their owners walk alongside holding the reins for timid riders. If you prefer you may walk the trail, which is well worth every step. We recommend the walk; it gives one time to stop and admire the fantastic rock formation. In any case, be sure to wear comfortable, flat walking shoes (sneakers are perfect). The distance through the Siq is less than two miles, and the walk or ride takes about 45 minutes. An occasional truck or jeep makes a trip through the Siq to carry food and supplies to workers at the camp or archeological sites, but there is no regular motor traffic into the Petra canyon.

WHEN TO GO. The best months to visit Petra are September through November and March through May. Many people make the excursion in one day, but to cover Petra adequately one should plan to spend at least two days. Petra is one of the few places in the world which can truly be called unique. It deserves a longer stay than most tourists devote to it.

PLANNING YOUR TRIP. In planning your first trip to Petra you should use a good travel agent in Amman, who can arrange for a car and driver for a one, two- or three-day visit. The fee is approximately J.D. 15 per person for overnight at the hostel and includes transportation to Petra by five-passenger car, meals, horses, entrance fee and guide.

Even if you decide to make your own arrangements for getting to Petra, you should have a guide to lead you around the ruins on your first tour. At Al-Ji Police Post and the Tourist Center English-speaking guides are available for J.D. 5 a day. The fee for a horse or donkey ride in and out of Petra is J.D. 2, and the owner will expect a tip. Also, bring along a guidebook. Iain Browning's *Petra* is the most extensive.

Jordan Tours and Transport (JETT) offers seat-in-bus tours twice weekly for J.D.10. The bus departs Fridays, Sundays and Tuesdays at 7 A.M. from Abdali Station and returns at about 7 P.M.

ITINERARIES AND PHOTOGRAPHY. If you leave Amman by 8 A.M. you can arrive in Petra for lunch at the hostel. Afterward, climb to the Monastery and return by sunset. This is an excellent time to photograph Petra to the east; the rocks glow in the light of the setting sun.

Early in the morning on the second day climb to the High Place of Sacrifice. This is the best time to take pictures to the west. Upon descending from the High Place continue to the Treasury for more picture-taking. The best hour at the Treasury is about 10 to 11 A.M., when the façade is in full sunlight, or about 4 P.M., when the stone is a deep pink—almost a raspberry color. After an early lunch, climb to the Urn, Palace and Corinthian Tombs.

You should plan to leave from inside Petra canyon by 4 P.M. in order to walk through the Siq in sunlight and to return to Amman by 8 in the evening.

For a one-day visit you must leave Amman by 6 A.M. to arrive in Petra by 9 A.M. Moving fast, you could make two climbs and leave the Siq an hour before sunset.

ACCOMMODATIONS. Restaurant facilities and over-night accommodations are available at the Government Rest House and at the Nazzal's Camp within the canyon. After the camp is removed in another year, it will no longer be possible to spend an overnight within the canyon. The Rest

House, situated outside the Siq, is built around an ancient tomb carved into the rock; guest rooms are in a modern structure and are large and comfortable with baths and hot water. There is a dining room and bar; the food is good and ample. If you plan to visit Petra from December through March, be sure to take along warm clothes. It can be very cold at night, and there is no heat in the guest rooms.

Construction is scheduled to begin this year on a 76-room hotel which is part of a project to upgrade Petra and Jerash with a $6 million loan from the World Bank matched by $6.1 million from the Jordan Government. In addition to the hotel, there will be an expansion of facilities for catering, shopping, reception and camping. One of the most important new features will be marked walking trails with printed descriptive itineraries. These will be a most welcome addition. It is now quite easy to get lost if one wants to strike out alone on a hike.

SUGGESTED READING. If you want to read up on Petra before your visit, several books offer excellent descriptions: G.L. Harding, *The Antiquities of Jordan;* Julian Huxley, *From an Antique Land,* and Iain Browning, *Petra.*

A last note: At your first sight of Petra you may be confused and even disappointed. It does not have the immediate impact of the colossal Temples of Baalbeck or Ramses' statues at Abu Simbel. Rather, Petra's effect is one of bewilderment and slowly developing fascination. Some temples are visible on the road as you enter but many others are not. The area inside the canyon is two miles square, so you do not get the whole effect until you have examined the temples, houses and rock at close hand, and climbed the mountains and cliffsides to look down on the sweeping panorama of the canyon. After that, Petra is sure to linger in your mind for years to come.

Beida: 2.5 miles north of Petra

Beida, a settlement dating back 9,000 years, is one of the oldest sites in the Holy Land and is considered by archeologists to be as important as Jericho for the evidence which has been uncovered from the Neolithic and subsequent periods.

Excavations were started in 1969 by Diana Kirkbride, one of the best-known archeologists working in the Middle East. She returned every two years for a period of two to three months until 1967. Six main building levels were uncovered and four different types of architecture, each with its own individual and significant techniques. Each village of the six main levels seems to have lasted an average of 75 years, judging from the amount and kind of debris that filled each level.

The oldest inhabitants of Beida, circa 7,000 B.C., were a Neolithic people who used stone tools in their daily life, before the invention of pottery. They built houses, developed crafts and ground grain. Later on, when Petra became the capital of the Nabataean Kingdom, the Nabataeans terraced the uneven ground for agriculture; remains can still be seen on the hilly surface.

The excavations conducted by Ms. Kirkbride are at about 3,000 feet above sea level. The first level dates from about 6,000 B.C. Proper identification of the top level was difficult due to erosion and the destruction caused by the terracing of the Nabataeans. Small rectangular houses with plastered floors were found.

The second and third levels date from about 6,600 B.C. Houses in these levels were all of the same size except for one large house in the second level, which was a single room measuring 27 X 21 feet with massive walls still standing to the height of three feet, and with a hearth in the center. Entrance was through doorways in the walls, which were thick enough to accommodate three descending steps to the plastered floor inside. South and west of this house were long rectangular buildings with wide unplastered walls, divided into six rooms by corridors. Artifacts suggest that they were workshops rather than dwellings, for crafts that show a certain degree of specialization even at this early date. One room contained a variety of heavy implements—grinders, polishers and axes. In another room an oval wooden box holding 114 choice flints was found. The big house was probably the meeting place and eating room for the workers.

Level 4 dates from about 6780 B.C. and was much damaged by later building activities. The structures were of circular walls broken by entrances. Walls and floors were plastered, similar to those of Jericho. In Level 5 there was strong evidence of an architectural evolution.

Level 6 is from 7,000 B.C. and contains the earliest Neolithic houses yet found. They are unique—circular in plan with stout posts set into the floor at regular intervals and united by beams to a strong central post. The scheme is similar to that of a wigwam. A wide stone wall was then erected around this scaffolding, with its interior face buttressing the posts. Across the upward slanting beams, brush or reeds were laid at right angles, like thatch. This supported a thick clay roof, which was probably given a fresh coat of mud annually. Interior walls, ceiling and floors were plastered. Three of these "clusters" were excavated. One of them provided valuable evidence not only regarding the construction but also of the crafts carried out in the rooms. One of these houses had been destroyed by a severe fire.

Under Level 6 appeared a mud brick wall with curved interior face and mud plaster surface. This produced purely Mesolithic artifacts.

Burial practices at Beida were somewhat macabre and resemble other sites, such as Jericho, Hacilar and Catal Huyuk in Turkey. Adults were buried without heads, while infants and small children were buried in an undisturbed state under the floors. A cemetery was found outside the village.

A road south of Wadi Musa leads west to *Gharandal*, where there is one of the most unlikely structures in the whole Middle East—a Chinese pagoda. Gharandal, which is 48 miles north of Aqaba via the new road through the Wadi Araba, is the site of a small village which was once a Nabataean settlement and is thought to have been the capital of the Edomites at one time.

From Petra to Aqaba one returns to the main road to join the Desert Highway north of Ras al Naqab.

THE DESERT HIGHWAY

The alternate route from Amman to Aqaba is the Desert Highway, which follows closely the railway line and the old pilgrim and caravan routes established during the Ottoman period. The drive takes about five hours.

The road out of Amman passes through Wahdat, beyond which the television station is located, and Umm al Heran, where there is a customs house for commercial trucks en route to and from Europe, Lebanon, and Syria to Saudi Arabia and the Gulf. Soon after, the road reaches a fork, with the road on the right continuing to Madaba, 8 miles, and that on the left to Aqaba, 192 miles.

On both sides of the road in the springtime the fields are green with a new crop of grass, which brings the Bedouin to graze their flocks of camels, sheep and goats. After 27 miles there is a cutoff on the right to Dhiban, and about one hour after leaving Amman you will be in Qatrana, which is a truck stop. There is also a pilgrims' camp—cement-block houses where pilgrims to Mecca are given lodgings.

On the right of the road there is a small fort, and a turnoff for Kerak, which is about 25 miles away. Noticing these turnoffs and distance, one cannot help but compare them with the road via the King's Highway. In every instance, 10 or 20 miles on the Desert

Highway represent two or three times the driving time on the King's Highway.

While the Desert Highway is not as scenic or dramatic as the King's Highway, it is not without interest. As the name implies, the road passes through desert, although it could more accurately be described as hard-packed earth. Here and there Bedouin and their low black tents can be seen, but what you are likely to see first are their camels and sheep. Drivers must be careful on this road; it is not unusual to come upon animals crossing the road, and no one has told them they are supposed to stop for traffic.

After about two hours out of Amman the road reaches Al-Hasa, the country's main center for phosphate mining. A few minutes more and a road on the west leads to Shobak and thence to Wadi Musa and Petra, about 25 miles away.

Approximately three hours from Amman you will reach *Ma'an,* the administrative capital of the region. On the northern outskirts of Ma'an is the government rest house (no overnight accommodations), where it is a good idea to make a rest stop. The road divides just south of here—on the right is the way to Aqaba; the left goes directly to El Mudawwara, the first town on the Jordanian-Saudi border. Ma'an is the major town of south Jordan, a stop on the railway line and a market center for the Bedouin of this region.

Further on, there is another turnoff on the west for Petra, about 19 miles away. From here Aqaba is about 63 miles further south.

At about 48 miles north of Aqaba the road reaches Ras el Naqab, the most scenic part of the road. From here all the way into Aqaba it is a downhill winding road and takes about one to one and a half hours to drive. There is a sign on the outskirts of Aqaba which tells you that this highway was built with U.S. aid.

On a hill overlooking Ras al Naqab at the head of the mountain pass there is a rest house where refreshments are served. It is worth the short detour for the view. There is a howling, chilly wind on this mountaintop, but there is also one of the most spectacular views in all Jordan. Here, in a flash, one can understand why in the olden days such high points were strategic to the control of the flow of goods and the march of armies. The location of ancient sites throughout Jordan—be it fort, castle, village or temple—was always related to survival, situated to take advantage of a water supply or an advantageous location.

This panorama will also tell you a great deal about erosion and what happens to land in the centuries that follow neglect or abuse.

As far as the eye can see there are mountains of rock, as at Shobak, but history tells us that at one time there were trees on these mountain sides. The Jordanian government is trying hard to reforest areas where there is enough soil to make it feasible, and has undertaken a "Green Plan" of reforestation in various regions of the kingdom.

On a clear day Wadi Rum, described later in this chapter, can be seen in the distance on the southeast.

Aqaba: 204 miles

At the southernmost tip of Jordan on the Red Sea is the country's only seaport, Aqaba, set in an amphitheater of rugged, stark mountains. The clear blue waters stretching along the Sinai Peninsula on the west and to Saudi Arabia on the east have some of the most beautiful coral reefs and fish to be found anywhere in the world. Scuba enthusiasts come from thousands of miles away, including the United States, to enjoy diving here.

Aqaba is probably the Biblical Eloth (1 Kings 9:26). Excavations at *Tell al Khalifa,* west of the present town, uncovered what some archeologists believe are King Solomon's copper smelters of Ezion Geber. Others place it on an island, Ile de Graye, three miles offshore, known since antiquity as Pharaoh's Island.

One of the earliest mentions of Aqaba dates from the tenth century B.C., and indicated that there was much sweet water only three or four meters beneath the earth's surface in some places. It is partly because of this water, and the strategic location at the end of the Red Sea, that Aqaba has been important so many times in history.

Aqaba engaged in extensive trade with South Arabia and the land of Sheba, and flourished up to the time of the Arab conquest. The great Roman road from Damascus via Amman and Petra extended south to Aqaba, where it turned west to Egypt.

During most of the 12th century the town of Aqaba and its immediate vicinity were held by the Crusader kingdom of Jerusalem as part of its fiefdom of Oultre-Jourdan. The crusaders built a fortress and placed a small garrison in the town; they made it a bishopric, and the title "Bishop of Aqaba" has survived in the Roman Catholic Church to this day. With the occupation of Aqaba the crusaders hoped to divide militarily the Moslems of Egypt from those of Arabia, and to be in a position strategically to levy tolls on the caravan trade.

Under the Ottoman Empire Aqaba was administratively part of the province of Hejaz, which encompassed Mecca and Medina and thus the western Arabian peninsula, rather than part of the Syrian district which was geographically closer.

From the retreat of the Crusaders to the 19th century little is known about Aqaba until its sudden prominence in World War I during the Arab Revolt.

During the 19th century Aqaba had become part of Egypt. The Egyptians constructed a road across Sinai during the 1830s and '40s, and Aqaba became a staging and boundary point on the pilgrim route from Egypt to Mecca. However improvements in navigation on the Red Sea after 1840 reduced the significance of the land route, and Egypt abandoned the town and the head of the Gulf of Aqaba to the Ottomans when the boundary between these two states was demarcated across the Sinai Peninsula in 1906.

Thereafter, Aqaba remained a sleepy oasis until 1917, when the British began using it as a supply route in their military offense against the Turks. After World War I the southern boundary of Britain's mandate of Transjordan was not defined. Leaders of the Arabian peninsula believed that the boundary was located 20 to 50 miles north of the town of Aqaba, since this had been the approximate boundary of the former Ottoman province of Hejaz. This would have allotted the southernmost part of Jordan, as well as Eliat, to the Kingdom of Hejaz, which in 1925 became part of Saudi Arabia.

Subsequently, Britain through a series of treaties with Saudi Arabia established the eastern boundaries for its mandate. However, no southern boundary was agreed upon, and Britain unilaterally marked one from a point on the Gulf just south of the town of Aqaba and running approximately east-south-east. This line gave about five miles of shoreline to Jordan. Britain's action was not accepted by Saudi Arabia which, however, agreed to maintain the status quo pending a solution of the matter.

Jordan had traditionally used Haifa and Jaffa on the Mediterranean as its ports. With the establishment of Israel in 1948, access to these ports was cut off. In the 1950's Jordan began developing a port at Aqaba, which had been connected by a paved road to the railroad terminal at Ma'an since 1936. Use of the port increased with the development of Jordan's phosphate and potash exports, and piers were constructed, but with the growth of traffic, land soon became insufficient for port development within Jordan's territory. A treaty with Saudi Arabia in 1965 finally provided a solution for both the 40-

year-old boundary question and the land requirements of the port of Aqaba. In exchange for about 4,000 square miles of Jordanian territory in the desert interior of the extreme southeastern corner of the country, Jordan obtained approximately ten miles of additional coastline south of the previous boundary on the Gulf.

The new boundary line on the Gulf of Aqaba is 330 yards north of the Saudi Arabian police post of Al Durra. The additional territory has enabled Jordan to expand both port and urban facilities as well as develop a resort area at Aqaba. Port facilities, however, have been expanded faster than tourist ones. These days about 50 ships a month are unloaded at new docks, compared to two or three 15 years ago. Furthermore, the port handles cargo ships not only for Jordan but also for Syria, Iraq and Saudi Arabia. The reopening of the Suez Canal in 1975 also created new business for the port.

As noted earlier, phosphate is the most important cargo loaded in Aqaba port. It is Jordan's main source of foreign currency. The phosphate comes from mines at Al-Hasa, on the railroad opened only a few years ago and already inadequate to handle the requirements. Trucks are used to help bring the phosphate from the mines to Aqaba.

The phosphate is unloaded from the rails into bins alongside Aqaba docks, located south of the town, and is powered from the bins through the pipes, across the docks and into open holds of ships.

Aqaba's population has grown from 1,700 at the end of World War II to about 20,000 today. In the old days the only way to reach the tiny fishing village from Amman was over a very bad road or by several days' trek through the desert—neither of which appealed to tourists.

Today, there are four ALIA flights a week to Aqaba from Amman. It is a 30-minute hop, and the cost is J.D. 10. By car, the drive is 5 hours on the Desert Highway, 8 hours or more via the King's Highway. There is taxi *service* and regular bus service from Amman.

Maximum day temperatures at Aqaba in December are in the mid-70's Fahrenheit. In March and April they are in the 80's; from June to August the temperature can exceed 100° F. There are 12 hours of sunshine a day in July, six in December, and about eight at Eastertime. The humidity, however, is low all through the year.

A trip to Aqaba can easily be combined with one to Petra. The cruise ships which call at Aqaba offer a day's excursion to Petra.

Aqaba is for the most part a new town. The old Crusader fort,

Qasr Aqaba, has been made into an archeological museum. It was built on the shores of the Gulf of Aqaba under Baldwin I, *circa* 1116. The Mameluks acquired it in 1320, and an inscription mentions Qansuh El Ghouri, a Mameluk who reigned in 1505. Above the double-arched portal flanked by towers is the Hashemite Coat of Arms, added in the early 20th century by the Sharif of Mecca.

Ile de Graye, or Pharaoh's Island (Jeziret Far'on), three miles offshore from Aqaba Port, is less than half a mile from Sinai. It is only a remnant of the fort built by Baldwin I and captured by Saladin. The island is a military zone and cannot be visited.

Along with improvements in roads, airport and port facilities have come new hotel accommodations. Out in front is the 113-room **Holiday Inn Aqaba,** P.O. Box 215, Aqaba. Phone: 2426. Telex 263. Opened in December 1976. Its owners, the Nazzals, also have the Philadelphia and Amman Holiday Inns. Its decor is a bit pretentious for a beach resort, but facilities include a swanky restaurant, coffee shop, cocktail lounge, swimming pool and meeting rooms. Rooms are furnished in the traditional Holiday Inn style with two double beds. All rooms are airconditioned and equipped with television, radio, telephone and private bath. Guest rooms are on two floors built around the swimming pool. Rates on the back side, away from the pool, are J.D. 12 single, J.D. 14 double; and on the seaside, J.D. 12.50 single, 15.00 double. To this should be added a 12% service charge. A drink in the bar costs J.D. 1. The hotel is set directly on the beach, and it has a discotheque.

Coral Beach Hotel, P.O. Box 71. Phone: 3521. Cable: Coral Beach. Several years old and being expanded, the hotel is built in a half-moon shape with guest rooms facing the sea and overlooking the hotel's private beach. Rooms are attractively furnished, comfortable, and airconditioned, with private bath and phone. There are a large dining room, bar and nightclub.

Aqaba Beach Hotel is government-run and the oldest of the group. Rooms in the main building are large and comfortable. Those in prefab cottages are adequate for a short stay, particularly if budget is a consideration. Meals are provided in a dining room facing the sea. The cottages do not face the sea, but they do have airconditioning. The hotel has been improved considerably since being taken over by new managers under the Grand Metropolitan Hotels' new 10 year contract to upgrade and operate all the government-owned hotels in Jordan.

Further along the waterfront at the eastern edge of town is the **Palm Beach Hotel,** which has a beach and a watersports center but not much else to recommend it. **Gulf Hotel** is under construction in the center of town.

The road west from the hotel cluster leads to King Hussein's villa on the beach where he is a frequent visitor. It is the last house before the demarcation line. Elath is on the western side of the Gulf.

King Hussein's active interest in sports has had a great deal to do with helping Aqaba develop as a resort. He has often been pictured water skiing and snorkeling at Aqaba. By leading the way he has made it popular with others.

A feasibility study of a $250 million sports and leisure complex in Aqaba has been completed by the Ministry of Tourism and Antiquities and Genstart Ltd., a Canadian firm. It envisions constructing a complete island lagoon resort at Aqaba as part of Jordan's overall plans to develop a modern resort on the Red Sea.

The focal point of the project is a central inland lagoon, connected with a series of narrow waterways, that will cover a 600-acre site along the northern shores of the Gulf. Facilities to be constructed on the man-made lagoon will provide for all types of water sports and will include four first-class hotels, 400 private homes, 500 apartments, and berths to accommodate 250 pleasure craft. A golf course is also planned, in addition to restaurants, shopping arcades, theaters, and other entertainment facilities.

Aqaba's Undersea Life

The Gulf of Aqaba has an unusual marine environment. Complex water movements, including chilled vertical currents, combine with the removal of warm surface water by the strong north winds. These leave the water surprisingly cool and invigorating—an ideal situation for coral growth and plant life. It also helps produce an incredible variety of fish, so abundant that divers do not need to use tanks, and the water is so clear that they can see up to 150 feet away. All one needs is a mask, snorkel tube for breathing and flippers. The variety includes chicken fish, clown fish, iron fish, crinoid, sea urchin, butterfly fish, stingray, trigger fish, goby, shrimp, grouper, scorpion fish, stone fish and more.

In addition to hundreds of species of fish, there are miles of reefs—a magnificent, living world under the sea only a few feet from the beach and easily seen by diving or from the comfort of a glass bottom boat. The boats belong to the hotels, which have jetties so that visitors can step into them easily. Some boats seat up to 12 passengers and have overhead awnings to protect them from the sun. Incidentally, spearfishing and the removal of coral are taboo.

If fish and reefs are not enough, there are shipwrecks to explore—no one knows how many. But when one remembers that the Red Sea has been an avenue of trade since ancient times, it's easy to speculate on the ships that never made their destination and are still lying at the bottom of this sea.

Aqaba has four diving clubs. The newest is the **Aqaba Aquamarina Club** on the beachfront between the Holiday Inn and the Aqaba Beach Hotel. It offers a wide variety of facilities for water sports in addition to hotel accommodation. It has a cinema, discotheque, cafeteria, bar/restaurant and gift shop. Equipment is available for skin diving, water skiing, fishing, sailing, rowing, surf sailing and pedal boating. The club has two annual water ski festivals: the first week of April and November 14, King Hussein's birthday.

Three other centers are the Jordanian Diving Center at the Palm Beach Hotel, the Aqaba Diving Center at the As-Samaka Restaurant and the Coral Beach Diving Center at the Coral Beach Hotel.

A Marine Science Station was established a few years ago by the Jordan Government to study the unusual marine environment of the area. The station provides facilities for scientific research as well as training of personnel in diving, underwater photography and boat handling. It also plans to have an outdoor aquarium, a museum and lectures on the area's sea life for visitors. The Station is located southeast of town near a solar energy experimental station operated in conjunction with a West German firm.

SCUBA DIVING IN THE RED SEA

Because of the enormous interest and attraction of Jordan's Red Sea waters for scuba fans, we are including here an article from Jordan Magazine *by Carl Roessler, underwater photographer and author of* The Underwater Wilderness. *Since 1974 Roessler has accompanied American scuba divers to Aqaba on trips organized by See and Sea, Inc. of San Francisco, a travel service specializing in diving programs.*

Regularly since 1974, our scuba diving groups have been traveling to Jordan for the excitement of photographing the hauntingly beautiful world that lies beneath the waters of the Gulf of Aqaba. This long and narrow finger of the Red Sea, which stretches north to Jordan, holds thousands of miles of fabulous coral reefs that house an abundant variety of fish and plant life. The water's transparency—you can see up to 150 feet away—makes it ideal for underwater photography.

From the moment we step aboard our boat, it is as though we embark upon a journey to another planet, so totally is it another world that opens up before our eyes. No more than a few meters out, we see through the clear water the shallow coral reefs along the coast. They are, both in their color and in the incredible variety of marine life that surround them, a dazzling sight.

No more than a snorkel and face mask or a glass-bottomed boat are needed to see intricate thickets of sculptured stony corals punctuated by the delicate branches of fire coral a few feet beneath the surface. Here and there, schools of tiny anchovy hover about, and occasionally a larger fish glides lazily by. All are bathed in the diamond sparkle of sunlight as it pierces through the water in prismatic pattern.

In some areas, the sea floor is an open sandy expanse with scattered coral heads. Here, each coral thicket becomes a sanctuary, sheltering brilliantly colored fish of many species. The fish hover near these free-standing coral heads for protection. The structures, with their many crevices and complexities, offer the smaller fish a handy place to take cover if a barracuda or other predator happens by.

For the photographer, this results in amazing assemblies of beautifully colored reef fish that require no swimming at all to find. Schools of vivid orange fairy basslets with purple eyes capture the sun's brightness in their own flashing dance, drawing the diver again and again to watch them.

Here and there on the coral reefs one may find a variety of unusual species: tiny pink coral clusters, delicate soft coral in rose, violet, and hazy pink, and gaudy red sponges, each of which is decorated with at least one tiny nudibranch (shell-less snail) ringed with blue, white and orange bands.

Each dive reveals new marvels. One pleasant morning we find a hawksbill turtle napping amid the corals. Right next to the turtle, a small moray eel with a yellow mouth snaps this way and that, as if carrying on a conversation with his larger companion.

On other dives we find many examples of the amazing relationship between the clownfish and the anemone. Anemones capture small fish by means of contact-actuated stinging cells lining their snaky tentacles. But the clownfish is exempt. The anemone chemically "recognizes" a mucus the clownfish secretes on his skin, and holds its sting. With this startling immunity the clownfish swims among the armed tentacles with flashing confidence, indeed uses them to protect himself from larger fish!

Other brilliantly hued fish on the Aqaba reefs include butterflyfish of several species, pufferfish, delicate pipefish, angelfish, and a rainbow of others. The colors of the king angelfish are arrayed in vertical slashes of blue, yellow and white. Usually one of the shyest of reef fish, these striking fellows will occasionally surprise the visiting photographer by swimming right up to the camera.

Each day we discover even more splendid undersea sites. One area was so beautiful we returned several times. Its appeal was an extraordinary population of the extravagantly designed lionfish. This is one of the world's most beautiful fish, and nowhere in the world have I seen more than here. In many locations in the Indo-Pacific a visitor may see one or two lionfish in a week of diving. In Aqaba, one will find at least a dozen on every dive. Indeed, on several dives we found as many as a dozen or more at a single coral head! At least six species of these plumed fish are seen regularly in Aqaba's waters. In what ranks as a personal thrill, on two of my trips I have managed to photograph a species which authorities tell me may be new to science. It does not conform to the defined fin structure and color patterns of the known species, and scientists are studying the pictures now to determine whether it is a species unique to Aqaba.

By the end of the two weeks, our divers have made perhaps thirty different excursions into the sea. Their films are carefully packed, and they dream of the photos with which they'll relive these incredibly beautiful days.

As we cruise for a last time along the barren coastline, looking down at the passing reefs, we are silent. We wonder how soon we may return to these serene reefs. Will they escape the damage to which reefs around the world have been subjected? Economic development is slowly spreading down Jordan's coastline as the needs of a busy nation translate into docks, highways and construction facilities.

To its great credit, the Jordanian government has recognized its marine resources as a national treasure and is moving to protect the reefs. Laws against spearfishing, coral collection and other damaging activities are already in place. The University of Jordan is carefully monitoring the impact of shipping and construction on the marine life of Aqaba and to date has detected only a minor effect.

Wadi Rum: 35 miles northeast of Aqaba, south of Ma'an

Those who saw the film *Lawrence of Arabia* will remember the magnificent desert scenery with towering cliffs of weathered stone.

The weirdly shaped rocks jutting up from the valley floor, the color of the stone and red sand, and the endless span of sky creates a panorama of strange beauty with an almost ethereal quality— scenery unsurpassed in the Middle East. This is Wadi Rum, a great valley lying northeast to southeast in the desert of southern Jordan; a vast, silent place that has been named the Valley of the Moon.

Wadi Rum was the route which T.E. Lawrence and Sherif Hussein took in World War I to fight the Turks. For those who take the same route it will seem a journey into another world.

Archeologists are certain that the area of Wadi Rum was one of the earliest inhabited sites in Jordan, and a holy site during Nabataean times. Excavations in the south have uncovered a small village dating from 4500 B.C., and on a hill in the center of the valley there are the remains of a small temple, probably Nabataean and probably built about the first century B.C. There are also slabs of rock throughout the valley with inscriptions in early Thamudic writing, recording the names of travelers of old who were apparently moved by what Lawrence called "this processional way greater than imagination," and who left their mark before vanishing in the vastness of time and the wadi.

Wadi Rum resulted from a great crack in the surface of the earth caused by an enormous upheaval that shattered mammoth pieces of granite and sandstone and heaved them upward in the form of great cliffs. The weatherworn rocks are like pale purple mountains rising out of infinity. As one gets closer to them, their purple color gives way to the tawny hues of sandstone ridges that tower a thousand feet in the air and are topped with domes worn smooth by a constant wind. Overhead the sky is pale and colorless; underfoot, the sand is rust. All around there is emptiness and silence—a silence so great, one can hear it; space so immense, man is dwarfed to insignificance.

To penetrate the heart of Wadi Rum takes less than an hour from the Desert Highway. It lies in the center of a vast plain between Jebel Ram and Jebel Um Ishrin, almost a mile away. Both are parts of the high cliffs which Lawrence described as being like "gigantic buildings along two sides of their street."

Wadi Rum can be reached by car in about an hour's drive from Aqaba. From the Desert Highway about halfway between the villages of Qwairah and Khirbet al Khalidi, about 25 miles north of Aqaba, a paved road turns east and crosses the desert for about 18 miles to the fort of the Wadi Rum Desert Patrol. The fort with its crenelated walls, gun towers, slit windows and swinging gates is itself out of a movie set, but an even greater treat—especially for photographers—are the men of the Desert Patrol, who wear the most handsome uniforms in the Middle East—and they know it! The splendid outfit is a long khaki kilt held by a bright red bandolier, a holster with a dagger around the waist, and a rifle slung over the back. The headdress is the traditional red-and-white checkered *kafiya* worn by the Bedouin of Jordan, but wrapped under the chin and tucked into the *egal* with a slightly cocky tilt. The patrolmen, in Bedouin tradition, are friendly and hospitable to travelers, and will probably offer you coffee and answer questions willingly.

Rum is the home of many Bedouin tribes. At the fort there are a school and two shops to serve the small settlement of Bedouin who set up their black tents in the vicinity. Water is available from the springs. Without it, the valley, whose summer temperatures reach 140° F. and where no more than four inches of rain fall in a year, would be uninhabitable.

To travel beyond the area of the fort one needs a Land-Rover, which can be rented in Aqaba. The driver or owner of the Land-Rover will know the routes and should accompany you. Do not try it alone, because you might lose your way, and in the desert that's a serious matter.

Normally the trip to Wadi Rum is a half-day's excursion from Aqaba and is best made from early fall through spring, although in early spring high winds sometimes create a dust bowl in the valley which obstructs viewing and all but eliminates photography.

Travel agents in Amman can arrange trips of two or three days by camel caravan through Wadi Rum. It is preferable to have a group of ten or more in order to keep down costs.

Approximately six miles east of Wadi Rum at Disih on the way to El Mudawwara an Italian excavation has uncovered a Nabataean site which was thought to be the capital a century and a half before the Nabataeans moved into Petra.

EAST OF AMMAN

Arab Palaces in the Desert

In the desert between Amman and Azraq stand the ruins of several seventh- and eighth-century castles. These desert retreats were fortresses, pleasure palaces, watch-posts and hunting lodges of the Umayyad Caliphs in the early days of the Arab Empire. Their ruins have furnished archeologists, historians, architects and tourists with a frame in which to picture life in the early Islamic era.

To see them all, one must make the trip in a circle, clockwise or counterclockwise from Amman. We did it the latter way and recommend it, because it takes in the hardest driving, over desert track, early in the expedition when one is freshest and most energetic, and leaves the easy part, the new asphalt highway from Azrak to Amman, for the last when, after a long day of sightseeing, it will be most appreciated. Also, taking the castles (known in Arabic as *Qasr*) by the counterclockwise route allows for early morning touring in the desert before the sun gets too high and hot.

The trip must be made in a Land-Rover or other car with four-wheel drive. The palaces are located in the desert where there are no roads, only desert track. Preferably, two cars should make the trip together. You should have a compass, full tank of gas, spare tire and equipment to change a flat. Chances are you will not need them, but it is wise to carry food, water, warm clothing and blankets for overnight camping in case your vehicle breaks down and you are unable to return to Amman the same day. For your own protection, you should check in at each Desert Patrol Post along the way.

With the new highway across the desert from Zerqa to Azraq, this part of the excursion is an easy two-hour drive from Amman and can be made as a half-day tour.

The Umayyads were the first of the Arab rulers to set up the capital of their new empire outside Arabia, and they chose Damascus, which had been one of the major cities of the Orient since antiquity. The Umayyads had come from the desert, and their first caliph, Muawiya, fearing that his son and heir might lose the desert virtues, returned with him frequently to the desert away from the crowded and polluted city. First they camped in tents, and then they built palaces where there was game, which they hunted with falcon, saluki dogs and trained cheetahs; and they raced their fine Arabian horses. In the evening they were entertained by poets, dancers and musicians.

Today these desert palaces stand lonely and eroded, dotting the landscape of sand and scrub, baking in the hot sun. There are five castles on the circuit, each with its own character, each bearing the mark of its builder or most illustrious occupant. Azraq and Hallabat are of Roman and even earlier construction, with overlays from Umayyad, Crusader and Mameluk usage. Amra, Kharanah and Mushatta are purely Umayyad. The last-named is thought to have been built by none other than Walid II, one of the greatest of the Umayyad caliphs.

Southeast of Amman a track of about five miles from Ziza on the

Desert Highway leads to **Qasr el Mushatta,** the biggest and once the most ornate, and today the most despoiled of all. Mushatta was a real palace. It is a large square, 450 feet on each side, with 23 circular towers built into its walls two stories high around an inner court surrounded by archways; a great trefoil hall; vaulting, now fallen—and all built on a grand scale. For some unknown reason the palace was never completed.

Only traces of the lavish carvings which once decorated the walls are left. Just prior to World War I the Turkish Sultan Abd-Al-Hamid gave the palace to Kaiser Wilhelm. Subsequently the carvings were stripped from the walls and shipped to a museum in Berlin. Lying about in the field are a few remnants of the elaborate carving and friezes of intricate design. In the south wall of the palace is a niche, thought to indicate the mosque.

From Qasr el-Mushatta the track leads northeast for 10 miles to a large Roman reservoir at **Al-Muwaqqar.** Traces of a palace built by Yazid II are visible. The site now has only a tiny village and a desert patrol post. In one of the ancient cisterns a hydrometer with Kufic lettering was found, suggesting that the area once had a large supply of water.

Qasr Kharana, one of the most interesting of the desert castles, lies east-southeast along the track of Al-Muwaqqar (or nine miles west of Qasr al-Amra over unpaved track). Apparently, it was the only one built for purely defensive purposes. A painted inscription dates the building A.D. 711. It was built of large undressed stone, with rows of smaller stones laid between the courses, and the outside walls were plastered over, emphasizing its solid appearance. This and its strategic position along the ancient caravan route suggests a fortress in the truest sense. It was also used as a caravanserai.

The only entrance to the castle is on the south. The long corridors on each side of the entrance housed the stables. The rooms of the castle were built around an open course in the center. The ruined columns in the courtyard once supported a second-story balcony. Stairways lead to corridors and rooms on the upper floor. Most of these rooms are decorated, domed and vaulted.

In the wadi about 1½ miles west-southwest of the castle is a site covered with thousands of flints from the Upper Paleolithic-Mesolithic Period.

Northeast of Kharana, 42 miles east of Amman, 14 miles west of Azraq over unpaved track, lie the best remains of all the desert castles, **Qasr Amra.** Built as a small hunting lodge early in the eighth century during the reign of Walid I, the building is composed of three parallel halls, each with a windowless room at the end. On the inside walls are examples of some of the earliest known painted frescos. Recently the frescos, which had been badly damaged over the centuries by smoke from the cooking fires of squatters and by the scribbling of careless visitors, were cleaned and restored by a team from the Madrid National Museum under the sponsorship of the Spanish government. The frescos are remarkable, rare examples of art that has survived from the Umayyad period.

The paintings, according to Prof. K.A. Creswell, are more representative of the Hellenistic art of Syria than of the art of Byzantium which prevailed in Syria at the time Islam came to that country. However, the nationality of the artist is recognized by art historians as Syrian rather than Greek. They point out that the desert area between Umm el Jimal and Azraq was inhabited by Arab tribes who were never converted to Christianity and thus were not influenced by Byzantine art. Many of their drawings on basalt stone depict nude women, dancing girls, and hunting scenes similar to the Amra paintings. Hence, historians conclude, the frescos of Amra represent the art of Arab tribes influenced by Greco-Roman civilization.

On the back wall of the middle room the painting shows the Caliph enthroned. On the south wall the enemies of Islam—Chosroes of Persia, the Byzantine emperor, the Negus of Abyssinia, and Roderick the Visigoth—are pictured. Other walls are painted with hunting and pleasure scenes. The Baths, too, are elaborately decorated. On the ceiling of the steam room is one of the earliest zodiac representations in Islamic art. The rooms at the back of the left and right halls have lovely mosaic floors.

Adjacent to the building is a large cistern and well which once supplied water for the lodge.

Azraq, 60 miles east of Amman over a new paved road (about 20 miles east of Qasr Amra)

In olden days the oasis of Azraq was strategic: it was the only oasis in the eastern desert, and it guarded the northern end of the caravan route through Wadi Sirhan, lying north-south along the western edge of the Arabian desert.

The castle of Azraq, a somber structure of black basalt, is now no more than the shell of what once must have been an imposing fortress. Its front gate is made of one huge black stone. Inscriptions date the fort to the time of Aziz ed-din Aybaq, who was governor of the area in the early 13th century. Other inscriptions, however, indicate that there were earlier Roman and Byzantine structures on the site. Since the Nabataeans used Wadi Sirhan as their main thoroughfare, authorities suggest that even earlier fortifications existed in the area. Here, as in Umm el Jimal, the use of basalt stone shows how man adapted to the lack of wood in the desert.

Because of its plentiful water from spring-fed pools and marshes, Azraq must have been a favorite of the Umayyads and desert tribes down through the centuries, especially for hunting of birds. It is in the migratory path of hundreds of species of birds traveling between Europe and Africa each spring and summer. The area has been made a National Wildlife Sanctuary by the Jordan Government.

Perhaps no one made better use of Azraq than T.E. Lawrence, who in his *Seven Pillars of Wisdom* described it as a "luminous, silky Eden." Modern travelers might find that a bit of an exaggeration, but Lawrence apparently loved the place, and used it as his headquarters during the final assault of the Arabs against the Turks in World War I. The room above the Arabic inscription near the entrance was his headquarters—reached now by a perilous stairway. Like all the castle, it is in a ruinous state, with fallen rafters from the roof and gaping holes in the walls. The upper level looks out on the lava-strewn desert in one direction and marshes in the other.

Azraq is a strange mix. There are two villages, one near the fort, one on the marshes. One is Druze, one is Shishani. The new highway to Saudi Arabia has brought a steady stream of traffic through an area which only a few years ago was a remote corner of the desert, and its character is changing rapidly.

The marshes of Azraq are the only permanent body of water in 12,000 square miles of desert, and hence, draw thousands of birds on migration. An expedition which included Julian Huxley counted 188 different species in one week during the migration season. Others have counted up to 200.

Although the Jordan desert has been decimated of almost all its native birds and animals, as late as 1900 there were roe deer, antelope, wild ass, bear, cheetah, ibex, oryx and herds of gazelle. Today there are only a few foxes and wolves here and there. However, if the scheme which was recently instituted by the government is successful, some day the animals natural to this area may roam the land again.

South of Azraq is the Shaumari Wildlife Reserve in the Azraq National Park, watched over by the Royal Jordanian Society for the Conservation of Nature. In the spring of 1978 four young male

Arabian oryx, all born at the San Diego Wild Animal Park, were re-introduced here. It is the first return of this rare antelope to the Middle East under a project known as Operation Oryx, begun 16 years ago when international organizations united to save the species from extinction by capturing the few remaining animals in the wild. If the four males thrive, young female oryx will join them soon.

THE BIRDS OF AZRAQ

The following is based on an article by J.B. Nelson *which appeared in the magazine* Jordan *in 1969. It is included here for the benefit of amateur birdwatchers, ornithologists and readers whose interest might be sparked by knowing more about the great variety of birds to be seen at Azraq at certain times of the year.*

Of the three migratory routes between Africa and Europe, the favored one has always been through Jordan, a crossroads for birds and other animals long before it became so for man. In the spring and autumn particularly, hordes of migrant birds flood through the country, stopping to rest and feed in the wide oasis of Azraq. The variety is wonderfully rich, and at the height of a season more than 200 species can be sighted.

Viewed from the top of a Jebel Aseikhim, where the ruins of a Roman castle now stand, the landscape is a delicately sculptured, subtly colored desert stretching out on all sides. Distantly, to the southwest, lies the vast Azraq depression—the Qa'. In spring the glint of its pools, the cool green of its meadows and marshes and the security of its trees and bushes beckon the high-flying birds. Here food, water, shelter and rest may spell the difference between life or death, particularly to the smaller creatures, despite their capability for astonishing flights across deserts and oceans.

From March to May, from the continent of Africa, they move north, pausing for hours, days or weeks at Azraq—warblers, swallows, flycatchers, chats, bee-eaters, rollers, wagtails, waders, ibises, storks, cranes, herons, falcons, eagles, hawks and many others. The ducks, which flock to Azraq in such numbers as to make this one of the world's foremost duck marshes, are also moving back to their Asian breeding haunts. In autumn, from August to November, all this will be reversed. But in spring, the pageantry is remarkable—many of the birds come through in full nuptial dress, the males in glorious plumage.

A list of the birds to be seen in a day at Azraq can hardly begin to describe, much less convey, the feeling of beauty one can experience in this unusual oasis. For those fortunate enough to visit Azraq for more than a quick sightseeing tour, there are three expeditions to make—at the end of April, in June and in January. It is a fascinating drama, full, varied and unforgettable—as much to the amateur birdwatcher as it is to the seasoned ornithologist.

If you can spend an April night in Azraq, strike out in the glorious early morning light, with the marsh glowing behind the Shishan Mosque and the tamarisk groves. Beyond, the brown Qa', beginning to dry, sweeps boldly toward the horizon and in the far distance, rising gradually from southeast to northwest, the barren hills lead on to Jebel Druze and Syria. In the marsh behind the pools, reed, marsh and Savi's warblers are singing and will nest, but the willow warblers, chiffchaffs, lesser whitethroats, blackcaps, garden warblers and many others feed silently and will move on.

Today happens to be a "shrike day." Hundreds of these "butcher birds" dot the bushes—masked, red-backed, in varied grays. You may see the remains of a willow warbler impaled on a sharp twig, the shrike's larder. Now you realize that, although you cannot see huge flocks of birds anywhere, the whole area is in fact alive with them. Down in the cultivated patches are beautiful ortolan and black-headed buntings, with scores of nondescript tree pipits and a gaudy hoopoe excitedly fanning its crest. A collared flycatcher darts out and returns to its perch, and hundreds of sand martins and swallows hawk for insects. A nightjar, cryptic brown and long in wing and tail, darts up from cover and twists away, while a cuckoo that may later charm an English copse flies off swiftly, reminding one of a hawk. A wryneck, whose English name stems from its habit of twisting its head around, was ringed at Azraq and recovered ten days later in Russia.

Walking along the canal, you approach reed-filled lagoons where squacco herons, egrets and storks are feeding on the abundant marsh frogs. Where there is mud and shallow water, you may have to puzzle out rare waders like broad-billed sandpipers among the more easily recognized stilts, avocets, green sandpipers, etc.. Among them run a bewildering variety of wagtails, for the many races of the yellow wagtail group, breeding in Asia and Russia, pass through Azraq. Water and red-throated pipits also like wet ground and will probably be there too. You will not fail to notice two or three marsh harriers quartering the reeds, and a smart gray male hen harrier or a pallid harrier may delight you.

Out on the Qa' proper you have a strange sense of spaciousness from the far shimmer of the flat sand stretches around you. A flock of short-toed larks feed on apparently bare ground, and scores of Kentish plovers sprint around you at high speed. If you have two or three hours in hand you can skirt the marshes and re-enter the nearby Druze village. On the way you will pass dozens of miniature lakes, very shallow but full of life, and much loved by storks, herons and waders, not to mention rarer visitors such as flamingoes, pelicans, gulls, terns and kingfishers.

A June expedition, to be enjoyed, should be early or late in the day when it is cooler. Most of the birds you will see now are breeding here in Azraq. Though most are difficult to find, there are about 60 different breeding species to look for. The marshes hold little bitterns, two or three kinds of rail or crake—small birds that run rapidly and secretively among the reeds—and marsh harriers. On the dry islands exotic blue-cheeked bee-eaters nest, gleaming bright green as they chase insects. In the summer heat, the Qa' is bone dry; even the lagoons where the duck shooters spread their decoys are shrinking or gone, and soon Bedouin tents will sit where the ducks and coot dabbled. Pratincoles and plovers are nesting on the dry edges, and there are crested larks everywhere. Depending on the year and the level of water, you may find avocets and stilts nesting. Bush chats and desert wheatears are conspicuous in the dry area, and in the hot desert beyond the oasis life is far from absent. An astonishing array of larks and wheatears manage to breed, sometimes even among the shiny black basalt boulders which stretch for miles and become blistering hot in summer. On sandier ground, coursers make their nesting scrapes, and in a very few favored areas houbara bustards still survive.

A winter visit to Azraq also has its rewards. In January the tamarisks glow orange and the reeds have turned brown. The water has risen again, and vast areas of wet mud and shallow lagoons shine on the Qa'. Hordes of duck have appeared, and it is the season for hunting. Teal, by the thousands or tens of thousands, feed in the rich ooze; solid masses of elegant pintails rest far out, or feed in the shallow water with wigeon, shoveler, mallard and others. Deeper water, in the heart of the swamp, may yield diving ducks—tufted, pochard, ferruginous. The hunters may bring home some rare items—perhaps a falcated teal, a red-crested pochard or even a cormorant, which should never have been shot at all. The winter sunlight is incredibly pure and lovely and the surrounding hills rise clear.

People who make the desert castle tour often plan to stop at Azraq for a picnic lunch. A shaded area by the oasis spring on the far side of Azraq village is the best place to enjoy a picnic. If you arrive in Azraq about 1 or 2 P.M. you will have ample time to picnic, to stop at other castle ruins on the way back to Amman and to arrive in the city before sunset.

On the left of the road, about a mile before the fort of Azraq, a secondary road leads to a new Government Rest House. When we last checked it had not opened, although it was almost completed. The structure is modern and includes a swimming pool with cabana-type rooms around it, and a large dining room in a large separate building. This guesthouse is much more elaborate than other hostels run by the government, and one might well ask why such a layout was built in the middle of nowhere.

About halfway between Amman and Azraq and only a few miles off the main highway is **Qasr Hallabat,** converted by the Umayyads into a defense post and pleasure retreat from earlier buildings of the Nabataeans, Romans and Byzantines. The original structure was probably built by the Nabataeans as a defense tower against desert raiders, and later enlarged by the Romans. After some rebuilding by Emperor Justinian in the sixth century, it served as a monastery. Most of the ruins are Roman, and only scattered carvings remain from the Nabataean period. Most of the carved stones are buried under heaps of fallen rock, but here and there decorative pieces are in evidence.

The hunting lodge and baths of **Hammam al Sarah** are located two miles east of Hallabat. These have been partically rebuilt. The desert road from Azraq to Amman joins the main highway near Zerqa, about 15 miles north of Amman.

WEST OF AMMAN

The Jordan Valley

Two main roads lead from Amman to the Jordan Valley. Either is a delightful drive through the ancient hills of Biblical history. From these heights of 2,500 feet above sea level the road descends to the lowest spot on the surface of the earth. Watch for a sign by the side of the road which marks the sea level point. Don't be alarmed if you feel dizzy or if your ears crackle from the sudden pressure. A few minutes' exposure to fresh air is all you need to make the adjustment.

As the road winds out of the Biblical wilderness into the valley, you see the Jordan River and the green valley floor stretching to the north and the silvery waters of the Dead Sea sprawling to the south. Here, in an area of ten square miles, are concentrated some of the world's most important sites of antiquity and Biblical history.

The Jordan River is only 200 miles long and less than a mile wide. It has no large cities on its shores. Yet, as the place of Jesus' baptism, the river has an immeasurable significance to Christians throughout the world. Visitors are often disappointed by the size of the Jordan, having imagined it as wide and majestic. Undoubtedly in Joshua's day the river was wider. Today, it would be easy to ford the stream in many places. But in Biblical times a miracle was required to roll back the waters so the people could cross by the Prophet's command.

Although there are no cities on the river now, archeologists believe its banks were the site of the earliest communal life of man. The Cities of the Plain were in the Jordan Valley, possibly at the mouth of the river. Authorities say that volcanic activity around 2000 B.C. completely changed the landscape of the valley.

The main source of the river springs from a grove on Mount Hermon, long considered sacred by the ancients. After leaving the little grove the stream drops through a basalt gorge for six miles until the waters enter Lake Tiberias, or the Sea of Galilee (600 feet below sea level). From Galilee the waters flow south through the Ghor region and finally empty into the Dead Sea. Several tributaries enter the mainstream as it winds slowly through the Jordan Valley. A narrow floor of rich earth borders the river from Lake Tiberias to the Dead Sea, and is known in Arabic as al-Ghor.

The Jordan Valley is the northern strip of the Great Rift, a deep and massive depression in the earth's surface that extends as far south as Mozambique in Africa.

Although the east valley narrows to a width of 2.5 miles in some places, it stretches to a flatland almost 10 miles wide as it approaches the Dead Sea. Here, the perennial dream of making the desert bloom has become a reality. Al-Ghor is Jordan's natural greenhouse. The climate is almost tropical with long, hot, dry summers and mild, briefly wet winters when rainfall averages between 3 and 16 inches. In this climate, crops ripen two months ahead of those in surrounding countries of the Middle East.

Annual production in the east valley has reached over 330 million pounds of tomatoes, 44 million pounds of cucumbers, 110 million pounds of melons and 36 million pounds of citrus fruits. The area that generates most of this output is a modest 30,000 irrigated acre a fraction of the 23,650,000 acres that Jordan encompasses. But tha. is only the beginning. Adjoining the land now being cultivated are an additional 62,500 arable acres waiting only for water. Here the government has set its highest priority, and has built dams, canals and irrigation systems and upgraded farming techniques. Through these improvements Jordan expects to increase its agricultural export income by 40 percent by 1982, and eventually to be self-supporting in food.

Already farmers are growing enough vegetables and fruits in the valley to send tons of it to countries throughout the area. To keep pace with demand, some farmers are growing many crops in mini-greenhouses of plastic that lie in long, low tent rows across the fields. The method has revolutionized output, and it increased production sevenfold the first year it was introduced.

In addition to the major crops of tomatoes and cucumbers, there are oranges, lemons, pomegranates, honeydews, cantaloupes, radishes, bananas, plums, cauliflower, green peppers, cabbages, olives, wheat, corn, lentils and beans.

At present there are two growing seasons for most crops, but al-Ghor has the potential for three crops a year with its hothouse climate and expanded irrigation. The government's current seven-year plan for agriculture calls for raising production by 300 percent, at the same time creating 40,000 new jobs in the valley.

Since ancient times the Ghor has been one of the richest areas of the Levant. According to the Bible, the vegetation was as dense and impenetrable as a jungle. Lion, wild boar, wolves and leopards roamed the river's shores; "Behold, he shall come up like a lion from the swelling of Jordan against the habitation of the strong." (Jer. 49:19). But over the centuries the land was denuded and ne-glected,and ultimately nature made it a wasteland. Now, it needs help.

Jordan began its first major development project to bring the valley under cultivation more than 25 years ago with the Yarmuk River Irrigation Scheme. Despite repeated setbacks, a great deal was accomplished.

The 66-mile-long East Ghor Canal is now the vital bypass artery of the river. Built in stages over the past 20 years, it begins at the Yarmuk River in the north and extends to Karameh in the south. Construction of its final ten miles to the Dead Sea is expected to start soon. During most of its course, the canal is only slightly to the east of and parallel to the Jordan River. Along the route of the canal there are dams and waterways to collect and divert into it the waters of the Jordan's tributaries. In turn, the East Ghor artery sends out smaller canals to reach farmlands along the way.

Four dams have been built and are in service; others are being constructed or planned. The $35-million King Talal Dam, the newest, was completed in 1977. It has brought the waters of the Zerqa River into the canal to begin irrigating an additional 15,000 acres of new prime land in the valley. The dam is also providing power to generate 5,000 kilowatts of electricity for valley residents, and eventually will supply fresh water to the Amman region.

The next major project is the construction of the long-postponed $150-million Magarin Dam on the Yarmuk River, where there is a tremendous source of water to be utilized. This 380-foot-high dam, along with an extensive sprinkler irrigation system, will bring the total number of irrigated acres in the valley to the goal of 90,000 by 1982.

The government's grand plan for the valley gives equal priority to human needs. Before the 1967 war, there were 100,000 people living in the valley. By 1970 that number had diminished to 3,000, who lived in the constant insecurity of a military zone. In recent years, encouraged by growing stability and the accelerated efforts of the government, thousands have returned, and today the valley's population is over 78,000.

As irrigated areas are expanded and more people are needed to farm them, the government hopes to entice them to the valley by good incomes, new housing and full community facilities. The optimum population is said to be 150,000 by 1983. Work on a social infrastructure began last year with construction on 28 schools, 10 health centers, a social community building, 8 government complexes and 300 housing units designed specifically to attract the teachers, doctors, nurses and other professionals required to run these facilities.

The government agency in charge is the Jordan Valley Development Authority (JVDA). It has dams and major irrigation schemes off the planning boards and building. It has completed a major highway that runs the length of the valley, and is building a secondary road network to serve outlying areas. Now, JVDA has turned its attention to a massive rural development program to provide farmers with the amenities of a good life. The plans include:

—Thirty-six communities to radiate in size and services from four primary to eight secondary to 24 tertiary settlements throughout the valley, all with an equitable distribution of drinking water, electricity and telecommunications.

—Nine educational zones, structured to provide all children with easy access to free schooling from primary through high school. JVDA is designing, building and equipping the schools, then turning them over to the Ministry of Education to staff and operate.

—Health services that include emergency health posts in small settlements, resident doctors and maternity and child care in secondary communities, and hospital facilities in the four major towns.

—Long-term low-interest mortgages, available from public funds to low-income groups for housing. The estimate is that 24,000 new units will be required over the next several years, and the government wants to facilitate private home-building.

—A land-redistribution law under which the government is buying up large tracts of land that it has irrigated. It permits the owner to retain 20 percent, and resells the other 80 percent in small holdings with long-term payment facilities. It wants eventually to divide all land holdings in the valley so that no one farmer may own more than 50 acres of irrigated land.

JVDA is also helping farmers boost production and get higher income from their crops. It runs training programs in the valley to teach new irrigation and farming techniques. It has set up, as well, the Jordan Valley Farmers Association, whose membership includes all the farmers in the valley, with an executive committee of 15 members, ten elected by the farmers and five appointed by the government.

The Farmers Association imports and distributes to farmers the equipment they need—seeds, fertilizers, tools and machinery. Another responsibility is grading and packing agricultural produce and then marketing it domestically and in foreign markets. To handle this operation JVDA has four centers planned, with the first already under construction in the central Ghor region. It was scheduled to open by the end of 1978, and will be able to handle 1,400 tons of produce daily.

Under this cooperative arrangement, all revenues return to the farmers. The Association also stands as a gilt-edged guarantor to any farmer seeking a loan; it can secure him quick credit with no other collateral than the potential produce of his land.

To accomplish all this, from dams to roads to housing, schools and public facilities, more than $250 million will be needed over the next several years. Most of the money is expected to come from international funds and from Arab, American and European aid.

It is an exciting development for Jordan and one that visitors can enjoy, too. The drive down to the heart of the valley can be combined with a picnic outing. It takes only an hour on the road northwest of Amman past Salt to the middle stretch of Highway 45 and Deir Alla, where every day (except Friday) is farmers' market day. Here you will find large quantities of freshly picked fruits and vegetables for a picnic or pictures.

Historic Sites

Deir Alla, which means "House of God," is the site of an ancient sanctuary overlooking the green fields of the Jordan Valley. Scholars who have excavated the site have found evidence which they believe is potentially so important it could cause the rewriting of history—or at least provide an alternate interpretation from the one on which so much of our history is based.

The tell, which is a square approximately 600 feet on all sides, was first excavated by a Dutch expedition under Dr. H.J. Franken, Director of the Department of Palestinian Archeology at the University of Leiden. It was found to be from the Late Bronze Age, c. 1500 to 1200 B.C., and the Iron Age, c. 1200 to 500 B.C., and much later a medieval Arab settlement.

On the northern slope of the tell the earliest settlers artificially heightened a temple mound on which to set their sanctuary—one that was so awesome, apparently, that it did not need protecting from the warring tribes of the valley, for there was no wall around it and no dwelling near it. The temple was active from the 16th to the 12th centuries B.C. In 1200 B.C., a date verified by an Egyptian faience vase bearing the cartouche of Queen Taouset found on the sanctuary floor, the temple was destroyed by an earthquake. It was abandoned and not rebuilt.

The site retained its character as a holy place, however, through the Iron Age, when remains of a large building with a different character appear. Here, many fragments of ritual vessels, particularly incense burners, were found. At the end of the second Iron Age the tell was abandoned for an unknown length of time. From artifacts discovered, it seems to have had a Persian settlement down to 330 B.C., and then was completely abandoned for centuries. During the medieval Arab era it was used as a cemetery by villagers who lived to the east of it.

In 1964 Dr. Franken came upon three clay tablets, inscribed in an unknown writing. The first tablet was in good condition. Its text was clearly incised in clay and divided into two registers, upper and lower, with dividing lines between the words. There are nine groups of letters. The second and third tablets are less well preserved. The third has lost its upper register, but the lower is complete and six words have been preserved.

Seven other tablets which bear mysterious dots in groups and series were also found. The writings are in an unknown type of alphabetic script, some letters having a likeness to the Phoenician Byblos script of Ahiram, others resembling a South Semitic writing.

An Aramaic text of the seventh century B.C. found written on a large fragment of plaster from a mud brick wall is very important. It speaks of a prophet named Bileam, son of Bear, as the head authority of the Deir Alla sanctuary. After studying the text, Dr. Franken declared that it confirms the archeological theory that Deir Alla was a sanctuary completely independent of the ancient Hebrew religion and of Hebrew cultural and political influence during the period of the Judean Kingdom.

In this region there seems to be an ancient site of historical or biblical significance at every turn in the road. **Tulul edh Dhahab,** the hills of gold, might be Phanuel, where Jacob struggled with the angel, according to the German Evangelic Institute which has surveyed the site. **Tell Hajjaj** is thought to be Mahanaim, where David fled when his son Absalom revolted. **Tell Amta** is Amathus, one of the towns of Perea and apparently an important place in ancient times. **Tell es-Saidiyeh** is thought to be Zaretan or Zarethan, where the waters of the Jordan stood still while the Israelites crossed over (Jos. 3:16). The site was excavated in 1964 by James Pitchard of the University of Pennsylvania, and subsequent teams have worked here. It was occupied from the early Bronze Age through about 700 B.C.

At **Tell Mazar,** also from the Bronze Age, the University of Jordan and the Department of Antiquities have been excavating for two seasons, trying to discover the relationship between the different ancient communities that were located in the area, and at the same time to give students at the university as well as foreign ones the experience of working on a dig. Upstream on the Wadi el Yabis, **Tell el Maqlub** has been identified as Abel-Meholah, the home of the prophet Elisha, where he was visited by Elijah.

Approximately 18 miles north of Deir Alla at Mashari a road on the right leads about two miles to the site of **Tabaqat Fahil,** which is ancient Pella.

The valley road continues north to Adasiya on the Yarmuk or

branches north east to Irbid. The valley road also continues south to meet a second road from Salt, which extends across a bridge to Jericho on the west bank of the river (it is not used by tourists).

Salt is the administrative center of the Balqa district, the second largest in the country, which extends from the Zerqa River to the Dead Sea. Salt has served as Jordan's capital several times in its history, and dates back to the Iron Age. A site nearby at **Tell Jadur** is said to be Gadara, capital of Perea at the time of Christ (but not the same as the Gadara of the Decapolis).

The road south of Salt leads to many sites which have been identified with the Old Testament—the Plains of Moab, Beth Nimrah near the village of Tell Nimrin and Tell Bileibil. Tell ar-Rama, which is Liviasi, may have been Beth-Haram.

At **Tuleitat Ghusul** (Teleilat Ghassul), recent discoveries identify it as one of the oldest sites in the Jordan Valley. Wall frescos were found which have been carbon-tested to be 6,000 years old, and may be the second oldest in the world. An Australian archeological team headed by Professor Basil Hennessy, under the auspices of the Jordanian Department of Antiquities, completed its final season of excavations at the site in 1978.

The paintings, which decorate the walls of an early Chalcolithic building, are rendered in strong colors of red, white, yellow and black. The frescos depict a group of figures standing before what is thought to be a religious shrine. Experts from UNESCO's School of Conservation in Rome will restore and mount the paintings for museum exhibition in Amman.

South of the main road to Jerusalem is Suweimeh, located approximately a mile northeast of the Dead Sea. A road leads to the sea.

The Dead Sea

The Dead Sea, 1,306 feet below sea level, is the lowest spot on the earth's surface. In Arabic is is called Bahr Lut, "Sea of Lot." The sea, 46 miles long and 3 to 10 miles wide, has no outlet. By day it is silvery blue, and by night it glistens in the moonlight. The Dead Sea is a scenic oddity unique in the world. For miles around, arid hills eroded by wind form a silent moonscape that is at once eerie and beautiful.

The heavy salt content (33 percent) of the water makes animal life impossible, and makes swimming an unusual experience. It is almost impossible to sink. You can lie on your back in the water and read a magazine. When divers were searching for the sites of Sodom and Gomorrah, their suits had to have special weights to keep them from bobbing to the surface. You can be photographed having a cup of coffee or reading a newspaper as you float on top. You'll need a shower when it's over; you will come out of the water with a nice, itchy coat of salt.

At Suweimeh there is a beach park with over a mile of seafront. Here there are facilities for a day's seaside outing—dressing rooms, indoor and outdoor showers, picnic area and snack bar. The Dead Sea Beach Club has a new restaurant. There are also cottages with kitchenettes, if you want to stay overnight. Sunset or moonlight on the Dead Sea is an extra bonus. If you want to avoid crowds, do not go on Fridays and Sundays.

An excellent article with magnificent photographs of the Dead Sea and surrounding area appeared in the *National Geographic,* February 1978.

In this region the effort to make the desert bloom is being followed by the even more colossal project of harnessing the power of the sun. A huge solar evaporation system is being readied to recover 1.2 million metric tons of potash a year from the Dead Sea. Located at Safi at the southern end of the Sea, it is a joint effort of the Arab Potash Company who will operate it, and Jacobs Engineering Group of Pasadena, California, who will design, engineer and construct the massive facility. The $425 million project is the largest in the history of Jordan and one of the most complex and challenging of its kind undertaken anywhere. It will make Jordan one of the world's primary sources of potash, and at the same time potash will be a major source of foreign exchange for Jordan. Potash is a key ingredient in the production of fertilizer, which in turn is vital to meet the growing food needs of the world. The mineral has been known since Biblical days when it was used as a fertilizer and in the making of soap.

Present plans call for the entire project to be completed within four years. The initial phase, which included field testing of the solar evaporation process, construction analysis of test dikes, and processing of test samples of potash in a pilot plant, was completed late in 1977. The second phase, now being accelerated, includes the construction of an elaborate network of evaporation ponds and dikes and related facilities. The third and final phase will involve building the processing plant and the actual production and marketing of potash.

Over the next few years about 25,000 acres of dikes and man-made ponds covering 40 square miles will be constructed at the southernmost end of the Dead Sea. When the facility is in full operation, 1.2 million tons of brine will be pumped daily through a six-mile-long canal leading into a network of evaporation ponds. It has been estimated that 1.25 billion gallons of fuel oil a year would have to be burned to achieve the same results by conventional methods.

A refinery plant to be built near Safi will be fed with the coarse potash salts through a floating pipeline. After being purified and dried at the plant, the potash will be hauled by truck along the newly constructed road from Safi to Aqaba, from where it will be shipped to its world markets.

Safi is accessible from Kerak as well as by the new road which runs through the Wadi Aqaba to Gharandal, Tel Khalifa and thence to Aqaba. Jordan plans to build a road from the north end of the Dead Sea which will connect with the new road at Safi. When this is completed, the country will have three parallel north-south highways: the Jordan Valley–Dead Sea–Wadi Araba; the Irbid–Jerash King's Highway, and the Mafraq/Azraq–Zerka Desert Highway.

THE WEST BANK

Jordan's Fertile Acres

Jericho: 22 miles northeast of Jerusalem, 853 ft. below sea level

> The area west of the Jordan River, which became part of Jordan in 1950 and is known as the West Bank, has been under Israeli military occupation since the war of 1967. In order to cross the Jordan River to the West Bank visitors must follow the procedures detailed in *Facts at Your Fingertips*.

Jericho (*Ariha* in Arabic) and its surrounding area is one of the oldest continuously inhabited sites in the world. On a mount overlooking the Jericho oasis excavations have uncovered settlements dating from 8000 B.C. and the oldest walled town (7000 B.C.) yet discovered.

Here, in the digs at Tell es-Sultan, many layers of ancient civilizations are visible. Joshua's attack, when he blew his horn and the "walls came tumbling down," was on Canaanite Jericho (probably about 1250 B.C.). In the center of the site a massive round Neolithic defense tower dating from before 7000 B.C. has been cleared to bedrock. The original entrance to the stairway is exposed, and those who are sure-footed can walk down to the bottom of the oldest known stairs in the world. For details of the site see K. Kenyon, *Digging Up Jericho*. Miss Kenyon was the archeologist in charge of the excavations which uncovered the tower.

In Roman times Jericho was a garden of fruit and palm trees, from which considerable revenue was derived. Mark Antony presented it as a gift to Cleopatra—and what a magnificent gift!

Jericho reached its peak under Herod the Great. His winter palace and new town were located south of present-day Jericho along Wadi al-Qilt, the Valley of the Shadow of Death in the 23rd Psalm. From the old road from Jericho to Jerusalem a road on the north leads down the ancient Roman road into the Wadi. In Biblical times shepherds led their sheep down the Wadi in autumn and came back up in spring. The danger of flash-floods made the route treacherous.

It was on a street in Jericho that Jesus healed the blind beggar. Later he was entertained at the house of Zaccheus the publican. Byzantines, Arabs and Crusaders also came to Jericho and left their mark.

Elisha's Fountain. At the foot of Tell es-Sultan is the main water spring of the oasis. Tradition says it is the fountain which Prophet Elisha sweetened by casting a handful of salt into it (2 Kings 3:21).

Mount of Temptation. West of Jericho and overlooking the Jordan Valley is the famous mountain where Jesus spent forty days and nights fasting, and where Satan tempted him "and showeth him all the kingdoms of the world, and the glory of them; and saith unto him, all these things will I give thee, if thou wilt fall down and worship me" (Matt. 4:8-9).

The path to the top of the mountain is very steep, and passes by a Greek Orthodox Monastery perched on one of the cliffs.

The road between Jericho and Jerusalem traverses the Wilderness of Judah, one of the most starkly beautiful landscapes that can be imagined. The muted pastels of the baked, barren hills rolling away as far as the eye can see are hauntingly lovely.

As you come from Jerusalem elevation markers on the side of the road pace your descent. Even after you pass the one saying "Sea

Level," you note that there's still a long way down . . . and the Dead Sea shimmers far below to your right.

The road forks, and Jericho is to the north; the other road continues to the Jordan River and the Dead Sea. A small road to the south leads to Nebi Musa (the Prophet Moses), which Moslems believed was the site of the prophet's tomb. The Bible, though, tells us that Moses' tomb is "unknown to this day" but lies somewhere in the Mountains of Moab. Tradition has placed it on Mt. Nebo, where it is marked by a chapel dating from the fifth century.

Hisham Palace, three miles north of Jericho at Khirbet al-Mafjar, was a country residence, probably built by the Umayyad Caliph Hisham Ibn Abdul Malik (A.D. 724-743). Hisham, like most of the early Arab rulers, preferred the freedom of the desert to city life. The palace is a complex of buildings, baths, mosques and colonnaded courts. Its mosaics and stucco ornaments are fine examples of Umayyad art and architecture.

Experts say an earthquake destroyed the buildings before they were completed. Thus the accumulated sand and debris helped to preserve the palace's lovely mosaics.

The mosaic floors of the baths are the major attraction for visitors. The Tree of Life (also called the Tree of Human Cruelty) is one of the most beautiful mosaics in the world. In the same room another mosaic pictures a Persian rug, complete with tassels.

Many of the carved stuccos from the palace are displayed at the Rockefeller Archeological Museum in Jerusalem. A great deal of the palace is reconstructed to provide an example of eighth-century Arab architecture.

In the Jordan Valley east of Jericho is the farm of the Arab Development Society. Its creation is the result of the courage and determination of its founder, Oxford-educated Musa al-Alami. The Society has given life, hope and education to hundreds of children orphaned by the Arab-Israeli wars. The major problem in setting up the farm was finding enough water. Experts said there was no water between Jericho and the Jordan River, but Musa Bey proved them wrong. The farm is fed from underground wells, and its high-quality products are sold throughout the area.

For the Christian world the most important site on the Jordan is **Makhad al-Hajla** (the Ford of the Partridge), six miles from Jericho, where tradition says John baptized Jesus. For centuries pilgrims have come to this peaceful, shaded bend in the river, and many take home water from the sacred spot. Water from the Jordan is used for baptisms in churches around the world. There are several churches near the spot, the most distinctive being the Greek Monastery of St. John. A special service of blessing the water is held annually on Epiphany Sunday.

It should be noted that, although the tradition has placed the site of Jesus' baptism here, there is considerable question in the minds of biblical scholars as to its accuracy. Eugene Hoade's *Guide to Jordan* devotes considerable space to the site on the east bank which he believes to be the correct one, based on reports of early pilgrims and, of course, the text of the Bible. It is northeast of the Hussein Bridge in the Wadi Kharrar, which is the site of Bethania *(Bethany)* beyond the Jordan. Hoade writes: "These things were done in Betania beyond the Jordan, where John was baptising" (John 1.28). "The site of the crossing of the Israelites under Josue is fixed at the same place as the Baptism of Jesus, and it is certainly the most probable of the fords suggested. The place is directly opposite Jericho and the land on both sides of the ford is more suitable than elsewhere for the crossing of a big number."

Khirbet Qumran and the Dead Sea Scrolls: 14 miles south of Jericho

The story of the Dead Sea Scrolls opened in 1947, when, by accident, a Bedouin found several scrolls in clay jars hidden in a cave on a rocky cliff high above the Dead Sea. After the sensational discovery Bedouin and archeologists, aided by the Jordan Department of Antiquities, searched every hole in these desolate hills and have turned up one of the most exciting discoveries of modern times: Biblical manuscripts 2000 years old, predating by some 1000 years the earliest known Hebrew text of the Old Testament. Also among the finds were books of an unknown religious community, identified as the Essenes, a pre-Christian, mystical Jewish sect mentioned in ancient writings. The discoveries were important as verification of Biblical text and for the study of Biblical history. The writings in these scrolls covered a period of 300 years, including the birth of Christ. Thus they have unveiled part of the background on which the teachings of Christ and the early Christian church were based.

The Essene community lived in caves and dwellings at a site known as Khirbet Qumran (the ruins of Qumran). The settlement has been termed the world's most ancient "monastery." Under strict rules of obedience and high ethical standards set down in their

Manual of Disciplines, the "brothers" spent their lives studying the Holy Writ and praying for the coming of the Messiah.

At Khirbet Qumran the oldest ruins are a cistern and a square building which date from the eighth century B.C. At this time the site was probably a fortress. Apparently it was deserted for a long period until the Essenes came in the late second century B.C.

The Essenes first erected small buildings around the earlier ruins. Later they expanded as the community grew. To cope with the problem of water on the waterless hilltop, an aqueduct was built to bring captured rainwater from nearby Wadi Qumran. Visitors will notice the large numbers of cisterns at the ancient site. Some were probably used for ritual ablution—a rule of the community.

In what was the upper story of a building excavators found long, narrow tables and benches along the walls and two large inkwells. This, then, they concluded, was the very room in which the Essenes sat to write their now-famous scrolls. Other excavations include the ruins of a storehouse, a communal kitchen, workshops, the community bread oven, an assembly chamber, a pantry in which hundreds of bowls, dishes, plates and jugs were found stacked in piles against the back wall, and a complete potter's workshop with a potter's wheel.

Experts believe the community fled the area during an earthquake in 31 B.C. After about thirty years they returned to repair their buildings and to settle again to a secluded life of prayer and study.

In A.D. 68 the settlement met an abrupt end. A Roman Legion en route to Jerusalem to put down the first Jewish Revolt destroyed it, and the members of the community fled after placing their precious manuscripts in the nearby caves for safekeeping. The site was not inhabited again except as a temporary hiding place during the second Jewish Revolt (A.D. 132). The settlement and its people were lost to history.

Among the thousands of scroll fragments which have already been identified most of the books of the Old Testament are represented. The task of cataloguing and assembling the huge collection was entrusted to an international group of scholars. Other scrolls have been found in caves at Wadi Murabbat about ten miles south of Qumran. These manuscripts include fragments from Genesis, Exodus, Deuteronomy and Isaiah.

Displays of scroll fragments may be seen in the Archeological Museums in Amman and Jerusalem.

A road continues along the Dead Sea to the southern end and hence to the Negev.

JERUSALEM

Shrine of Three Faiths

Few places in the world have commanded the devotion of so many people for so long a period as has Jerusalem. From your first day in the Holy City you will be awed by a sense of history and spiritual significance. Jerusalem is a city with a special destiny. Its effect on visitors is unique.

The origins of Jerusalem are lost in the remote past. Recent archeological excavations reveal that it is at least as old as the 15th century B.C. In Egyptian and Babylonian literature it is called Urusalimu. The first mention of it in the Bible is probably under the name of Salem, the city of Melchisedek, "Priest of the Most High God" (Gen. 15:18). It is afterwards referred to as Jebus. When David captured the Jebusite fortress of Zion, he made the city his capital and there placed the Ark.

Under Solomon the first great Temple was built upon Mount Moriah. After Nebuchadnezzar, King of Babylon, overran the city

Jordan's most prized tourist destination, the Treasury at Petra, as seen emerging from the Siq, the narrow canyon which is the ancient city's only entrance.

Powerful statements of old and new in Jordan's capital, Amman.
Above, designed to represent a bedouin tent, the Cultural Center
at the Hussein Sports City; below, a well-preserved Roman amphitheater, dating from the 2nd or 3rd century A.D.

Ancient inhabitants of Jordan took great care of both the living and the dead—a Roman forum for the former in present-day Jerash (below), and elaborate Nabataean temples and tombs for the latter (above) embellishing the canyon inside Petra.

From atop the Crusader castle at Shobak, 12th-century knights and present-day travelers see the same sight—a mountainside exotically eroded by time and ever-present winds.

in 586 B.C., the Jews were taken into captivity. A half-century later Cyrus, King of Persia, allowed them to return and to rebuild the Temple and city on a modest scale. Among the city's subsequent conquerers were Alexander the Great in 332 B.C. and Antiochus Epiphanes in 168 B.C. Under the Maccabeans, and later the Herods, Jerusalem was independent to a certain extent, although the Herodians were Roman vassals.

Under Herod the Great the Temple was rebuilt on a more grandiose scale and Jerusalem was enlarged and beautified. It was in the 36th year of his reign that Jesus Christ was born in Bethlehem.

Following a Jewish revolt in A.D. 70 the Temple and city were destroyed by the Romans under Titus, son of the Emperor Vespasian. After a second revolt in A.D. 132 the Jews were expelled. On the ruins a pagan city was built by Emperor Hadrian and named Aelia Capitolina.

In the third century under the reign of Constantine, Jerusalem became a Christian shrine. The Emperor's mother, Helena, ordered the construction of the Church of the Holy Sepulchre on the site she determined was the site of Christ's crucifixion. From established traditions, advice of the bishops and revelations in her dreams, Helena established a number of "official" sites connected with the life of Christ. These sites are still recognized today by most Christians. Many have been confirmed by archeological research; many have not.

Early in the seventh century the city was sacked by the Persians, but by 637 the Arab armies had taken all the major towns from the Tigris to the Mediterranean, except Jerusalem, from the Byzantines. As they moved to take that city, the Greek Patriarch sent word that he would surrender Jerusalem without a struggle but only to the Caliph Umar in person.

As the story goes, Umar, who was in Damascus, hurried to the scene and entered Jerusalem alone, except for a servant. The priests mistook the servant for the caliph, much to Umar's amusement.

Once the confusion was cleared up, Umar asked the Patriarch to show him the city's holy places. He was led first to the Church of the Holy Sepulchre, where the Patriarch invited him to pray. Umar declined, saying that it might encourage his followers to convert the church into a mosque. Instead, he prayed outside. Today the spot is commemorated by a mosque in his name.

Umar offered the Byzantines the same treaty he had proferred to the Christians in Damascus. It stated that Umar "grants them security of their lives, their possessions, their churches and crosses

. . . they shall have freedom of religion and none shall be molested unless they rise up in a body . . . They shall pay a tax instead of military service . . . and those who leave the city shall be safe-guarded until they reach their destination . . ."

The religious tolerance established by Umar was continued by the Umayyads but deteriorated under later caliphs and disappeared under the Crusaders who captured Jerusalem in 1099. The European conquerors massacred most of the city's Muslims, burnt the small Jewish community in its synagogue, and slaughtered large numbers of the local Christians. They converted Muslim shrines to churches, including the Dome of the Rock.

A century later the Crusaders were driven out by the Arabs under Saladin, who restored the covenant of Umar. Jerusalem remained Arab for the next 800 years.

In 1517 the Ottoman Turks occupied Jerusalem, and governed the city until World War I, when it surrendered to the Allied troops under Allenby, the British commander. During the rule of Turkish Sultan Sulayman the Magnificent the present walls of the Old City were constructed in 1542.

After World War I, Jerusalem and Palestine were placed under British Mandate. When the British withdrew in 1948, hostilities broke out between the Jews and the Arabs. The United Nations Armistice line, drawn in 1949 as a result of this conflict, divided Jerusalem.

Following the war in 1967, Israel occupied all of Jerusalem and the West Bank of the Jordan. The area which had divided it from Israel, known as No Man's Land, has since been intensively built up with modern high-rise apartment buildings, greatly changing the timeless character of the area surrounding the ancient walled city. The area east of the old armistice line is known locally as East Jerusalem or Arab Jerusalem. The modern Jerusalem of Israel is west of the line.

In this section of the book we will concentrate on East Jerusalem and the West Bank, where the majority of holy places are located, plus other sites and cities of particular religious significance. Travelers who are planning an extended visit can refer to *Fodor's Israel*.

THE OLD CITY OF JERUSALEM

Within an area of about one square mile of Old Jerusalem are concentrated some of the most important historical and religious shrines of the world's three great monotheistic religions, Judaism, Christianity and Islam.

The Ancient Walls and Gates

The 16th century walls which enclose the Old City contain eight gates: Jaffa (west), New (north), Damascus (north), Herod's (north), St. Stephen or Lion's (east), Golden (east), Dung (south), and Zion (south). The Golden Gate was closed by a Turkish governor in 1530. Legends say that the governor hoped to postpone the final judgment and the end of the world by closing the gate, which according to tradition would be the place of the first trumpet call and the resurrection of the dead.

Within the walls on the east and north are the Moslem quarters, containing the Haram esh-Sharif, or Dome of the Rock, the Aqsa Mosque, the Islamic Museum and the Wailing Wall. On the north and west are the Christian quarters, where the Church of the Holy Sepulchre and the Via Dolorosa are located. The southwest contains the Armenian Quarter and the Jewish Quarter.

Outside the present walls of the Old City on the south is the city of David, ancient Ophel. It is bounded on the east by the Valley of Kidron and on the south and west by the Valley of Hinnom, which meet at the Pool of Siloam. Opposite the east wall of the Old City is the Garden of Gethsemane, and across the Kidron Valley is the Mount of Olives.

In the great wall overlooking Gethsemane and the Mount of Olives stands the stately Gate of St. Stephen, or Lion's Gate. Entering the Old City from this gate will orient you best; the road leads directly into the Via Dolorosa and passes the main shrines.

St. Stephen's Gate is the legendary site of the stoning of the martyr Stephen. It is also called Bab Sitti Miryam, or St. Mary's Gate, since several sites nearby are connected with the Virgin. The Crusaders named it the Gate of Jehoshaphat because it overlooked the valley of the same name. Many claim the present gate was built by the Crusaders because of its architecture. Others say the gate dates from the 16th century, citing as proof a tale about the Turkish Sultan Sulayman the Magnificent.

The Sultan dreamt he was being torn apart by four lions. When he asked for an explanation of the dream, a sheikh replied that the Sultan proposed to punish the inhabitants of Jerusalem for refusing to pay their taxes. The Sultan, intrigued by the dream and its explanation, made a pilgrimage to Jerusalem. There he was seized with an urge to do something for the city. As a result he had the walls rebuilt—and, as a reminder of the dream, he had the lions carved over the portals of the gate.

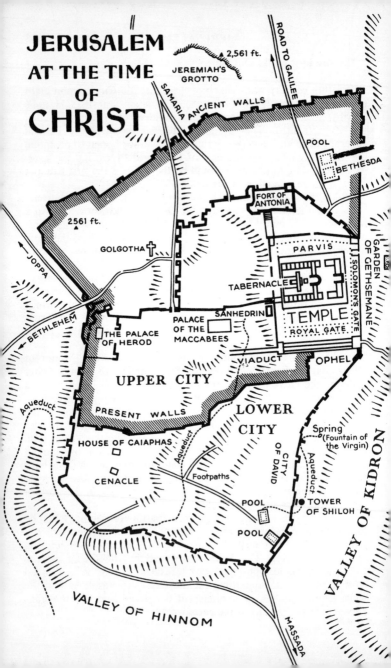

JERUSALEM
AT THE TIME
OF
CHRIST

▲ 2,561 ft.
JEREMIAH'S
GROTTO

ROAD TO GALILEE

SAMARIA

ANCIENT WALLS

POOL
BETHESDA

FORT OF
ANTONIA

JOPPA

2561 ft. ▲

GOLGOTHA ✝

PARVIS

SOLOMON'S GATE

GARDEN OF GETHSEMANE

TABERNACLE

TEMPLE

SANHEDRIN

ROYAL GATE

BETHLEHEM

THE PALACE
OF HEROD

PALACE
OF THE
MACCABEES

VIADUCT

OPHEL

UPPER CITY

PRESENT WALLS

LOWER
CITY

Spring
(Fountain of
the Virgin)

Aqueduct

HOUSE OF CAIAPHAS

Aqueduct

CITY
OF
DAVID

Aqueduct

CENACLE

Footpaths

POOL

TOWER
OF SHILOH

VALLEY OF KIDRON

POOL

VALLEY OF HINNOM

MASSADA

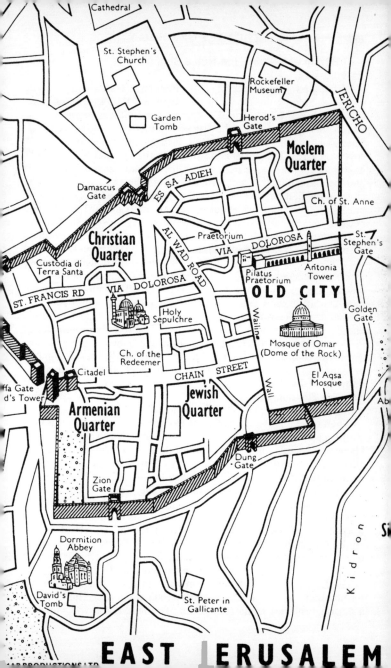

EAST JERUSALEM

Al-Haram esh-Sharif, the Noble Sanctuary

On the left after entering St. Stephen's Gate is the sacred enclosure holding the Dome of the Rock and the Aqsa Mosque on the summit of Mount Moriah. It forms the southeast corner of the Old Walled City and was the site of the first and second Temples. The area with its colonnades and surrounding walls and gardens covers 30 acres. The site is associated with the Prophet Muhammad's nocturnal journey to Jerusalem and his visit to heaven. During his lifetime Muhammad faced Jerusalem while he prayed. Hence, the city was the first *qiblah* (the direction toward which Moslems face to pray) in Islam. The Rock acquired early sanctity in Moslem eyes and became second only to Mecca and Medina as a Moslem shrine.

Tradition holds that Mount Moriah is the site where Abraham prepared to sacrifice his son. Here at a later time Ornan (Araunah) the Jebusite had his threshing floor, which David bought and upon which he erected an altar. David's altar was superseded by Solomon's Temple, which was destroyed by Nebuchadnezzar in the sixth century B.C. A smaller temple was rebuilt by Zorobabel. On the same site Herod the Great built an enormous and splendid temple. Herod's temple was the one Jesus knew, and his prophecy of its destruction was fulfilled in A.D. 70 at the hands of the Romans. The lower course of the second temple on the southwest side came to be known as the Wailing or Western Wall after the temple's destruction by Titus in 70 A.D. After the second Jewish revolt Emperor Hadrian rebuilt Jerusalem and erected a temple dedicated to Jupiter on the site of the previous temples.

When Queen Helena, mother of Constantine, came to Jerusalem in the early fourth century she had all pagan shrines, including Hadrian's Temple on Mount Moriah, destroyed. The area was then abandoned because Christians believed it was cursed by God. Eventually it became the city's rubbish heap.

Early in the seventh century, when the Caliph Umar Ibn al-Khattab conquered Jerusalem, he helped clear with his own hands the accumulated refuse of centuries and had a simple mosque of wood built on the site. A half-century later the Umayyad Caliph Abdul Malik Ibn Marwan built the Dome of the Rock. It remains one of the most magnificent examples of Moslem architecture and one of the most beautiful monuments in the world.

The Dome has undergone reconstruction many times. The most recent repairs were made in the early 1960's when King Hussein took a personal interest in its restoration. The lead dome was removed altogether with its wooden supports and replaced by another made of gold-colored aluminum. The building's famous 16th-century tiles have been replaced with copies of the originals.

The focal point of the mosque is the Rock, from which Mohammed is said to have made his nocturnal visit to heaven. You can discern the spot from the railing around the Rock; there appears to be an imprint of a human foot. A small box near the footprint holds a few hairs of the Prophet. The cave dug into the Rock is called "The Well of Souls."

On the east side of the Dome of the Rock is the miniature Dome of the Chain, which is said to have been the model for the larger mosque.

South of the Dome, going through arched portals and past a large, ornamental fountain called El-Kas (The Cup), is the Mosque of al-Aqsa, built by Walid, son of Abdul Malik Ibn Marwan. Inside the mosque are some of the finest oriental rugs in the world. It was here that King Abdullah was assassinated in July 1951 as he was entering the mosque.

A curious legend attends two pillars standing cheek-by-jowl near the front of the mosque: those of the faithful who can squeeze through the space will also be able to pass through the gates of heaven. It's a pretty tight squeeze.

Next to El-Aqsa on the southeast corner are the subterranean Stables of King Solomon. These were used later by the Romans and the Crusaders.

One of the eight gates of the Old City is within the Noble Enclosure. This is the Golden Gate, sealed up about five centuries ago.

On the northwest corner is a tall tower, the site of Herod's Antonia Fortress and the place where tradition says that Pontius Pilate condemned Jesus to death.

The area of the Haram also has smaller domes, minarets, fountains, shrines, a library and the Islamic Museum.

Visiting hours for the Dome of the Rock are 8:30–11 A.M., 12:15–2 P.M. and 3–6 P.M.. The shrine is closed on Fridays and Moslem holidays. There is an entrance fee.

Across from the Haram esh-Sharif on the right after entering Lion's Gate is the Church of St. Anne. It stands on the traditional site of the house of Anne and Joachim, parents of Mary, at the time of her birth. Within the precincts of the church is the Pool of Bethesda, where Jesus healed the sick man who had waited faithfully for 38 years to be cured by its waters. St. Anne's Church was built during Crusader days on the remains of a fifth-century shrine. Northwest of the church are the remains of earlier Byzantine and Crusader churches.

The Via Dolorosa

The Via Dolorosa (Way of the Cross, or Way of Sorrows) is the road Jesus walked carrying his cross from the Praetorium to Calvary. The street winds through the narrow cobblestoned alleys of Old Jerusalem, past churches, chapels, bazaars and ancient archways. The fourteen Stations of the Cross are indicated by inscriptions in Roman numerals. Every Friday at 3 P.M. the Franciscan fathers retrace these steps accompanied by pilgrims of all denominations. (The present-day level of Jerusalem is 20 feet above that at the time of Christ, and the authenticity of the route is questioned by many Christian sects; but it has been accepted and made holy from centuries of pilgrims' devotion.)

First Station: Jesus was condemned to death, scourged and crowned with thorns (John 19:2-16).

The station starts at the site of Pilate's Praetorium (200 yards beyond the Church of St. Anne). In this courtyard Pilate placed the judgment seat and interrogated the populace. Christ was presented, scourged, to the public with the words "Ecce Homo" (Behold the Man). Pilate then washed his hands and condemned Jesus to death on the Cross.

El-Umariye School marks the first station and the Franciscan Convent of Flagellation stands on part of the site of the Praetorium. It has a rich museum and a special library for Biblical and archeological studies.

Second Station: Jesus received the Cross (John 19:17).

The station is fixed outside on the street, opposite the Chapel of Condemnation.

The Chapel stands on the Gabbatha or Lithostratas (the street by which Christ went out of the Praetorium to Calvary). A large part of the original pavement is visible in the Chapel of the Condemnation and in the Convent of the Sisters of Zion. The sisters will show you the flagstone street on which you can see traces of games played by the Roman soldiers. This is one of the few accessible places in Jerusalem which has been authenticated as the Jerusalem of Jesus' time. It is very likely that Christ actually passed along this pavement. The Chapel of the Flagellation, where Jesus was scourged, has a beautiful stained glass window behind the altar.

Third Station: Jesus fell the first time.

Marked by a small chapel which was once the main entrance to the baths. In back of the third station is a small museum.

(Here the Via Dolorosa turns sharp left onto al-Wad Road.)

Fourth Station: Jesus met his mother.

The station is marked by an altar outside the Armenian Catholic Church. On the altar rests a marble statue of Jesus meeting his mother.

(Twenty yards beyond the fourth station the Via Dolorosa turns sharp right on Tariq as-Serai.)

Fifth Station: Simon of Cyrene helped Jesus carry his Cross.

The station is marked outside on a building on Tariq es-Serai.

Sixth Station: Veronica wiped the face of Jesus.

The traditional site of the house of Veronica is marked by a fragment of column inserted in the wall. (The incline to Calvary begins here.)

Seventh Station: Jesus fell the second time.

The station is marked by a Franciscan chapel at the Souq Khan ez-Zeit. Apparently there was a city gate here where Jesus' death notice was posted.

Eighth Station: Jesus spoke to the daughters of Jerusalem.

At the Greek Orthodox Convent of St. Charalambos the station is marked by a stone with a Latin cross and the Greek word NIKA inserted in the wall. It is opposite the Station VIII Souvenir Bazaar.

Ninth Station: Jesus fell the third time.

At the Coptic Church the shaft of a column enclosed in a pillar of the door marks the station.

Stations 10 through 14 are located in the Church of the Holy Sepulchre. Just inside the church a red slab stone on the floor, the Stone of the Unction, covers the spot where the body of Jesus was anointed.

Tenth Station: Jesus was stripped of his garments (John 19:23).

Eleventh Station: Jesus was nailed to the Cross (Luke 23:33).

The station is located in the Latin chapel.

Twelfth Station: Jesus died on the Cross (John 19:30).

The station is located in the Greek chapel.

Thirteenth Station: The body of Jesus was taken down from the Cross (Luke 24:53).

The station is the Latin altar of the Stabat Mater Dolorosa between the eleventh and twelfth stations. The Chapel of the Discovery of the Cross is said to be the place where St. Helena discovered the original cross. The Chapel of the Division of the

Raiment is supposed to mark the place where the Roman soldiers distributed the Savior's clothes.

Fourteenth Station: Jesus was laid in the sepulchre (John 19:40).

This is the spot which marks the burial place of Christ.

The Church of the Holy Sepulchre is the holiest church in Christendom, erected upon the traditional site of the crucifixion, burial and resurrection of Jesus Christ. The site on which the church stands was outside the city walls at the time and included Calvary and the garden of Joseph of Arimathea where Jesus was buried.

The early Christians worshipped secretly at these places. When Titus attacked and destroyed the city in A.D. 70 Christians in Jerusalem fled across the Jordan. After the war they returned and continued to worship at Calvary and the Tomb.

In an attempt to wean Christians away from their faith and holy places, Hadrian built a temple dedicated to Venus on the site of Calvary. Ironically, his deed marked the spot forever. Upon Constantine's conversion to Christianity, his mother, Helena, ordered the erection of a magnificent basilica on the site. Over the centuries the church was destroyed and rebuilt several times. Today the building is approximately the same as the one restored by the Crusaders in the 12th century.

By a tradition established by Saladin to avoid misunderstandings among the different Christian sects, the keys of the Church were kept by the Moslem family of Joudeh, and the opener of the door was a member of the Moslem family of Nuseibah. At Easter, three sects are allowed to have the long, curiously-shaped key. On Holy Thursday it goes to the head of the Franciscan Monastery; on Good Friday, to the chief Dragoman of the Greek Orthodox Monastery, and on Holy Saturday to the head of the Armenian Orthodox Church.

An 18th-century decree gave six churches to the right to share the sanctuary: Latin (Roman) Catholic, Greek Orthodox, Armenian Orthodox, Coptic, Syrian (Jacobite) and Abyssinian. The latter two are allowed the privilege only for special ceremonies during the year. No Protestant sect has the right to share the sanctuary.

The status quo and the designation of space within the sanctuary are jealously guarded by each denomination, and regrettably have often been obstacles to restoration of the church.

The chapels in the church are elaborately decorated and the altars are cluttered with a bewildering array of statues, pictures, candelabra, and silver, gold and bejewelled gifts.

Some people come to Jerusalem expecting to find the city as it was during Jesus' time. They imagine Calvary as a barren hilltop—even picturing it with the Cross of Jesus still standing. Upon entering the Church of the Holy Sepulchre, they are astonished and distracted by its glittering contents, the international parade of clergy, and the heavy air of burning incense. Their guides often rush them past crowded altars and through dimly lighted chambers so quickly there is little time for reflection or meditation. As a result, visitors are often critical and disappointed. If you find yourslef in this situation, it will help to recall Mark Twain's visit to the Holy Sepulchre a hundred years ago, which he described in *The Innocents Abroad* (Hartford, Conn., The American Publishing Co., 1869). Upon entering Jerusalem, Mark Twain wrote, "One naturally goes first to the Holy Sepulchre. It is right in the city, near the western gate; it and the place of the Crucifixion, and in fact, every other place intimately connected with the tremendous event, are ingeniously massed together and covered by one roof—the dome of the Church of the Holy Sepulchre . . ."

After describing the church and its history, he notes that "When one stands where the Saviour was crucified, he finds it all he can do to keep it strictly before his mind that Christ was not crucified in a Catholic Church."

Mark Twain ended his description with this paragraph:

> And so I close my chapter on the Church of the Holy Sepulchre—the most sacred locality on earth to millions of men, and women, and children, the noble and the humble, bond and free. In its history from the first, and in its tremendous associations, it is the most illustrious edifice in Christendom. With all its clap-trap side-shows and unseemly impostures of every kind, it is still grand, reverend, venerable, for a god died there; for fifteen hundred years its shrines have been wet with the tears of pilgrims from the earth's remotest confines; for more than two hundred, the most gallant knights that ever wielded sword wasted their lives away in a struggle to seize it and hold it sacred from infidel pollution. Even in our own day a war, that cost millions of treasure and rivers of blood, was fought because two rival nations claimed the sole right to put a new dome upon it. History is full of this old Church of the Holy Sepulchre—full of blood that was shed because of the respect and the veneration in which men held the last restingplace of the meek and lowly, the mild and gentle, Prince of Peace!

The Church of Alexandros Nephki is near the Church of the Holy Sepulchre, to the southwest. This church, better known as the Russian Excavations, will help you understand the orientation of the original Church of the Holy Sepulchre. Ruins dating from the time of Hadrian include the Triumphal Arch and part of the enclosure walls of the Temple.

Near Jaffa Gate stands the Citadel, known as David's Tower. The fortification was built during the 14th century on the base of a 12th-century Crusader castle, which in turn had been built on an ancient foundation. The huge stones at the bottom of the big tower on the right of the entrance are the oldest part and are said to date back to the time of Herod the Great. It has a small museum on the history of Jerusalem. A weekly Sound and Light show is held here.

The Cathedral of St. James, an Armenian Orthodox Church, is located in the Armenian quarter near the Citadel. It was erected in the 12th century on the site where, tradition holds, St. James was beheaded by Herod Agrippa. Architecturally the church is very beautiful. One must be modestly dressed to enter; hours are 6–7 A.M., and 3–3:30 P.M. daily and 2:30–3 P.M. Sundays. Nearby the Church of St. Mark stands on the traditional site of the house of Mary, mother of John surnamed Mark. Across the Armenian compound is the Gulbenkian Library.

Opposite Zion Gate on the south side is Mt. Zion, the hill that is crowned by the Church of the Dormition and its monastery, dedicated at the beginning of the 20th century. They stand on ground presented by the Turkish sultan to the German emperor. According to tradition, this was the spot where the Virgin Mary "fell into eternal sleep." The sanctuary is ringed by chapels, the walls are covered with medallions commemorating the kings of judea, and the floor is adorned with symbols of the months, saints and prophets. The crypt contains a stone sepulchre representing Mary in her last sleep. The inscription around the wall is from the Song of Solomon (II.13): "Arise, my love, my fair one, and come away." The chapels surrounding the crypt were donated by different countries.

The Cenacle, or Upper Chamber, is a Gothic room built on the site of the Last Supper. Seven weeks after the Passion the Holy Ghost appeared here to the assembled disciples. This was the origin of the Pentecost, as recorded in the Acts of the Apostles.

A medieval building leads to the Tomb of David. The cenotaph contains an impressive sarcophagus. Brocade hangings adorn the walls and the solid silver crowns of the Torah provide decoration. Although this site was not discovered until the 12th century, during the preceding 200 years people had been claiming that David's remains lay buried here.

The valley below once was forest land. On a certain day in that forest a tree was felled from which a heavy cross was fashioned. This event is commemorated by a medieval fortresslike structure called the Monastery and Church of the Holy Cross.

The road along the old walls from Zion Gate leads to Dung Gate, so called because the city's garbage was taken out through it in olden times, to be dumped down the slopes of the Valley of Kidron.

Dung Gate is also closest to the Wailing Wall, where Jews came to pray and bewail the destruction of the Temple.

The lower layers of the Wall are a section of the retaining and supporting wall of Herod's temple extension, while the upper layers were added by Sir Moses Montefiore in the middle of the 19th century. The claim that the huge lower blocks were from Solomon's temple has no foundation. Men and women pray at different sections of the Wall in accordance with Orthodox Jewish custom.

South of Dung Gate is the Church of St. Peter's in Gallicantu, built by the Assumptionist Fathers to commemorate St. Peter's denial of Jesus and the former's repentance. The site, within the Armenian Convent, is believed to be the place of Caiaphas' Palace where Jesus was taken on the night of his arrest.

From Dung Gate at the southeast corner of the city wall the road drops down and crosses the Valley of Kidron (Kedron), or Valley of Judgment. Below lie many tombs. Most prominent among them are Absalom's Pillar and the Tombs of St. James, Zachariah and Josephat. In the walls of the city overlooking the valley is the Golden Gate. According to tradition this is the gate through which Jesus rode into Jerusalem on Palm Sunday. The tradition is substantiated by underground chambers and stonework dating from Herodian times. It was the only gate of the outer city wall which would have led directly into the area of the Dome of the Rock, *i.e.* the site of Herod's Temple.

Farther down the valley road, on the right, is the Virgin's Fountain. Here, it is said, the Virgin Mary took water to wash the clothes of Jesus. The fountain is fed by the Spring of Gihon.

Gethsemane and the Mount of Olives

Across the Valley of Kidron and facing the Golden Gate lie Gethsemane and the Mount of Olives. On the north of the road before climbing the hill stands the Tomb of the Virgin, or the Church of the Assumption. According to tradition, this is the site of the Virgin's resting place before her ascent into heaven. The church in its present form was built by the Crusaders in 1130 to replace an earlier fifth-century basilica.

Further up the hill on the right is the Garden of Gethsemane. Here, in this peaceful grove of ancient olive trees, Jesus spent the night with his disciples when he visited Jerusalem. The Grotto of Gethsemane is traditionally believed to be the cave mentioned in the Bible where Jesus was betrayed by Judas and arrested by the soldiers. The Basilica of the Agony, or the Church of All Nations, is built over the Rock of Agony, where Christ is believed to have prayed and wept before his arrest. It is one of the loveliest churches in the Holy Land. Many nations contributed funds to build it, and their coats of arms are displayed in the cupolas.

The Church of St. Maria Magdalena with its onion-shaped domes was built by Tsar Alexander III in 1888. It is open Tuesday, Thursday and Saturday, 9 A.M.–12 noon and 2–7 P.M., Sunday 10–2. There is an entrance fee.

On the road to the summit of the Mount of Olives you come to the Church of the Ascension, said to mark the spot from which Jesus ascended into heaven. The chapel dates back to Crusader times and stands on the site of an earlier fourth-century church. After Saladin's recapture of Jerusalem in 1187 the church was made into a mosque. Inside there is a rock bearing what tradition holds is the footprint of Christ. Nearby, the Church of the Pater Noster marks the traditional site where Christ taught his disciples the Lord's Prayer. It was built for the Carmelite Nuns in 1875 by Princess de la Tour d'Auvergne on the ruins of a Crusader church. In the church are tablets of glazed tiles on which the Lord's Prayer is written in 44 different languages; these tiles were donated by Christians around the world.

At the summit of the Mount of Olives the Church of the Dominus Flevit rests on the traditional site where Jesus wept over Jerusalem before his entry into the city on Palm Sunday. The road rises to a crest here and stops in front of the Jerusalem Inter-Continental Hotel. From the top of the hill there is a view of the walled city of Jerusalem, the Judean Hills to the west, and the Judean wilderness and the little village of Bethany to the east.

Damascus Gate

On the north side of the city walls is Damascus Gate, the largest and most impressive of the entrances to the Old City. From ancient times it led to the road to the Syrian capital. The road stemming out from it today is called the Nablus Road.

The Damascus Gate is a beehive of activity inside and out. In front of it is the bus terminus of East Jerusalem. From here buses leave for all parts of the West Bank. Most of the nine buslines going between East and West Jerusalem start here, too.

Within the great gate itself there are stalls and shops and the fantastic souks of the Old City. On the way to the Street of Spices there are moneychangers, souvenir shops, and coffee houses where men in partly Western, partly Oriental attire spend their social hours sipping Turkish coffee, smoking their narghilis and noisily playing backgammon, as their fathers and grandfathers have done for centuries before them.

The Garden Tomb: A short walk up Nablus Road from Damascus Gate outside the old walls there is a small path on the east side leading to an ancient tomb in a garden. Some Protestant groups believe this to be the place of Jesus' crucifixion and burial because it more accurately fits the description in the Bible. The site was located and excavated by General Gordon (of Sudan fame) in 1883. Nearby, a hill still used as a graveyard is believed to be the site of Calvary. (It is best seen from the garden.) It is known that Christ was crucified at "the place of a skull." Immediately in front of the Garden Tomb is a rock formation resembling a skull, which Gordon believed to be an obvious identification of the original site. The Garden is a lovely and quiet place for meditation.

Farther along, where Nablus Road intersects with Saladin Street, is the Tomb of Kings. This is a misnomer; it is actually the tomb of a queen and her family who came to Jerusalem in the first century A.D.

Back toward the walls on the corner of Nablus and Saladin is St. George's Cathedral, the largest Anglican edifice in the country and the Anglican Commission's center for the Holy Land.

Before you reach Herod's Gate (also called the Flower Gate) there is a small iron grill door leading down to King Solomon's Quarries. From these labyrinthine caves the stones for Solomon's Temple are believed to have been cut. The Masons consider it the birthplace of their order. The quarries have numerous galleries covering thousands of feet and, in a direct line, the quarry penetrates more than 700 feet into the Old City. Some people are convinced it stretches even farther. An alternate name for the quarries is Zedekiah's Cave. Legend has it that the last king of Judah fled into the cave to escape his Babylonian enemies. He emerged miles from Jerusalem, in the Plain of Jericho, only to be caught anyway.

Opposite King Solomon's Quarries, down a narrow street, is Jeremiah's Grotto. It is supposedly the dungeon into which the prophet was cast and whence he was rescued by Ebed Melech the Ethiopian.

Rockefeller Archaeological Museum. Northeast of the city walls near Herod's Gate is one of the finest museums in the Middle East. Built in the 1930's and maintained by a gift of John D. Rockefeller, Jr., it houses many treasures from years of excavation in the Holy Land. Only the best samples of each item are on display. The exhibits are arranged chronologically.

Among the most interesting is a collection of jewelry dating from 1700 B.C. to A.D. 700, a coin collection dating from 500 B.C. to A.D. 1600, and a group of oil lamps from the early Bronze Age to the Islamic period. Exhibits of the Stone Age include objects 200,000 years old. Wooden panels of the seventh and eighth centuries from the Aqsa Mosque in Jerusalem and carved stuccos and frescos of the same period from the Hisham Palace in Jericho are also on display. In a corner of one exhibit room you will see a copy of a tomb with skeletons and artifacts exactly as they were found in Jericho. Samples of the Dead Sea Scrolls are displayed in a separate room. You need at least two hours at the museum for even a brief look at all the exhibits.

Hours: 10 A.M. to 5 P.M. daily; Friday and Saturday, 10 A.M. to 2 P.M. Entrance fee.

North of the Museum is the area known as the American Colony, so named because of the American missionaries who settled here in the mid-nineteenth century. Located here are the U.S. Consulate, Y.M.C.A., St. George's Cathedral and the **American Colony Hotel,** one of the oldest, best and most attractive in the Middle East. The original building dates from about 1850 and was the palace of a pasha. It is built around a beautiful old courtyard where, weather permitting, guests can dine or enjoy a drink and coffee. The upstairs sitting room with an elaborately painted ceiling is lovely. Saturday brunch is an all-you-can-eat buffet for about $10. Winter rates are $12.95 single, $31 to $33 double. Phone 282421.

The Y.M.C.A., built in 1933, is probably the most beautiful "Y" in the world. It is also the best bargain in town: $11 single, $19 double. Phone 282375. It has a restaurant and sports facilities. There is an excellent view of the Old City from its tower. It houses the Herbert Clark collection of Middle East Antiquities, open Monday through Friday, 10 A.M.–1 P.M. Entrance fee.

Other Sites

In addition to the Dome of the Rock and al-Aqsa Mosque, there are 29 mosques within the Old City of Jerusalem; and there are dozens of churches in addition to those named.

From the roof of Notre Dame de Sion or the Tower of the Lutheran Church near the Church of the Holy Sepulchre you can get the best view of the Old City of Jerusalem.

The French School of Biblical and Archeological Studies in Jerusalem conducts specialized tours of the Old City. A different place is selected each week as the focal point. The school also sponsors trips outside Jerusalem. The tours are led by professors from the school, and lectures are in French.

At the Pilgrim Office of the Franciscans on St. Francis Street in the Old City you may obtain a "Pilgrim Certificate" as a memento of your visit to Jerusalem. The tradition was established during the Crusades, and the certificate is given to pilgrims of all denominations.

Holy Days

The traditional holy days of Christianity are observed throughout the year by both Eastern and Western churches in Jerusalem.

The Eastern Church follows the old Julian calendar, which is 13 days behind the Gregorian. Consequently Eastern and Western religious feasts seldom coincide. Christmas and Easter are the major celebrations in which thousands of pilgrims and tourists from all over the world participate. Programs listing the major celebrations and services are available from churches, the Tourism office, leading hotels and travel agencies.

Christmas in Bethlehem

Christmas has three dates in the Holy Land: Western Christmas is celebrated on December 25, the Orthodox one on January 6, and the Armenian Christmas on January 19.

Christmas Eve, December 24, in the little town of Bethlehem is a memorable experience. About 1 P.M. the Latin Patriarch makes his ceremonial entrance into Bethlehem. He is followed by a colorful procession of churchmen and choirboys, and is met upon arrival by church organizations in Bethlehem of all denominations, by groups of school children, and by a large crowd of townspeople and visitors.

At dusk the YMCA holds a service in English and other languages at Shepherd's Field, where the angels appeared to the shepherds "as they sat watching their flocks by night." The congregation joins the choir in singing well-known Christmas carols. It is a beautiful moment to hear the familiar words of "Silent Night" as the first stars of evening appear overhead. At the end of the service, a traditional supper of bread and meat is served to the congregation. For the service at Shepherd's Field buses leave from the YMCA in Jerusalem at 3 P.M. and return about 7 P.M. Sometimes the weather is cold and windy. Wear warm clothing and comfortable shoes.

At nine o'clock in the evening you may join the community carol singing in the Church of the Nativity courtyard. Bethlehem is gaily lighted and a festive spirit is in the air.

At midnight, a Pontifical High Mass is celebrated in the Franciscan Church of St. Catherine, adjacent to the Church of the Nativity. At the moment the choir sings the Gloria, a huge star over the altar is set aglow and the bells of Bethlehem are rung. The little town's special message of "Glory to God in the highest, and on earth, peace and good will toward men" is carried throughout the world.

Tickets for the service are limited; be sure to request yours far in advance. They may be obtained through travel agents and the Pilgrim Office. The church always overflows its capacity, so plan to arrive early. The Mass is long and most of the congregation stand throughout the service. Wear warm clothing and comfortable shoes.

On Christmas morning, services are held in almost every church in Jerusalem. A pamphlet listing the hours of services at the major churches is available from the Tourist Office.

Christmas cards mailed from Bethlehem on Christmas Day bear a special postmark. You may also arrange in advance to have cards mailed from Bethlehem.

Easter in Jerusalem

Few ceremonies rival in pomp, pageantry and piety the Easter services in Jerusalem. The very names associated with the celebration—the Washing of the Feet, the Exposition of the Column of the Flagellation, the Service of the Imperial Hours, the Ceremony of the Holy Fire, the Bridegroom's Arrival, the Abyssinian Search—intensify the devotion of pilgrims.

During Holy Week many processions are held. On Palm Sunday the Anglican procession begins at the ruins of the Crusader Castle in Bethany and proceeds along the ancient footpath over the Mount of Olives to Gethsemane, and then to the Anglican Cathedral of St. George in Jerusalem.

Among the most splendid rituals of Holy Week are those of the Roman Catholic Church. They begin at 6:30 A.M. on Palm Sunday with the ceremonial entry of the Latin Patriarch into the Church of the Holy Sepulchre, followed by his Blessing of the Palms. Each member of the congregation carries an olive or palm branch to symbolize the reception of Christ entering Jerusalem. After blessing the Palms, the patriarch leads a procession three times around the Rotunda of the Holy Sepulchre, once around the Stone of Unction, and concludes with the Pontifical Mass before the Holy Tomb.

The Exposition of the Column of the Flagellation (a three-foot cylindrical column to which Christ was bound when He was scourged) takes place on Holy Wednesday in the Chapel of the Flagellation.

At 1:45 P.M. on Maundy Thursday in front of the Holy Tomb in the Church of the Holy Sepulchre, the patriarch, divested of his miter and cope, performs the Washing of the Feet, as did Jesus before his last Passover (John 12:5). (The ceremony is colorful and crowded; be sure to arrive early.) In the evening at 8, Mass is said at the Garden of Gethsemane. The Lutherans walk from their Church of the Redeemer near the Holy Sepulchre along the Via Dolorosa to the Garden of Gethsemane.

The next day, Good Friday, at 11 A.M. the Franciscan Fathers lead a procession from the site of Pontius Pilate's court along the Via Dolorosa, pausing for brief service at each of the fourteen Stations of the Cross. Many orders of priests and nuns carry heavy crosses.

This service is widely attended and is very crowded. The pilgrimage is divided into sections according to language. You should join the section you wish to attend at the first station. The procession inches along at a snail's pace. Persons in weak health should stay near the back.

In the Burial Service later in the day at 7 P.M., a procession visits the Stations of the Cross within the Church of the Holy Sepulchre. When the procession reaches the Cross, an effigy of Christ is taken down and wrapped in a winding sheet. It is then carried to the Stone of Unction where it is anointed, spiced and scented with incense. The effigy is laid to rest in the Holy Tomb, and the Good Friday services are concluded with a memorial sermon.

The Russian Orthodox Good Friday begins with the Service of the Imperial Hours ("Imperial" refers to the universal empire of the Lord) at the Church of Alexandros Nephki, and ends in the evening with the Burial Service in St. James Cathedral. Between these two services a solemn procession begins at the Greek Orthodox Convent of the Prison of Christ and traces Christ's steps along the Via Dolorosa to Calvary.

The Armenian Church has special ceremonies for the Holy Week.

They are held in the Armenian Chapel of St. John and the Chapel of the Second Calvary.

The Coptic Ceremony of the Washing of the Feet is held in the Coptic Church of St. Anthony. The feet of the "disciples" are not actually washed. Instead, the Coptic Patriarch marks with olive oil a cross on one knee of each of the twelve, and afterwards on the knee of any member of the congregation requesting anointment.

The Syrian Orthodox Church is entitled by custom to hold its Burial Service in the Church of the Holy Sepulchre. Other services of the Church are performed in the Chapel of St. Nicodemus and the Church of St. Mark in the Syrian Orthodox Convent. In the latter the Ceremony of the Bridegroom's Arrival is celebrated on Palm Sunday.

The Abyssinian Orthodox Church, established in Ethiopia sixteen centuries ago and having rights to the sanctuary of the Holy Sepulchre, does not have an altar inside the Church. Its tiny altar is located on the roof of St. Helena's Chapel near the entrance to the Church of the Holy Sepulchre. There, in the Chapel of the Saviour, the Abyssinian Orthodox Church celebrates the services of Holy Week. The most colorful is a small procession known as the Abyssinian Search. The group moves about in a symbolic search for the risen body of Christ. The service is held on the night of Easter Sunday; the ceremony is unique.

The Roman Catholics celebrate another Pontifical High Mass on Holy Saturday before the tomb and hold the Blessing of the Fire.

At the same time, in the Greek Orthodox Church the congregation moves in procession to the tomb of Lazarus (Lazarus Saturday) in the town of Bethany on the road to Jericho. There Lazarus lay for four days in his tomb until Christ raised him from the dead (John 12:1).

The Ceremony of the Holy Fire is the major service of the Eastern Churches and one of the most ancient. It symbolizes the Resurrection, when Christ, the Light of the World, rose from the tomb. The ceremony is at least a thousand years old, for it was mentioned by Bernard the Wise in the ninth century. Although the Syrian, Armenian Orthodox and Coptic Churches participate, the ceremony is mainly Greek Orthodox and is conducted by the Greek Orthodox Patriarch.

At 11 o'clock on Holy Saturday the door to the empty Tomb of Christ in the Rotunda of the Church of the Holy Sepulchre is closed. A white ribbon passed through the door handles is sealed with a large piece of hot wax.

Exactly at noon on Easter Sunday the Greek Orthodox Patriarch enters the crowded Rotunda. The ribbon and seal are removed, and the unlit silver Holy Lamp is placed in the Tomb. At 12:30 the service begins. The Patriarch, preceded by members of leading Greek Orthodox families of Jerusalem carrying thirteen banners, leads a solemn procession three times around the Rotunda. The Patriarch removes his cope and miter and enters the Holy Sepulchre, accompanied by the Bishop of the Armenian Church. At this moment the crowd in the tiny Chapel of the Angel is silent.

The Patriarch prays before the Holy Tomb of Christ. The Holy Lamp is lighted, and from it torches are ignited by the Patriarch and the Bishop. Their flaming torches are raised to small openings above the Holy Sepulchre, where the fire is received on one side by the Greek Orthodox congregation, on the other by the Armenians. The instant the fire is seen the crowd rushes frantically forward with candles and torches to receive it. Lasting honor is bestowed on the one whose candle is lit first. As the light of the Holy Fire appears, the massive bells of the church are rung, and the fire passes rapidly from candle to candle until the entire church is aglow.

The candles of churches in the Jerusalem area, which are extinguished on Good Friday, are lighted on Easter from this fire. All year one candle in each church is kept lit from the holy flame.

On Easter Sunday, Roman Catholics hold mass in the Holy Sepulchre without pause throughout the day.

 HOTELS: Hotels in East Jerusalem range from luxurious American style such as the Jerusalem Inter-Continental to simple and inexpensive, and are rated from five stars to'one.

A complete list of five-star hotels is available from the Tourist Office in Jerusalem. Hotels range from $26 to $47 for a double room. Generally hotels in East Jerusalem are lower in price than those in West Jerusalem. Four-star hotels charge $21 to $31 and three-star ones run about $17 to $25. Two-stars are $13 to $16 double. There are also youth hostels and hospices. (See list at the end of this section.)

SOUTH OF JERUSALEM

The sites described in the following section can be covered in a half-day; however, those who want to spend time in Bethlehem should allow a full day.

Bethany: 1¼ miles

Bethany was the home of Lazarus and his sisters, Mary and Martha, and Simon the Leper. On the site where Jesus called forth Lazarus from the tomb (John 11:43) stands a Franciscan church built on the foundations of earlier Byzantine and Crusader churches. The latter was used as a mosque at the end of the 16th century.

Jesus sent two disciples from Bethany to Bethpage on the Mount of Olives to fetch a donkey, which he rode into Jerusalem on Palm Sunday (Matt. 21:1). Today the exact site of Bethpage is no longer known, but the name is given to the enclosure of the Franciscans. Its chapel contains a cubical stone with paintings and Latin inscriptions, discovered in 1876. Past the church, going up a hill, is the entrance to the Tomb of Lazarus. The key is with the people who run the souvenir stand opposite. For a small fee you are taken down 24 slippery steps into a dark cave which is always cool no matter how warm it may be outside. There you may view the tomb, which rests in a lower vaulted room. Above is the Greek Orthodox Church of Lazarus.

On Palm Sunday, following a tradition set in the fourth century, Bethpage is the starting point for the procession that ends at the Church of St. Anne in the Old City.

Rachel's Tomb: 10 miles

On the right of the road before Bethlehem a small 19th-century domed building marks the traditional site of the tomb of Rachel, wife of Jacob. The structure was originally built by the Crusaders, but in subsequent years was altered many times.

Bethlehem: 11 miles

As the birthplace of Christ, the charming town of Bethlehem has a sweeter meaning to Christians than any place on earth. Its origins are lost in history. The first mention of it in the Bible is in connection with the death of Rachel. Bethlehem was the scene of the idyll of Ruth the Moabite and Boaz. In Bethlehem Samuel anointed David King of Israel.

The Church of the Nativity, facing Manger Square in the center of Bethlehem, stands above a cave, the traditional site of Jesus' birth. The first Church of the Nativity was built at the time of Constantine about A.D. 326. It was destroyed two centuries later, but rebuilt in the sixth century by Justinian. The present-day structure is basically the same as the sixth-century one.

The length of the church is divided by four rows of columns in reddish limestone. The wooden ceiling is made of stout English oak, a gift of King Edward IV. The vast amount of lead the monarch donated to cover the roof is said to have been melted down by the Turks to use as ammunition.

Three Christian denominations share rights in the church—Roman Catholic (Franciscan), Greek Orthodox and Armenian. Each has its own chapels and altars. Rivalries in the past have been so intense that fighting has broken out among the religious orders. The status quo which is now adhered to was the result of compromises worked out by the British Commissioner during the Mandate. Peace is maintained by the three communities' strictly observing their schedules. For example, the Greek Orthodox must have finished censing the Altar of the Nativity by 4:30 A.M., when the Catholics hold their first mass. The Armenian mass begins at 8 A.M., after which the Grotto is open to the public.

Beneath the protective floor boards of the church are fragments of the beautiful mosaics of the church built by Justinian. During the Persian conquest of Palestine in A.D. 614, most Christian places were devastated. According to legend, the Persians spared the Church of the Nativity because its mosaics pictured the Magi dressed as Persians. (These mosaics were only uncovered in 1933.) Fragments of other mosaics dating from the 12th century decorate the inside walls of the church.

On each side of the altar steps descend to the Grotto of the Nativity, wherein lies the manger (Luke 2:7). A silver star marks the birthplace. Seventeen lamps burn day and night above the altar. The original star was placed here by the Roman Catholic Church in 1717 but was removed by the Greeks in 1847. The Turks replaced it, but the incident was said to be a contributing factor to the outbreak of the Crimean War.

Next to the grotto is the Chapel of the Manger. Catholics are forbidden to use the Altar of the Nativity, but they may burn incense over the star. They use the Altar of the Manger, which is marked by a Latin inscription saying that the newborn Jesus was placed here by his mother.

North of the Basilica is the Church of St. Catherine. On Christmas Eve, the Latin Patriarch takes a wooden image of the infant Jesus from the Franciscan Church of St. Catherine and solemnly places it on the Altar of the Manger, where it remains until Epiphany. Here on Christmas Eve the church bells are rung during the midnight mass, announcing the dawn of Christmas around the world.

All the outside entrances to the Basilica are closed except one, which is entered from the courtyard. According to tradition, the passages were blocked to prevent Turkish soldiers in bygone days from entering the church on horseback. The one door remaining open, called the Door of Humility, was made smaller so that visitors must bow upon entering the small passageway.

The Milk Grotto is near the Church of the Nativity. Tradition holds that while Mary was nursing Jesus, drops of her milk fell on the rock and turned it white. The original church is said to have been built in the fourth century.

A description of Bethlehem's history with Biblical references and details on the Church of the Nativity are available in Eugene Hoade's *Guide to the Holy Land*.

A road to the east just before Manger Square in Bethlehem leads down to Beit Sahour and Shepherd's Field (Luke 2:8-10). On Christmas Eve before sunset services are held in the field next to the YMCA Hostel. Services of the Catholic and Orthodox Churches at the nearby Shepherd's Field are held earlier in the day.

On the Jerusalem–Bethlehem road immediately after Rachel's Tomb the south road leads to Hebron.

Qala'at el Burak (Castle of the Pools): 13 miles

Two miles beyond Bethlehem on the Hebron road on the east is a fortress built by the Turks in the 17th century for the protection of Solomon's Pools. These three ancient reservoirs are set in a beautiful grove of pine and cypress trees. The enormous pools collect rain from the surrounding hills and the water from the nearby springs. Upon seeing the reservoirs empty, you may wonder if enough water could ever flow from the surrounding area to fill them. To appreciate their size, you should walk the length of the three pools, which are set in a row.

According to scholars, the pools are misnamed. Solomon probably came to the spot to enjoy the gardens and springs, but history records that Pilate, not Solomon, built the great aqueduct which supplied water to Jerusalem. It is possible, of course, that an earlier water supply system existed. The reservoirs still provide Jerusalem with part of its water.

Herodion and Mar Saba

Five miles southeast of Bethlehem lie two interesting and historic sites: the fortress and burial place of Herod and the Monastery of Mar Saba.

Herodion, a huge circular bastion, was one of a string of fortresses built during Herod's reign and was apparently one of his proudest, for he was buried here. Built on a height of 2,500 feet above sea level, it commands a view of the Judean Wilderness and the Dead Sea. The defensive walls were built over 70 feet high and the great towers over 100 feet from the floor of the fortress.

Closer to the Dead Sea, clinging to the very wall of a high canyon, is Mar Saba, a monastery founded by St. Saba of Cappadocia in the fifth century. Long a center of theological literature and poetry, the monastery has had as many as 5,000 monks in residence at one time. Today it is tended by only 14.

Isolated as it is, the monastery was destroyed many times through the centuries by invading armies and bandits. It was sacked for the last time in 1835 and was rebuilt by the Imperial Russian Government in 1840. The fantastic, fortresslike complex has 110 rooms with living quarters on five stories.

Only men are permitted to visit the monastery. Women—and even female animals, it is said—are forbidden to enter. Women may, however, look out on the monastery from a special tower to the south of the building.

West of Bethlehem is the village of Beit Jalla, set among olive groves and vineyards, where the Cremisan Monastery is located. The friars make a popular wine, bottled under their name, which can be sampled and bought here.

Continuing toward Hebron, the road passes through some of the highest parts of the Judean hills. At the village of Halhul on the east there is a tall tower which local tradition claims is the tomb of the prophet Jonah, Nebi Yunes, who is revered by Moslems as well as Christians.

At Mambre, the Mamre of the Bible, on the east one mile before Hebron, stand the ruins of Haram Ramet el-Khalil (Enclosure of the High Place of the Friend). It is the traditional site of the Oak of Mamre, where Abraham received the three angels of God (Gen:18). Ruins from the Abrahamic period have been excavated, although only those from the times of Herod, Hadrian and Constantine are visible.

Hebron: 28 miles

Al-Khalil, as Hebron is called in Arabic, means "the Friend [of God]," *i.e.,* Abraham. In ancient times it was known as Kirjah Arba, "the town of four," because of its position on four hills. Situated at an altitude of 3,000 feet, Hebron has been continuously settled for 5,000 years. It lies in a valley identified with the Biblical Valley of Ephron (Gen.24:17) as well as the Valley of Eshkol, where Moses sent his scouts to spy out the fields near Hebron. They returned with pomegranates, figs and grapes in clusters so large that it took two men to carry them (Num. 13:21-24).

The Bible relates that Abraham "moved his tent and came and dwelt in the plain of Mamre, which is in Hebron, and built there an altar unto the Lord." After the death of his wife Sarah, Abraham bought the Cave of Machpelah from a Hittite and buried her there (Gen. 24:17). Later, Abraham was buried beside her. In the years that followed, Isaac and Rebecca, Jacob and Leah were also buried there.

Hebron was captured by Joshua, and later was David's capital. The story of the cave disappeared from history until the time of Herod, when a temple was built on the site.

After the Moslem conquest of Palestine in the seventh century, Hebron, because of its association with Abraham, became one of the four sacred cities of Islam. To the Moslems, Abraham was the first Moslem.

In 1100 the Crusaders took Hebron, but later it was recaptured by Saladin. It has remained predominantly Moslem since that time. Today it is the seat of government for the southern district of the West Bank.

Al-Haram al Ibrahimi al Khalil (The Sanctuary of Abraham, the Friend) is a mosque built on the traditional site of the Caves of Machpelah. The building is massive; the wall is about 50 feet high and almost ten feet thick. The lower part dates from the time of Herod. The main part of the building was formerly a Crusader Church which was an enlargement of the original Byzantine basilica used by Christian pilgrims en route to Abraham's Oak at Mamre. The upper part and four minarets (of which only two remain) were added by the Mameluks.

The mosque is divided by four pillars into a nave and two aisles. The cenotaph on the right as one enters the mosque is that of Abraham; the one on the left, that of Sarah. The cenotaphs are enclosed in chapels above the tombs, which lie in the cave below.

The cenotaphs are covered with green velvet tapestries embroidered with golden threads, presented by a Turkish sultan over a century ago. The stained-glass window over the main entrance dates from the 12th century.

The *mihrab,* or prayer niche facing Mecca, is made of multi-colored marble and fine mosaics. Next to it the carved walnut *minbar,* or pulpit, is a masterpiece of intricate workmanship. It was constructed without a single nail. An inscription on it explains that it was made in the 11th century by order of the minister of the Fatimite Caliph of Egypt.

In front of the *mihrab* stand the two black-and-white marble cenotaphs of Isaac and Rebecca, and to the north are the two similar tombs of Jacob and Leah. The bodies of the patriarch and their wives lie in the cave below. The cave itself may not be visited, but you may look through an opening in the floor by the dim light of a suspended oil lamp into the eerie subterranean chambers below. Visiting hours: Sunday-Thursday, Saturday and holidays, 7:30–11:30 A.M.; 1:30–3 P.M.; 4–5 P.M. Closed on Fridays.

The mosque is approached on foot. You leave your car or bus in a parking lot and climb up a road which is lined with shops, all eager to sell to tourists. Along the way you will have a view of the wares of the town—Hebron glass, sheep and goat skins and woodcarvings.

As the place of David's anointment and the burial of the patriarchs, Hebron is holy to Jews as well as to Moslems. Because of the religious fervor which this town inspires, it has frequently been the scene of conflict between Arabs and Israelis.

Hebron is a conservative town. Some of the Moslem women were veils of flowered material which, when viewed from afar, are weird and startling. You should be cautious about photographing in Hebron. Ask your guide about taking pictures, especially in the area of the mosque.

In the bazaar near the mosque as well as on the road into Hebron there are small glass factories where hand-blown glass is made. It has been a trade of Hebron since the Middle Ages. You may watch the men at work around their ancient furnaces, turning and blowing the green, blue or amethyst glass into vases, pitchers, candlesticks and beads. The glass items can be bought here for half the price for which they sell in Jerusalem.

NORTH OF JERUSALEM

The trip from Jerusalem to Sabastiya (Sebaste), with stops at major Biblical and archeological sites along the way, can be made in a hurried half-day. For the trip as far north as Jenin one should allow a full day. The trip to Nazareth and the Sea of Galilee is an overnight excursion.

Going north from the Damascus Gate on the Nablus Road, a tall minaret on a high rise can be seen on the left. This is Nebi Samwil, one of the sites where the prophet Samuel is said to be buried. From the top of this mosque one can see the entire breadth of the Holy Land, from the Mediterranean to the Mountains of Moab. From this vantage point, over 3,000 feet above sea level, pilgrims in medieval times often caught their first glimpse of their goal—Jerusalem. The height was thus dubbed Mount of Joy. Before Ramallah, a side road to the west leads to Jerusalem Airport.

Ramallah: 15 miles

In the year Columbus discovered America a small Christian community in Shobak in southern Jordan fled north to avoid the marriage of one of their daughters to the son of the chief of the Moslem tribe. As a child, the daughter had been promised by her father to the chief's son. The little community settled near Bireh, a Moslem village north of Jerusalem. Today the Christian town of Ramallah and the Moslem town of Bireh form a single adjacent community.

Situated at 2,900 feet above sea level with a view of Jerusalem and the Mediterranean in the distance, Ramallah means "Height of God" in Arabic. Traditionally it has been a popular summer resort. It is connected with Jerusalem by a four-lane highway and is a 20-minute drive through rolling hills and green valleys.

Ramallah has several good hotels and restaurants. The town is known for the chocolates and ice cream made there. The American Friends (Quakers) opened their first school in Ramallah in 1866.

While Ramallah itself does not have known sites of antiquity, the town is surrounded by places familiar to us from the Bible.

Bireh (Bira), mentioned above, was the first stopping place for caravans from Jerusalem to Galilee, and is therefore believed to be the place where Mary and Joseph missed the 12-year-old Jesus. Afterwards they returned to Jerusalem to find him in the Temple. *Rentis,* a village near Bir Zeit northeast of Ramallah, was said to be the home and burial place of Samuel.

East of the road from Jerusalem to Ramallah, *Tel el-Ful* is the site of Gibeah or Gabaath, the birthplace and residence of Saul. At *Er-*

Ram, ancient Ramah, the prophet Jeremiah was freed from the convoy of captives on its way to Babylon. At *Tel en-Nasbeth,* the site of Mizpah, Saul was elected the first king of Israel.

About ten miles from Jerusalem on the Ramallah highway a road leads west to the village of *El-Jib,* identified as Gibeon, "where the sun stood still" (Josh 10: 12-13). Excavations are located south of the village. In his book *Gibeon Where the Sun Stood Still* James Pritchard provides valuable diagrams and descriptions which aid in viewing the site.

About three miles further along this road is *Qubeibeh,* traditionally believed to be ancient Emmaus, where Jesus appeared to the disciples Cleophas and Simon on the third day after his burial. Later Jesus broke bread with them in the house of Cleophas. A Franciscan church, reconstructed on the foundation of an earlier Crusader church, stands on the traditional site of Cleophas' house.

The German Hostel in Qubeibah provides food and sleeping accommodations. The hostel is famous for its preparation of *musakhan,* a local chicken dish.

One mile before Latroun is the small village of *Amwas* (Imwas), believed by many Biblical scholars to be the correct site of Emmaus; the name of the present village is almost identical to the ancient one. Further on at Latroun the *Abbey of the Trappist Monks,* built about 40 years ago, stands on the ruins of a 12th-century Crusader castle. The abbey is known for its good wines bottled under the name of Latroun.

A mile or so north of Ramallah a small road to the right leads to the village of *Beit-el,* thought perhaps to be biblical Beth-El (House of God). It is repeatedly mentioned in the Book of Genesis, first as the place by which Abraham pitched his tents and built an altar to the Lord in the land of Canaan, later when Abraham returned here from Egypt with his nephew, Lot.

Beit-El is most closely associated, however, with the story of Jacob and his dream of a ladder reaching to heaven. Jacob took the pillow of stone he had rested his head on when he slept and set it up as a pillar (Gen. 28: 18-19).

North of Ramallah and Bireh en route to Nablus the road passes through the fertile *Wadi el-Haramiyah* (Valley of the Robbers). The area is dotted with Biblical sites, and the ruins of a khan at *Ain al-Haramiyah* (the Robbers' Spring) mark the major pass on the route from Jerusalem to Nablus. From earliest times small forts were used to defend the pass against robbers; hence the name.

About halfway to Nablus a road on the right leads to *Kirbet*

Seilun, the site of ancient Shiloh (Silo). After the conquest of Palestine, the tabernacle and the Ark of the Covenant were placed in Shiloh, where they remained for two centuries until the Ark was captured by the Philistines. From excavations at the site authorities believe that Shiloh was destroyed by the Philistines about 1050 B.C.

Further along the Nablus road *Ain Berkit,* near Khan al-Lubban, marks the traditional frontier between Judea and Samaria.

Jacob's Well: 34 miles

The famous well dug by Jacob near his camp outside *Shechem* is located less than one mile south and east of Nablus. Here Jesus met the Samaritan woman and asked her for a drink of water. He revealed himself to her as the Messiah and she believed (John 4:5-25).

In the early fourth century a church was built over the well. Apparently destroyed during the Samaritan revolts of the fifth century, it was later restored under Justinian. In Crusader days a new church was built over the old one.

The area containing the Crusader church ruins was acquired by the Greek Orthodox Church in 1860. Reconstruction was begun in the 19th century but had to be stopped after World War I, when funds from the Church of Russia were discontinued.

The Greek Orthodox monk in attendance will lower a bucket into the well and bring up clear, fresh water for you to drink.

Joseph's Tomb

Joseph had requested that upon his death his body be buried in the Land of Canaan. Four centuries later Moses brought Joseph's mummy on the Exodus and buried him near the site of Jacob's well. The tomb is marked by a white dome. Northeast of the tomb is Askar (Sichar), the village home of the Samaritan woman.

On the east of the road immediately before reaching Nablus, the small town of Balata is the site of ancient Shechem (Sichem), the first capital of ancient Samaria. Behind the village at Tel Balata excavations reveal the ruins of two city gates and a large temple built about 1600 B.C. Apparently the temple was used for four succeeding centuries. About 800 B.C. a granary was built over the temple site. Shechem was probably first settled by the Canaanites in the fourth millennium B.C. It is mentioned in the Bible in connection with Abraham and Jacob.

Nablus: 35 miles

Between Mount Garizim and Mount Ebal lies Nablus. The town is located in an area that has an abundant water supply. Its gardens and fields are irrigated from sixteen springs. The Nablus area is known for its olive crop and the production of oil and soap. Kanafa, one of the best oriental sweetmeats, is also a specialty of Nablus. If you have time, stop in one of the town's pastry shops to enjoy the delicious dessert.

Nablus, the largest town of the West Bank, was founded in A.D. 72 by Roman legionaries under Titus. In 636 the town was taken by the Arabs and, except for a brief period during the Crusades, has remained predominantly Moslem to the present day. The town's main ancient building is the Great Mosque. It was originally a Byzantine basilica, rebuilt as a church by the Crusaders.

In addition to its small Christian minority, about 300 Samaritans live in Nablus. Their high priests (Cohanim) are the direct descendents of Levi, the descendant of Aaron, the son of Jacob. A modern synagogue has replaced the ancient one, which was destroyed by an earthquake in 1927. Here you can see an ancient Pentateuch Scroll or Torah written in Samaritan script, akin to Hebrew. (These are the five books of Moses and the only part of the Scriptures accepted by the Samaritans.) The Samaritans claim that the document is the original copy of the words of Moses—hence the oldest one in existence. In fact, however, scholars say the oldest part of it goes no farther back than the 10th or 11th century A.D..

Mount Garizim, the holy mountain of the Samaritans, is located southwest of Nablus. The Jews, after their return from captivity (538 B.C.), refused to consider the inhabitants of Samaria as Jews because they had intermarried with Gentiles. The Samaritans, on the other hand, had retained the old Judaic teachings and rejected the new ideas acquired by the Jews during their forty-nine years in Babylon. Therefore, the Samaritans, believing that Mount Garizim fitted Abraham's description better than Mount Moriah, built a rival temple to the one in Jerusalem. Although the temple has long since been destroyed, the Samaritans celebrate the feasts of the Passover, Pentecost and Tabernacle on the site. Also on the summit are the ruins of a mosque and an octagonal church, the earliest known one dedicated to Mary. The panoramic view of the Holy Land from the summit of Mount Garizim is magnificent.

In the valley between Mt. Garizim and Mt. Ebal the twelve tribes of Israel assembled. By Joshua's orders the six nobler tribes stood for blessings on the side of Mt. Garizim, while the lesser nobility stood on Mt. Ebal. The priests, judges and elders gathered around the Ark of the Covenant placed in the valley between the two mountains.

The Samaritans point out a rock on Mt. Garizim that, they say, was the place where Abraham prepared to sacrifice Isaac, rather than Mount Moriah in Jerusalem. They also show the twelve rocks Joshua was supposed to have set up for the tribes of Israel, although the Bible puts this on Mount Ebal.

To the Samaritans Moses is the only prophet and God is one and incorporeal. Mount Garizim is the chosen place on earth. Annually, at the summit of the mountain, the Samaritans hold their unique Passover feast on the evening before the full moon of Nisan (April), following every word of the Mosaic Law literally, up to and including the slaughter, roasting and eating of the Paschal lamb on the night of the feast. A year-old lamb is struck with a knife. If it is not killed on the first blow, another one is presented. Only a Samaritan is allowed to touch the sacrifice. The blood of the lamb is poured into bowls and used to mark the first-born son of each family. The carcasses of the lamb are boiled after the entrails have been removed and burnt. After defleecing, the lambs are oven-roasted and the meat is distributed to Samaritans to eat.

Sabastiya (Sebaste): 48 miles

At a fork in the road northwest of Nablus the route west leads to Tulkarm; the one to the north proceeds to Sabastiya, the site of ancient Samaria. On a hill above the new town lie the ruins of many ancient civilizations.

History tells us that Omri, the sixth king of Israel, bought an isolated and defensible hill for two talents of silver from Shemer. There he built a city called Samaria and made it his capital. The city was embellished by his successors, one of whom was Ahab. Under the influence of his Phoenician wife, Jezebel, Ahab built a temple in honor of Baal. For Ahab's blasphemy the prophets foretold that Samaria would be "a heap of stones in the field." After Israel's defeat by the Assyrians and later Babylonian captivity, the prophecy came to pass. The area was subsequently settled by the Chaldeans, but destroyed again by Alexander the Great in 331 B.C. and later by John Hyracanus in 108 B.C.

After the Roman conquest the town was rebuilt by Pompey. Later Augustus bestowed it on Herod the Great, who called it Sebaste and embellished it to its former opulence. According to one legend, here

Salome danced for the head of John the Baptist. Other legends, however, say it was at Jericho, and still others claim it was at Machaerus, south of Madaba. Ruins of a fifth-century church built on the traditional site contain frescos representing a beheading.

In the present-day village of Sabastiya ruins of the Crusader Church of St. John the Baptist may be visited. The church was built on the remains of a Byzantine basilica, in the crypt of which were found relics of several prophets. The presbytery and the apse were made into a mosque called Nebi Yahya (Prophet John). On the hill above the village the site of ancient Sebaste includes the ruins of a Roman forum, a colonnaded street, a theater and a temple to Augustus. South of the temple are ruins of the palace of Omri. The walls of the town, many times enlarged by successive conquerors, are also visible in the excavations.

About 14 miles north of Sabastiya is the site of ancient *Dothan,* where Joseph was sold by his brothers and taken to Egypt (Gen. 37:17-28).

About 27 miles north of Nablus is the town of Jenin, ancient Engannin. There, according to tradition, Christ cured the ten lepers. At Jenin there is an excellent view of the Plain of Esdraelon and a glimpse of Nazareth.

The road leads through cultivated fields into the Esdraelon (Jezreel) Valley to Afula, ten miles away, believed to be the site of ancient Ophir.

Galilee

The border of the West Bank ends above Jenin. The editors have included Galilee, however, because of its important Christian sites.

Galilee, the country of Jesus, is one of the most fertile and highly cultivated areas of the region. But for all its lushness and religious significance, it was also one of history's bloodiest battlefields. A natural trade and migration route between Europe and Asia, it was fought over for thousands of years by the Egyptians, Canaanites, Philistines, Israelites, Romans and Crusaders, to name a few.

All roads in this region of craggy hills and cultivated valleys lead to an inland freshwater lake known as the Sea of Galilee, whose waters spring from Mt. Hermon and cascade in a torrent or trickle in a stream into the basin. At the southern end of the Sea of Galilee (or Lake Tiberias, as it is also known) the waters flow southward through the Jordan Valley.

Galilee is a region of extremes, from green riverbank farmland to parched hillsides strewn with basalt boulders to grand mountain peaks such as Mount Meron (3,964 feet), Mount Canaan (3,150 feet) and Mount Tabor (1,929 feet).

On the east is *Mount Gilboa* where Saul and his three sons died in battle with the Philistines (1 Sam. 31). Nine miles west of Afula is Megiddo, a stronghold on the Via Maris, the ancient caravan route between Egypt and Mesopotamia and the key to controlling the valley and the trade and supply route to and from the sea and the hinterland. In the Bible the very sound of its name was a trumpet call to war. Armageddon is where St. John predicted the last great battle between good and evil will be fought (Rev. 16:16).

The great Egyptian pharaoh Thutmose III ordered his victories over Megiddo in 1478 B.C. to be carved in detail upon stone. Solomon considered it necessary to maintain a garrison there, and the tax he levied for the walls of Jerusalem also had to finance the fortification of Megiddo. As a shrewd soldier he was aware that the outcome of battle on a plain depended on the cavalry, and he kept the garrison well stocked with horses and chariots. Josiah was killed here in 610 B.C. trying to stop the advance of Nechao, king of Egypt, who had nevertheless told him, "My quarrel is not with thee."

Twenty levels of settlement have been brought to light by scholars at Megiddo since 1925, covering the period from 4,000 to 400 B.C. The oldest remains uncovered so far are those of the Canaanite temples, built to face the rising sun. A museum at the foot of the mound houses the unearthed pieces on display, together with models to help visitors understand the site. The museum is open 8 A.M.–5 P.M. daily, Fridays to 4 P.M. The archaeological site is open April–September 8 A.M.–5 P.M.; October–March 8 A.M.–4 P.M.

From the top of the hill there is a magnificent view of the entire valley.

A road from Afula continues north to Nazareth and the Biblical sites of Kafr Kana (Cana) and Mount Tabor overlooking the Sea of Galilee.

Nazareth

Nazareth is a Christian Arab town. Its greatest site is the Basilica of the Annunciation, the biggest and richest in the Middle East, and the Mosque of Peace. Both were completed in 1965. The Basilica stands over the grotto where the Archangel Gabriel appeared to

Mary to announce the coming birth of Christ (Luke 1:26-35). A Greek chapel now stands on the site where Jesus preached.

In this cradle of Christianity all sects are represented, and their members here, as elsewhere, wage a cold war. Outside of the Basilica there is the Roman Catholic Church of St. Joseph, built on the traditional site of his carpenter's shop. The oldest Church of the Annunciation (300 years), dedicated to St. Gabriel, is Greek Orthodox and built over the well where Mary is said to have drawn water. The Greek Orthodox also believe it is the site where Gabriel appeared to Mary. It is open daily 8 A.M.–6 P.M.

The Melchite community has a Greek Catholic church near the marketplace. The Maronites, originally from Lebanon, have in the Latin quarter of Nabaa a Maronite church where Mass is said in Arabic and Aramaic. The Anglican Church is located near Casanova Street. The Southern Baptist Convention built their temple next to the Greek Orthodox church about 40 years ago, and a small Coptic church was added in the eastern part of the town in 1952.

The Salesian Order of St. John Bosco has a beautiful church, also known as the Church of the Boy Jesus, on a hill above the town. It can be seen from afar, but one must climb the hill on foot to reach it. Lastly, west of Nazareth on another summit stands the Greek Church of St. Joseph.

Nearly all the streets of Nazareth slope downhill. Casanova Street in the center of town gets its name from the Latin words *casa* and *nova* and has nothing to do with the amorist. In olden days the Franciscans had a hospice in Nazareth to house pilgrims. When it began to deteriorate they built another and called it the new house, *casa nova,* to distinguish it from the old one. The town has a dozen hospices, convents, monasteries and hostels of denominations which lodge pilgrims and travelers.

In the time of Jesus the town had a somewhat bad reputation. The people of Galilee looked down on it: "Can any good thing come out of Nazareth?"

Today the Temple where Jesus spoke is a Greek Catholic Church. A chapel, Our Lady of Fright, belonging to the Franciscan Order of Nuns, the Holy Clairs, was built on a hill south of town at the place where Mary was supposed to have been seized with fear for her son's life. A mile or so from Nazareth at Jebel-el-Qafse you will be shown the hill from which angry townsmen wanted to push Jesus.

The cave where the annunciation was said to have taken place, a site hallowed by tradition, is under the present Basilica. For 1,600 years chapels, churches and basilicas have been built and rebuilt here. The site was confirmed only a few years ago by an archeological discovery: an inscription reading "Hail Mary" in the ruins. The old Greek Orthodox Church of the Annunciation had laid claim for 300 years to the glory of standing on the site of the miracle.

The present Basilica was built over a very old altar bearing the words "And the Word was made flesh" (John 1, 14). That alone matters. The early Christians, the Crusaders, generations of pilgrims for the past 2,000 years have knelt here in awe. Four times in the course of centuries the Byzantines, the Crusaders, and twice the Franciscans have borne witness to their faith and that of millions by building a church here.

One should allow a minimum of an hour to tour the Basilica of the Annunciation. It contains many works of art. Masses are said at 7, 8, 9, 10:30 A.M. and 6 P.M. Entry is forbidden to persons wearing shorts. Photographs cannot be made of the interior. The Tourist Information Office is located on Casanova Street, phone (065) 54144.

Seven miles to the east of Nazareth on the main road is Kfar Kana, old Cana, where Jesus attended a wedding feast with his mother and turned the water into wine (John 2: 1-11). As in Nazareth, two churches lay claim to the spot. A first chapel was built in the fourth century by Constantine. Later, the Crusaders built a church on the ruins, and even later the Franciscans added the church which now stands on the site. There is a water jar on display which they claim is one of the originals. On the other hand, the Greek church also claims to stand on the ruins of the old house where the water was changed to wine. And still another tradition places Cana eight miles north of Nazareth!

A few miles to the west on a hilltop lies Zippori, which means "bird." A simple village now, it is said to have been the most important town in Galilee in Jesus' time. A church, built on the ruins of a Crusaders' church, marks the birthplace of Mary in the house of her mother, Ann, and her father, Joachim.

Tiberias, 18 miles northeast of Nazareth, was built by Herod Antipas in honor of his emperor. One can take a boat to the northern shores of the lake where Christ preached and where so many of the miracles took place.

Sea of Galilee

The Sea of Galilee, thirteen miles long and seven miles wide, lies 686 feet below sea level. Its waters appear calm, but they are deceiving. Unexpected violent storms can whip up from nowhere.

Like Jerusalem and Nazareth, the sea is linked with the name of Jesus. He walked on its waters (Mark 4: 45-56); He becalmed the storm (Mark 4: 35-41); He filled the empty fishing-net (Luke 5: 4-7); He gathered together His followers Simon, Andrew, James and John (Matt. 4: 18-22). We meet Him everywhere—in Tabgha, in Migdal, in Capernaum; but He avoided the town of Tiberias.

In the fourth century, beginning with Constantine, the first emperor to be converted to Christianity, churches went up among the temples of Tiberias; afterwards the Arabs built their mosques. The earthquakes of 749 and 1033 destroyed the town. The survivors moved nearby to settle in what is now the old town. After defeating the Crusaders, Saladin captured Tiberias in 1187. It was again leveled by earthquake in 1837.

The landscape around Tiberias is beautiful and the weather unbelievably mild.

The main road along the lake, heading north, leads to famous New Testament locations. Each year thousands of pilgrims visit these shrines. Three are at lakeside—Migdal, Tabgha and Capernaum—and another, the Mount of Beatitudes, is on a beautiful hilltop. Mount Tabor, which is reached by following a southwesterly route, is a half-hour's drive away.

Following the shore of the lake northward, one should see the Monastery of St. Peter, kept by the Franciscans. The apse of the old Church of the Crusaders is still shaped like a ship's prow, a reminder of Peter the Fisherman. Further on there is an Antiquities Museum.

Migdal, the old Magdala, four miles from Tiberias, gave its name to the renowned sinner Mary Magdalen, who was born here. Having fled from Nazareth, Jesus stopped near a tower, *migdal,* and met the woman who, through Him, was to see the light. The meeting place is marked by a small whitewashed dome.

Formerly the people of Migdal salted fish from the Sea of Galilee. Now the village is a mere suburb.

There is a camping ground and, on the shore of the lake, a youth hostel.

Tabgha, four miles north, is the site of the multiplication of the loaves and fishes. Here the Benedictine Order has a monastery built in the gray stone of Galilee. The monks make a very good dry wine, and show the traveler the magnificent mosaics in the old Byzantine basilica. It pictures the miracle in a wonderful setting of plant and animal life.

When Jesus heard of the death of John the Baptist, "He departed thence by ship into a desert place apart." This place seems to be Tabgha, or Tabigha, from the Greek word *heptapegon,* "seven springs." "When the people had heard thereof, they followed Him on foot." Evening came, and the crowd had no food. The disciples had "but five loaves and two fishes." Jesus handed them out, "and they did all eat, and were filled: and they took up of the fragments that remained twelve baskets full. And they that had eaten were about five thousand men, beside women and children" (Matt. 14: 13-21).

It would also be in Tabgha that the Lord appeared, and "this is now the third time that Jesus shewed Himself to his disciples, after that He was risen from the dead" (John 21: 14). And "when they had dined"—following a second catch of fish—"Jesus saith to Simon Peter . . . Feed my lambs . . . Feed my sheep." A Franciscan church in honor of St. Peter was built there during World War II.

Mount of Beatitudes

The Mount of Beatitudes is two and a half miles from Tabgha. On the hill top, at about 330 feet there is a hospice kept by an Italian Order of Franciscan nuns, and a chapel. The shrine was built in 1937. Within, the eight sides of the dome list the beatitudes uttered by Jesus in the opening to His Sermon on the Mount (Matt. 5). The signs of the seven virtues are inlaid in the floor. The view from here is lovely, with the Sea of Galilee spread out below, a fitting end to the rolling landscape. Farther away, Mount Hermon lifts its snowy peak.

According to tradition, it was on the Mount of Beatitudes that Jesus chose His twelve apostles from among His followers: "And He goeth up into a mountain, and calleth unto Him whom He would . . . and He ordained twelve, that they should be with Him" (Mark 3: 13-14). On going down, Jesus went into Capernaum.

Capernaum is today a graveyard of old stones worked by the hand of man. There are traces of a second- or third-century temple, probably built over the one where Jesus preached. For, on coming from Nazareth (Math. 4:13), He made of Capernaum the "center of His teaching." The "village of Nahoum," on the road from Syria to

Egypt, must have been of some importance, since it called for a Roman garrison and a customs house. In spite of His prodigies of healing there—Simon's mother, the man possessed of an unclean spirit, the centurion's servant—the people of Capernaum mocked Jesus, who proceeded to denounce them: "And thou, Capernaum which art exalted unto Heaven, shalt be brought down to hell."

There is a Franciscan monastery, open daily 8:30 A.M.–4:30 P.M. Entrance fee.

Mount Tabor

The best road to Mount Tabor is from the southern tip of the lake. The climb up the mount is steep, with many hairpin bends, and so narrow that if two cars meet, one has to back off to a widening in the road to allow the other to pass.

As you drive up the sun beats fiercely down onto the treeless, stony path. But, having labored for 1,900 feet, the traveler is rewarded at the top by a panorama of tranquility. Mount Tabor is topped by a tableland on which stand the Basilica of the Transfiguration and the Hospice Casa Nova, both kept by the Franciscan Order. There is also a Greek church named for St. Elias. The Mount is the site where Christ was transfigured before Peter, James and John (Matt. 17). The Basilica is open daily 8 A.M.–12 noon and 3 P.M. to sunset.

The hill has a historic past, but it owes its renown to St. Cyril of Jerusalem, who in the fourth century named it the scene of the Transfiguration. The evangelists had merely spoken of a high mountain, which many had thought was Mount Hermon (Luke 9:28).

Two passages in Luke have served as the starting point for the architects who over the centuries have been called upon to rebuild the Church of the Transfiguration. The latest one has three triangles on the front, recalling the three tabernacles (Matt. 17:1-8). The effect of the Transfiguration can be seen at sundown when the rays of the setting sun, falling slantwise through an opening, shine on the golden mosaics of the rounded vault.

The first Church of the Transfiguration was built in the fourth century in the form of three chapels. The present altar is said to be on the former site of the biggest chapel, that of Jesus. The two others are today marked by chapels daubed with frescos; one recalls the meeting of Elias with the priests of Baal.

From the terrace of the Hospice Casa Nova there is a breathtaking view stretching from Upper Galilee to Mount Gilboa. One can make out the town of Na'ine (Nain), where Jesus raised a widow's dead son (Luke 7:11-16).

At the foot of the hill lies Ein Dor, famous in the story of Saul, who came there to speak with the witch on the eve of the battle that was to cost him his life (1 Sam. 28: 7-25).

Dabburiya is the town where 2,000 years ago nine followers waited with Peter, James and John for Jesus to come down from the "high mountain."

The road leads to the Arbel Valley, wedged between the Horn of Hittin on the left and Mt. Arbel on the right. Here is the place where Saladin defeated the Crusaders in a decisive battle. One may continue from here to Tiberias.

The Pilgrim's Map of the Holy Land (See Reading List) lists the Biblical references to the sites and is particularly helpful in touring Galilee.

CHRISTIAN HOSPICES

For Christian visitors making a pilgrimage to the Holy Land, hospices of all denominations are available. They offer board and accommodation at reasonable prices. Facilities vary greatly from hospice to hospice. In addition, each hospice has its own rules regarding length of stay, who may be admitted, etc. You should write to them directly.

JERUSALEM

Casa Nova PP. Franciscans (Roman Catholic)
Near Jaffa Gate (Buses 1, 19, 20)
P.O.B. 1321
Tel. (02) 282791.

Christ Church Hostel (Anglican—British)
 Jaffa Gate (Buses 1, 19, 20)
P.O.B. 14037
Tel. (02) 282082.

"Ecce Homo" Convent; Notre Dame-de-Sion (Roman Catholic)
Via Dolorosa (Buses 3, 12, 27)
P.O.B. 19056
Tel. (02) 282445.

Evang. Lutheran Hostel (Lutheran—German)
St. Mark's Street

Old City (Buses 1, 5, 20)
P.O.B. 14051
Tel. (02) 282120.

Filles de la Charite (Roman Catholic—French)
Bethany Shiya (Buses 36, 43, 63)
P.O.B. 19080
Tel. (02) 284726.

Sisters of Nigrizia (Roman Catholic—Italian sisters)
Bethany Shiya (Buses 36, 42)
P.O.B. 19054
Tel. (02) 284724.

Sisters of Notre Dame de Sion (Roman Catholic—French)
En Karem (Bus 27)
Tel. (02) 69665.

Sisters of the Rosary (Roman Catholic—Arab)
14 Agron Street (Buses 22, 30)
P.O.B. 54
Tel. (02) 228529. Meals only during the summer.

St. Andrew's Hospice, (Church of Scotland)
near railway station
(Buses 4, 6, 7)
P.O.B. 14216
Tel. (02) 37701.

St. Charles Hospice; Order of St. Karl Borromaeus (Roman Catholic—
German)
German Colony (Buses 4, 6)
P.O.B. 8020
Tel. (02) 37737.

St. George's Hostel (Anglican/Episcopal)
Nablus and Saladin Streets (Buses 3, 12, 27)
P.O.B. 19/0018
Tel. (02) 283302.

MOUNT TABOR

Franciscan Convent of the Transfiguration; Roman Catholic (Italian)
Tel. (065) 54355.

NAZARETH

Casa Nova Hospice; Franciscan (Roman Catholic)
P.O.B. 198
Tel. (065) 54355.

Greek Catholic St. Joseph Seminary (Greek Catholic)
P.O.B. 99
Tel. (065) 54224.

Religieuses de Nazareth; Roman Catholic (French)
306 Casa Nova Street
P.O.B. 274
Tel. (065) 54304.

St. Charles Borromaeus (German Sisters; Roman Catholic)
316 12 Street
Tel. (065) 54435.

TIBERIAS

Church of Scotland Centre; Church of Scotland (British)
Old Town
P.O.B. 104
Tel. (067) 20144.

Franciscan Sisters (Roman Catholic)
Old Town Near Northern Wall
P.O.B. 207
Tel. (067) 20782.

Terra Sancta; Franciscan (Roman Catholic)
Old Town, on shore of the Sea of Galilee
P.O.B. 179
Tel. (067) 20516.

Y.M.C.A.—on western shore of Sea of Galilee
Make advance reservations through Jerusalem Y.M.C.A., P.O.B. 294
Tel. (02) 227111.

CHURCHES IN JERUSALEM

Name/address	Phone	Denomination
JERUSALEM		
Armenian Patriarchate III Station Chapel Via Dolorosa	(02) 289262	Catholic
Basilica of the Holy Sepulchre	(02) 284213	Franciscan
Basilica of all Nations Gethsemane	(02) 283264	Franciscan
Church of the Dormition P.O.B. 22	(02) 39927	Benedictine
Church of St. Anne St. Stephen's Gate	(02) 283285	Catholic
Church of St. Stephen Nablus Road	(02) 282213	Catholic
Church of the Agony Gethsemane	(02) 283964	Catholic
Church of the German Hospice German Colony P.O.B. 9020	(02) 37737	Catholic

Name/address	Phone	Denomination
Dominus Flevit Mt. of Olives		Franciscan
Flagellation Convent (Via Dolorosa)	(02) 282936	Franciscan
Franciscan Convent Close to the Cenacle (Mount Zion)	(02) 33597	Franciscan
Greek Patriarchate Jaffa Gate	(02) 282023	Catholic
Grotto of Gethsemane		Catholic
Latin Patriarchate of Jerusalem Jaffa Gate	(02) 282323	Catholic
Maronite Vicariate Maronite Convent Rd.	(02) 282158	Catholic
Pontifical Biblical Institute 3 Emil Botta Street P.O.B. 497	(02) 222843	Jesuit
Saint Saviour's Church Saint Francis St.	(02) 282354	Franciscan
Seventh (VII) Station of the Way of Cross		Franciscan
St. James Beit Hanina	(02) 254694	Catholic
American Gospel Church 55 Habevi'im Street	(02) 234804	Protestant
Anglican Services St. Abraham Chapel Holy Sepulchre		Anglican
Association for Unification of World Christianity P.O.B. 14015		Protestant
Baptist House 4 Narkis Street P.O.B. 154	(02) 225942	Baptist
Baptist Southern Worship Rashid St.	(02) 284165/ 281415	Baptist
Christ Church Anglican Jaffa Gate P.O.B. 4037	(02) 28202	Anglican

Christian Assembly	(02) 31178	Protestant
Church of Christ Al-Zahra St. near New Victoria Hotel P.O.B. 19529	(02) 282723	Protestant
Church of God Mt. of Olives near Palace Hotel	(02) 284436	Pentecostal
Church of the Nazarene Centre 33 Nablus Road P.O.B. 19426	(02) 283828	International
Church of the Redeemer P.O.B. 194076	(02) 282543	Lutheran

Collegiate Church of St. George
  the Martyr, commonly called
  St. George's Cathedral
Nablus Road and Saladin St.
P.O.B. 190018
	(02) 282253/
	287708
		Anglican/
		Episcopal

First Baptist Bible Church Salah-el-Din St.	(02) 282118	Independent
Garden Tomb near Damascus Gate P.O.B. 19462	(02) 283402	Interdenominational
Pentecostal Church 33 Hanevi'im Street Zion House		Protestant (American)
Seventh Day Adventist Advent House, near Y.M.C.A.		Protestant
The Scottish Church of St. Andrew Harakevet Street	(02) 37701	Protestant
Armenian Orthodox Patriarchate St. James Cathedral near Jaffa Gate	(02) 292331	Armenian
Gethsemane (Tomb of the Virgin)		Armenian
Holy Sepulchre		Armenian
St. James Tomb	(02) 292331	Armenian
Blessed Virgin Mary Chapel (room on façade)		Coptic
Coptic Orthodox Patriarchate Old City	(02) 282343	
Holy Sepulchre		Coptic
St. Anthony (Main Church Patriarchate)	(02) 282343	Coptic

Name/address	Phone	Denomination
St. George (St. Mitri)		Coptic
St. Helene (before Patriarchate on right before the one leading to 9th station)		Coptic
Der es-Sultan (Holy Sepulchre)		Ethiopian
Ethiopian Orthodox Church Ethiopia Street	(02) 28671	Ethiopian
Paradise Ethiopia St.		Ethiopian
Patriarchate Church (Harat el Nasara)		Ethiopian
Church of the Holy Sepulchre	(02) 284202	Greek
Parish Church of St. James (beside Holy Sepulchre)		Greek
Orthodox Patriarchate of Jerusalem Convent of Patriarchate	(02) 284917	Greek
St. Michel of Arch (St. John Chrysostom)		Greek
St. Nicolas Church		Greek Orthodox
St. Simeon Church Katamon		Greek
Russian Orthodox Church (outside of Russia) St. Mary Magdalen (Mt. of Olives)	(02) 282897	Russian
Russian Orthodox Church (outside of Russia) St. Alexander 25 Dabbagha Street	(02) 284580	Russian
Gethsemane Tomb of the Virgin		Syrian
Holy Sepulchre		Syrian
St. Marks Church St. Marks St.	(02) 283304	Syrian

SUPPLEMENTS

SUGGESTED READING LIST

AIDS TO SIGHTSEEING

Awwad, Marian (ed.). *Welcome to Jordan*. Amman: American Women's Club, 1977. A basic introduction to life in Jordan for newcomers planning to live in the country. It is especially useful for its shopping guide, with detailed maps, and its classified telephone directory—the only one available in English.

Fistere, John and Isobel. *Jordan, The Holy Land*. Beirut: Middle East Export Press, 1965. An inexpensive travel and picture book to take home as a souvenir of your visit to Jordan. The authors are American writers who have lived in the Middle East for the past 20 years and have been closely associated with Jordan tourism.

Harding, G. Lankester. *The Antiquities of Jordan*. London: Praeger, 1967; paperback, 1974. An absolute must for anyone going to Jordan and a guide to be used while there. The book is well written and easy to read. It will generate an interest in Jordanian antiquities, even though you may have had no previous attraction to the subject. Mr. Harding was the Director of Antiquities in Jordan for 20 years, and his enthusiasm for his subject is contagious.

Hoade, Fr. Eugene, O.F.M. *Guide to the Holy Land*. Jerusalem: Franciscan Press, 1962. Although written as a guide for Catholics, this is the standard and most thorough guidebook available. It is indispensable for its detailed information on Biblical sites. The book includes maps, diagrams, mileages, and itineraries.

Father Hoade's later book, *East of the Jordan* (1966), was revised and released in 1977 under the name *Guide to Jordan* by the Franciscan Fathers. It is available in Amman bookstores, and is particularly valuable for those who are exploring Jordan on their own.

Huxley, Julian. *From an Antique Land*. New York: Crown Publishers, 1954. As an introduction to the Middle East this is one of the best books available. The writer was a scholar, an enthusiastic traveler, and a keen observer. The photographs are excellent.

Morton, H.V.C. *Through Lands of the Bible*. London: Methuen, 1959. *In the Steps of the Master*. London: Methuen, 1962. *In the Steps of St. Paul*. London: Methuen, 1959. *The Women of the Bible*. New York: Dodd, 1941. The first-named book has the widest general interest, but a Morton fan will want to read them all. It is a painless and entertaining way to absorb vast amounts of information on the Holy Land. Some of the books are out of print and are now collector's items.

Nelson, Bryan. *Azraq: A Desert Oasis*. London: Allen House, 1973; Ohio University Press, 1975. A specialized book on one of Jordan's important historic and naturalist sites.

BIBLICAL/ARCHEOLOGICAL/HISTORICAL

Albright, William. *The Archaeology of Palestine*. New York: Penguin Books, 1960. A basic treatment of the subject by one of the world's leading scholars.

The Archeological Heritage of Jordan, Part 1: The Archeological Periods and Sites (East Bank). Amman: Department of Antiquities, 1973. Published to mark the 50th anniversary of the Department of Antiquities, this volume reviews the archeological work done during this period. The Department also publishes annual reports which include summaries of all activity by foreign expeditions excavating in Jordan.

Avi-Yonah. *The Holy Land*. New York: Holt, Rinehart &

Winston, 1972. An architectural survey from an historic point of view of the major buildings and sites in the Holy Land.

Baly, Denis. *The Geography of the Bible,* rev. ed. New York: Harper and Row, 1974. Indispensable as a reference book; one of the most authoritative available.

Browning, Iain. *Petra.* London: Chatto & Windus, 1973; Noyes, 1974. The most extensive book in print on Jordan's major tourist attraction, this is a wonderfully detailed volume that can be used as a guide as well as for pleasurable background reading. It is available in Amman bookstores.

Cross, Frank Moore, Jr. *The Ancient Library of Qumran,* The Haskell Lectures, 1956-1957. New York, 1976; *Qumran and the History of the Biblical Text.* Cambridge: Harvard University Press, 1975. The first is readable and authentic, although it is now a bit out of date, since subsequent research has augmented the early work on the scrolls.

Fosdick, Harry Emerson. *A Pilgrimage to Palestine* (1926) 1977 reprint. A readable account of a trip through the Holy Land.

Glueck, Nelson. *The River Jordan.* New York: Philadelphia Publication Society of America, 1945 (out of print). For those seriously interested in the archeology of the Holy Land, Glueck's books are standard reading. The author is recognized as one of the leading scholars of this century. His survey of the Holy Land was the first scientific one undertaken. Subsequent works by the author are *Dieties and Dolphins: The Story of the Nabataeans,* Farrar, Strauss & Giroux, 1965, and *The Other Side of the Jordan,* American School of Oriental Research, Cambridge, Mass., 1970.

Grollenberg, L.H. *Shorter Atlas of the Bible.* Penguin, 1977. Valuable for reference and background reading.

Guillaume, Alfred. *Islam.* Penguin Books, 1956 (paperback). A standard introduction to Islam.

Hitti, Phillip. *History of the Arabs.* London: Macmillan, 1970 (paperback). The classic work, indispensable for serious students of the area. A shortened version by the author, *The Arabs: A Short History* (Chicago: Henry Regnery, 1956), is also available in paperback and is recommended as a primer.

Keller, Werner. *The Bible as History.* New York: Morrow, 1956. Also available in paperback: Bantam, 1974. The standard work on the subject, and the one to read for a Holy Land visit.

Kenyon, Kathleen. *Digging up Jericho.* New York: Praeger, 1957. *Archaeology in the Holy Land.* New York: Praeger, 1960; London:

Ernest Benn, 1970, paperback. *Digging Up Jerusalem*. New York: Praeger, 1974. *Royal Cities of the Old Testament*. New York: Schocken, 1973. Miss Kenyon was one of the leading archeologists to work in Jordan. To her goes the credit for uncovering the oldest walled city in the world. The story of that dig is described in the first book; the second is a good one for beginners.

Lambert, Michel John. *Jerusalem*. New York: Putnam, 1958. (Out of print.) The leading book on the history of Jerusalem. It contains photographs, maps, and charts; and it will provide pleasurable reading after you get home.

Moore, Elinor. *The Ancient Churches of Old Jerusalem*. Beirut: Khayat, 1961. *Early Church in the Middle East*. Humanities Press, 1968. The author traces the origins and history of some 50 churches in Jerusalem, based on accounts written by pilgrims from the years A.D. to 1750. The first title is out of print and difficult to find in the U.S.

Pritchard, James. *Gibeon: Where the Sun Stood Still*. Princeton: Princeton University Press, 1962. *Archaeology and the Old Testament*. Princeton, 1958. The author was head of the excavations at Gibeon during the 1950s. He has authored many books on archeology in the Middle East.

Runciman, Steven. *History of the Crusaders*. 3 vols. Cambridge University Press, 1954. The standard treatment of the subject.

Sanger, Richard. *Where the Jordan Flows*. Washington, D.C.: Middle East Institute, 1963. Provides extensive Biblical and historic chronological data, and is a valuable guide for visitors with academic interests.

Sheen, The Most Rev. Fulton. *This Is the Holy Land*. Conducted by Rev. Sheen, photographed by Yusuf Karsh and described by H.V. Morton. New York: Hawthorn Books, 1961. (Out of print.) Three famous men combine their knowledge and abilities to take the reader on a pilgrimage through the Holy Land.

Thubron, Colin. *Jerusalem*. Boston: Little, Brown, 1969. With 64 pages of color photographs by Alistair Duncan. *Jerusalem* Great Cities Series. New York: Time-Life, 1976. An esthetic description of Jerusalem and nearby holy places.

MODERN HISTORY

Antonius, George. *The Arab Awakening*. New York: Putnam, 1965. A necessity for anyone who plans to stay in Jordan for an extended period and wants to understand the background of the modern Middle East.

Glubb, John B. *A Soldier With the Arabs.* New York: Harper and Bros., 1959. *The Story of the Arab Legion.* Da Capo, 1976. *Peace in the Holy Land.* London: Hodder & Stoughton, 1971; Verry, 1971. Few foreigners have known Jordan and the Jordanians better than Glubb, who for many years was head of the Arab Legion and Chief of Staff of the Jordan Army. And fewer persons were as close to events in the Middle East during the 1940s and 1950s.

Harris, George. *Jordan: Its People, Its Society, Its Culture.* New Haven: Human Relations Area Files, 1958. A thorough treatment. Especially good background reading for anyone planning to live in Jordan.

Hussein, Ibn Talal, King. *My War With Israel.* New York: William Morrow, 1969. *Uneasy Lies the Head.* Toronto: Heinemann, 1962. Jordan's tumultuous history as seen by the man at center stage is indispensable reading for all who are genuinely interested in the country and the Middle East.

Johnston, Charles. *The Brink of Jordan.* London: Hamish Hamilton, 1972.

Knowles, John. *Double Vision.* New York: MacMillan, 1964. (Out of print.) A journalistic account with many human interest stories, for background reading.

Lawrence, T.E. *Seven Pillars of Wisdom.* New York: Penguin, 1976. (Paperback.) If seeing the film *Lawrence of Arabia* didn't lead you to read this book, a trip to the Middle East should. Read it before you go.

Memoirs of King Abdallah. Gives a picture of the country from 1920 to 1945.

Peake, F.G. *A History of Jordan and Its Tribes.* Coral Gables: University of Miami Press, 1958. (Out of print.)

Snow, Peter. *Hussein: A Biography.* London: Barrie & Jenkins, 1972.

Sparrow, Gerald. *Hussein of Jordan.* Toronto: George Harrop, 1960.

P.J. Vatikiotis. *Conflict in the Middle East.* London: Allen & Unwin, 1971. The author is one of the leading scholars of modern Middle Eastern history today.

MISCELLANEOUS

Foley, Rolla. *Song of the Arab: The Religious Ceremonies, Shrines and Folk Music of the Holy Land Christian Arabs.* New York: Macmillan, 1953. The major religious folk rites of the Christian Arabs are described. The book provides background information on the pageantry, traditions, and folklore of the Holy Land.

Gubser, Peter. *Politics and Change in Al-Karak,* Jordan. London: Oxford University Press, 1973.

Montfort, Guy. *Portrait of a Desert: The Story of an Expedition to Jordan.* London: Collins, 1965.

Mufti, Shawkat. *Heroes and Emperors in Circassian History.* Beirut: Librarie du Liban, 1972.

Nevins, Ed, and Theon Wright. *World Without Time—The Bedouins.* New York: John Day, 1969. (Out of print)

Pilgrims's Map of the Holy Land for Biblical Research; The Journeys and Deeds of Jesus Christ. Details the Holy Land at the time of Jesus and locates the sites mentioned in the Old and New Testaments, together with an index of the Bible references. The map is on sale at bookshops in Amman and other major towns and antiquities sites.

GLOSSARY

There are many systems for the transliteration of Arabic words into English equivalents. In the following glossary the system has been made as simple as possible.

— All long vowels appear as double vowels except "a" which is written with a circumflex: â.

— The letter *ain* in Arabic has no English equivalent. Its presence (when necessary to avoid confusion with other words) has been indicated by: '.

— The *hamza,* a glottal stop, is indicated by: '.

— H, h: the first is hard, the second is like the English "h" in *hat.*

— T, t: the first is hard, the second is like the English "t" in *tip.*

— D or th (like the "th" in *this*) are almost the same sound in Jordanian speech: hatha, ooDa.

— The sound indicated by "kh," pronounced gutturally, as the German "ch" in *Bach.*

Greetings

Good morning	*SabaH el khair*
(reply)	*Sabah el noor*
Good evening	*masa-l khair*

Good night	*laileh sa'eedi; tisbaH 'ala khair*
Good day	*nahârak sa'eed*
(reply)	*nahârak sa'eed wa-mbârak*
Hello	*marHaba*
(reply)	*marhabtain*
Greetings (Peace be with you)	*as-salâm 'alaikoom*
(reply)	*'alaikoom salâm*
Goodbye (the one departing)	*b-khatirkum*
(the one remaining)	*ma'-salâmi; fi amân illah*
How are you?	*keef Hâlak*
Well, thank God	*mabsut (a) elHamdu lillâh*
Welcome, (host says)	*ahlan wa-sahlan*
(reply)	*ahlan bekum*

Useful Phrases

Yes	*na'âm*
No	*lâ*
Please	*min fadlak, min fadlik (f.)*
If you please	*a'mel ma'roof*
After you, I beg you	
to (enter, eat, take)	*tfaDDal, tfaDDali (f.)*
If God is willing	*inshallah*
Thank you	*shukran; mamnoonak, mamnoonik (f.)*
What is your name?	*shu ismak? Shu ismik? (f.)*
My name is	*ismi ....*
Do you speak English?	*btiHki ingleezi*
I do not speak Arabic	*ana ma baHki 'arabi*
How? (In what way)	*keef?*
How much? (cost)	*adaysh?*
How many?	*kam?*
What?	*shu?*
What is that?	*shu hatha?*
What is it? What's the matter?	*shu fee?*
What do you want?	*shu biddak?*
Who?	*meen?*
Why?	*laish?*
For what purpose?	*min shân aish?*
I do not want	*ma biddi*
I do not have	*ma fee, ma 'indi*
I am hungry	*ana ju'an, ana ju'ana (f.)*
I want to eat	*ana bidee akul*
Give me	*'ateeni*
Bring me	*jibli*
Excuse me	*mut'asif, ma ta'aKhizni*
Take care, watch out	*ou'a*

Go away!	*imshi, rooh*
Hurry up	*Yallah*
Get up	*qoom*
Stop	*waqqif, uqaf*
Stop, enough	*bass*
Slower please	*'ala mahlak minfadlak*
Slowly	*shway, shway*
Take me to the hotel	*khudni 'al otel*
Wait here!	*istenna hoon*
Open the door!	*iftaH el bâb*
Shut the door!	*sakkir el bâb*
Let me see!	*farjeeni, warreeni*
Come here!	*ta'a la hoon*
I do not know	*ma ba'raf*
See!	*shoof!* I saw *shuft*
Never mind	*ma'laish*
Again, also	*kaman*
Another time	*marra tâni, kaman marra*
Once	*marra*
Twice	*marratain*
Everything	*kull*
All of us	*kulna*
Together	*sawa*
Here	*hawn*
There	*hoonak*
Yet	*lissa*
Not yet	*ma lissa*
When	*emta*
After	*ba'd*
Later	*ba'dain*
Never	*abadan*
Always	*daiman*
Perhaps	*yimkin*
Is it possible	*mumkin?*
Please wash these	*minfadlik, ighsil hatha (f.)*
Please press these	*minfadlik, ikwi hatha (f.)*

At the Airport

Airport	*maTâr*
Car, taxi	*arabiyeh; taxi; sayyara*
Customs	*gumruk*
Handbag	*juzdan*
Money	*fuloos*
Porter	*hammal, attâ*
Office	*maktab*
Suitcase	*shanta*

| Ticket | *tezkara* |
| Trunk | *sanduq* |

In Town

Bridge	*jisr, qantara*
Church	*kaneesah*
District	*Hye, Hara*
Harbour	*mena*
Market	*souq*
Mosque	*jami*
Museum	*matHaf*
Place	*maHal*
Hospital	*mustashfa*
House	*bait*
Shop	*dukkân, makhzen*
Square	*midân*
Street	*shâri'*
Town	*medineh; balad*

At the Hotel

Ashtray	*manfatha, mtakkeh*
Bed, mattress	*farsheh*
Bath	*hammam*
Blanket	*hrâm*
Door	*bâb*
Doorman	*bawwâb, concierge*
Floor (storey)	*tâbiq*
Hotel	*otel, lukanda*
Hot water	*mye sukhni*
Lamp	*Daw*
Light	*noor*
Lightbulb	*lamba*
Pillow	*makhadda*
Room	*ooDa*
Sheet	*sharshaf*
Soap	*saboon*
Towel	*manshafa, bashkir*
Window	*shubbâk*
Is there air-conditioning?	*fee tabreed?*
Is there heat?	*fee tadfi'a*
Show me a room	*farjeeni ooDa*
Where is the toilet?	*wain bait-el-mye?*

On the Road

| Above, up | *fooq* |
| Behind | *wara* |

Under	*taHt*
East	*sharq*
Far	*ba'eed*
Gasoline	*benzeen*
Go down	*inzal*
Go up	*iTla'*
In front	*'uddam*
Inside	*juwwa*
Left	*shemal*
Near	*'areeb*
North	*shamâl*
Over	*'ala*
Outside	*barra*
Right	*yameen*
Road, highway	*tareeq*
South	*jannub*
Straight ahead	*dughri*
Village	*day'a, qarya*
Where	*wain*
Where is the road to ....?	*wain et-tareeq 'al ....?*
Is the road far from here?	*et-tareeq ba'eed min hoon?*
How many kilometers?	*kam kilometer?*

In the Restaurant

Bill	*fatoora, hisab*
Breakfast	*ftoor*
Cigarette	*sigara, sagayer (pl.)*
Dinner	*'asha*
Fork	*shokeh*
Glass	*kubbayeh*
Knife	*sikkin*
Lunch	*ghada*
Matches	*kibreet*
Plate	*saHn*
Restaurant	*mat'am*
Spoon	*mal'aqa*
Table	*tawla*
Table napkins	*foota*
Waiter	*walad; garçon*

Food

Apricot	*mishmish*
Banana	*mooz*
Beef	*laHm baqar*
Beer	*bira*
Bread	*khubz*

Butter	*zebda*
Cabbage	*malfoof*
Cheese	*jibneh*
Chicken	*djâj*
Chick peas	*Hummos*
Coffee	*'ahwi*
Cracked wheat	*burghul*
Cucumber	*khiyar*
Cutlet	*castaletta*
Eggs	*baid*
hard boiled	*baid maslooq*
soft boiled	*baid brisht*
omelette	*'ijje*
Eggplant	*batinjan*
Figs	*teen*
Fish	*samak*
Fruit	*fawakeh*
Garlic	*toom*
Grapes	*'enab*
Green beans	*loobiyeh, fasulia*
Honey	*'asal*
Ice	*talj*
Lamb	*kharoof*
Lemon	*limoon*
Lentils	*'adas*
Lettuce	*khass*
Meat	*laHm*
Roast	*rosto*
Skewer	*meshwi*
Melon (yellow)	*shammâm*
Milk	*Haleeb*
Olive	*zaitoon*
Olive oil	*zait*
Onions	*basal*
Oranges	*bortuqâl, bort'ân*
Peaches	*durrâq*
Pepper, black	*filfil aswad*
sweet	*bhâr hellu*
Pistachio	*fustuq halebi*
Pine nuts	*snobar*
Plums	*khûkh*
Preserves	*murabba, tatli*
Rice	*ruzz*
Salt	*milH*
Salad	*salata*
Soup	*showraba*
Squash	*koosa*

Sugar	*sukkar*
Tea	*shy*
Tomatoes	*banadura*
Veal	*laHm 'ijl*
Vegetables	*khudra*
Vinegar	*khall*
Water	*mye*
Watermelon	*baTTeekh*
Wine	*nbeed*
Yogurt	*leban*

Useful Words

Antiquities	*athar*
Baker	*khabbâz, farrân*
Barber	*Hallâk*
Bedroom	*ooda-t noom*
Book	*kitâb*
Bookseller	*maktabji*
Bookshop	*maktabeh*
Camel	*jamal*
Candle	*sham'a*
Caravanserai	*khân*
Carpet	*sijjâda*
Castle	*qasr, qal'a*
Chair	*kursi*
Coat	*kaboot*
Column	*'âmood, 'awamid (pl.)*
Consul	*'unsul*
Diarrhea	*is-hâl*
Dining room	*ooda-t sufra*
Doctor	*Hakeem, doctoor*
Dog	*kalb*
Dome, cupola	*qoobah*
Donkey	*Hmâr*
Dress	*fustân*
Elder man	*sheikh*
Eyeglasses	*naDDarat*
Fever	*harâra; Humma*
Fire	*nâr*
Girl	*bint, benât (pl.)*
Headache	*waja' râs*
Heaven, sky	*sema*
Holiday	*'eed*
Horse	*Hosân*
Iron (metal)	*Hadid*
(instrument)	*makwa*

Jar	*jarra*
Judge	*qâDi*
King	*malak*
Kitchen	*matbakh*
Letter	*maktub*
Living room	*sâlon*
Monastery	*deir*
Money-changer	*sarrâf*
Moon	*qamar*
New moon	*hilâl*
Pain	*waja'*
Pilgrim	*Hâjji*
Pilgrimage	*Hâjj*
Policeman	*bolees*
Police station	*markaz bolees*
Prophet	*nebi*
Prayer-niche	*miHrâb*
Pulpit	*minbar*
Reception room	*diwan, dar*
Religion	*deen*
Seamstress	*khayyâta*
Servant (maid)	*khadmi (f.) khaddam*
Shirt	*qamees*
Shoes	*kundara*
Shrine	*mezâr*
Stone	*Hajar*
Sun	*shams*
Tomb	*qabr*
Toothpick	*miswâk*
Trousers	*bantalon*

Numbers

zero	*sifr*	six	*sitte*
one	*wahad*	seven	*sab'a*
two	*etnain*	eight	*tamanya*
three	*talata*	nine	*tis'a*
four	*'arba'*	ten	*'ashra*
five	*khamseh*	eleven	*hedasher*

INDEX

(The letters H and R indicate hotel and restaurant listings.)

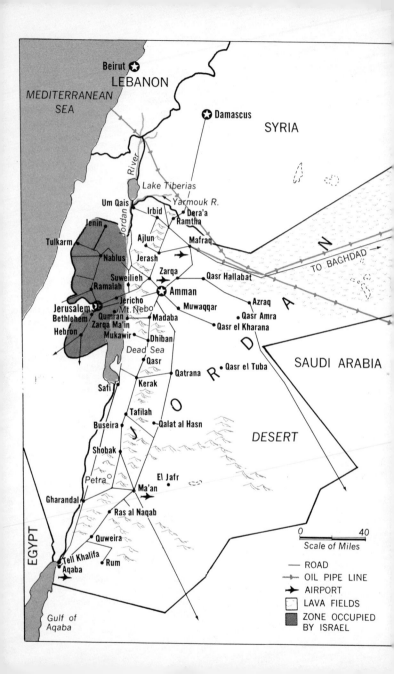

Lovingly restored

Garden proper

Good, wide, open space lawn

Party of rainbow colours summer flowers.